‖‖ ‖‖‖ ‖ ‖‖‖‖‖ ‖ ‖ ‖‖ ‖‖ ‖ ‖ ‖ ‖‖ ‖‖

D1617337

COMPARATIVE PUBLIC POLICY

COMPARATIVE POLITICAL ECONOMY AND PUBLIC POLICY SERIES
Volume I: Comparative Public Policy:
Issues, Theories, and Methods

Series Editors:
CRAIG LISKE, *University of Denver*
WILLIAM LOEHR, *University of Denver*
JOHN F. McCAMANT, *University of Denver*

COMPARATIVE PUBLIC POLICY
Issues, Theories, and Methods

Edited by
CRAIG LISKE
WILLIAM LOEHR
JOHN McCAMANT

SAGE Publications

Halsted Press Division
JOHN WILEY & SONS
New York – London – Sydney – Toronto

Copyright © 1975 by Sage Publications, Inc.

Distributed by Halsted Press, a Division of
John Wiley & Sons, Inc., New York

Printed in the United States of America

Library of Congress Cataloging in Publication Data

Liske, Craig.
    Comparative public policy.

    Bibliography: p.
    1. Policy sciences—Addresses, essays, lectures.
I. Loehr, William, joint author.   II. McCamant, John F., joint author.
III. Title.
H61.L54   300   73-91354
ISBN 0-470-54116-4

FIRST PRINTING

*Read:
Chapters
2, 3, + 10*

CONTENTS

Introduction

"THIRSTING FOR THE TESTABLE"

I recommend this book highly to anyone who wants to get a good general idea of what the younger generation of political scientists and political economists thinks and does. In the last few years the generation gap has been very wide in political science between the older tradition of historical, literary, and philosophical research and the newer tradition of quantitative and statistical work, which might almost be called "politicometrics." I am not quite sure that the new tradition has reached the critical age of thirty yet, but it is at least old enough to have a good deal of maturity, and we can begin to see where it is going. This book is an excellent sample of the workers in this new tradition. It is a sample and not an encyclopedia. The studies are confined to North and South America, East and West Europe, and a part of one study on India, so that Africa, the Middle East, the Islamic world, China, Southeast Asia, and Australasia find no place in it. Nevertheless, as a sample of interests and methodologies it is probably representative. The geographical limitations illustrate, however, the problem of a data-oriented methodology—that it has to go where the data are—and the parts of the world that are not covered in these studies tend to be those which are data-poor.

Some other foci of interest of these papers may be noted. They are all involved with problems of governmental decisions and governmental policies. Comparative politics apparently still does not spill over into the study of decision-making and policy of non-governmental organizations, even where these are strongly "affected by the public interest," like large corporations, especially international corporations, large trade unions, and even churches. Six out of the twelve papers deal with some aspects of military budgets and government decisions about the military; they do not deal with the level of military or strategic decisions themselves in any great detail. Budgets, indeed, are the prime data source and object of statistical manipulation. Ten out of the twelve papers attempt some sort of statistical analysis of data, and the data, almost without exception, consist of budgets or expenditures on the part of governments. Expenditure records, after all, are where the great underground worms of politics emerge into the topsoil and can be picked off by the beaks of early researchers.

Finally, there is great interest and devotion to theory construction. At least eight of the papers devote considerable attention to theory, and two of them, by Wagner and Sandler, are entirely devoted to theory without even a libation toward statistical testing other than a hope for the future. Most of the papers, however, are concerned with attempts to test theoretical propositions by means of statistical analysis of some body of data.

This "thirst for the testable" is one of the most engaging and encouraging features of the new generation of social scientists. They recognize that social systems are extremely complex, so much so that they are beyond the intuitive grasp of any participant in them. We do have a good deal of intuitive knowledge of the social systems in which we are a personal participant, though even here our experience may be highly biased and may lead to unrealistic images of the system. As we move into larger and more complex systems the dangers of generalization from personal experience become greater, and the problem of reducing the complexity of the relationships to some kind of model which can be grasped by the limited capacities of the human nervous system becomes overwhelmingly important. It is not surprising, therefore, that faced with large, complex, and partly inaccessible systems the researcher turns to numbers, that is, to data which can be expressed in quantitative form, and to the statistical analysis of these numbers, which have the delightful property that they can be added and subtracted, multiplied and divided, and hence they are much easier to manipulate and analyze than sentences.

It should never be forgotten, however, that the very concept of number involves an abstraction for the n-dimensional sets of the real world, a process which itself involves a massive loss of information. When we say that the population of the United States is 207,000,000, or whatever it is, we have abstracted from all the richness and complexities of persons, so that each person is represented only by the number "1," which is pretty close to being a cipher. Dollars of expenditure represent an almost equal degree of abstraction; what is real is what is purchased with the dollar, and this can be anything from an idea or ritualistic act, some ergs of energy, or some transformations of material, to a pound of tea or a small fraction of a missile. The numericalness of dollars, like the numericalness of population, is a ghost of a vast, rich, bodily, and spiritual complexity which we can apprehend only through a glass darkly.

I am not, of course, against either quantification or statistical manipulation as such. It is my firm conviction that all knowledge, and even perception, is gained by the orderly loss of information, and that the abstractions which are involved in quantification are often necessary in the reduction of information to manageable proportions. The fact that quantification does involve large reductions of information, however, should never be forgotten. Quantification should never be regarded as an end in itself. Statistical significance is a mere milestone on the road to epistemological significance, which is something much more fundamental. The critical question is, "When we have a number do we know any more than we did before we had it?" and the answer is often, "Yes, but not very much." Many of these papers convey a proper sense that numbers are an abstraction from the real world, a kind of crutch, as it were, in the hobbling search for images of complex systems of greater realism. There is always a danger, however, particularly with well-trained social scientists, that the training is in the rituals of the craft and that epistemological significance may sometimes be submerged in the sheer delight of statistical numerology.

If we ask ourselves, therefore, what do we learn from the perusal of a group of papers like this, one answer is nearly always that the world is more complicated than we thought and that simple generalizations are frequently wrong, especially, one is tempted to add, about Latin America. Military regimes do not always spend heavily on the military, and civilian regimes sometimes do. Leftist regimes do not always favor education and rightist regimes sometimes do. Homeowners are sometimes more stingy in regard to public goods than renters, but not always. On the theoretical side, also, the implications are all for eclecticism. Empirical studies in this field tend to have been guided by two apparently competing theoretical views, the structural and the behavioral, a division which delightfully identifies as the difference between causes and reasons. Statistical research has the tendency to go in for causes, or at least antecedents. What characteristics of a situation is it which makes some polities spend more on some particular objective than others? This stance tends to abstract from the decision-making processes themselves and the political institutions and role structures which surround them, perhaps because it is harder to get at these. Many of the papers, however, suggest that both approaches are necessary; that while political decisions operate within boundaries which are drawn by the total social and economic environment, these boundaries do not completely eliminate the decision space, so that decisions may make a difference as they move from one boundary or another. Occasionally it matters who is the occupant of a powerful role, though the implication now is also that it matters much less than unsophisticated political enthusiasts might predict.

One has the impression, also, that the kind of theory which gives rise to interesting statistical analyses is rather crude theory and it is perhaps significant that the papers which expound the most elegant and refined theories, namely Wagner's and Sandler's—both derived incidentally from economics—did not lead into much in the way of statistical analysis. In political science as well as economics I have argued that there is a lot to be said for what I have called the "bulldozer theory," which can push large problems around in rather crude ways, as against the "scalpel theory" of elegant intellectual refinement, which is not much use in the face of a large pile of dirt.

One wonders, finally, what will emerge cumulatively out of the mass of studies of which those in this volume are quite a small sample. A large number of statistical data-oriented studies is now beginning to appear. What is still lacking, however, is an integrated framework which can weave these studies into a comprehensible image of a total world system. Each of the studies in this volume is an analysis of part of a very large system. What is still lacking is some framework by which the parts may be related to the whole, something like, for instance, the periodic table in chemistry. At the moment there is no place where all these different studies are collected, collated, and stored not merely in a data bank, which after all is a pretty static concept, but into a "results bank" in which similar things should be identified as similar and diverse things as diverse. In a sense this volume is only a milestone or a very long road that leads to the reality-testing of the total world system. The number on the milestone, however, is a little closer to the goal, and on a long hike a milestone can be a very cheering encounter.

Kenneth E. Boulding

A STATISTICAL PREFACE

WILLIAM LOEHR

Much of the work in this volume is exploratory. Theory has led several authors to expect associations among certain variables in the complex politico-economic systems under study. Indeed, this is the first step in most empirical research. Once theory has led to the expectation of some association, we attempt to reinforce that expectation before proceeding. If a reinforcement is not found, then we must reformulate our thinking before we can go on.

The simplest search for an association among variables usually begins with some form of correlation analysis. The measure of association most often employed, the correlation coefficient (r),[1] indicates the degree to which variables are linearly correlated. It does not address how they are related; this is the task of regression analysis.

Several important factors must be kept in mind in the interpretation of correlation coefficients. First, no causal relationship is implied. The correlation coefficient between X and Y (r_{xy}) can be calculated whether X affects Y, Y affects X, both affect each other, or there is only indirect relationship between X and Y through other variables. Second, the r_{xy} only measures linear association between X and Y, and becomes rather useless when linearity is not a good approximation of the true relationship between them. Third, as with other statistical measures, the statistical significance of a calculated r may be in question. Almost any random variable will correlate statistically with some other random variable, despite the lack of true association between them. Therefore, we must be particularly careful to test our results for statistical significance before proceding further.[2] It is important at this stage to be as careful as possible to choose only variables which show significant correlations *and* have some theoretical likelihood of being causally connected.

REGRESSION

If preliminary theorizing leads one to the hypothesis that there exists a causal relationship among variables under consideration, then the technique of regression analysis may be used to test for the hypothesized relationship. At this point the researcher commits himself to designating a variable as being "dependent" and related in a causal sense to other "independent" variables. While any relationship might be postulated between a dependent variable (Y) and any number of independent variables (X_1, X_2, ' ' 'X_n), not all functional forms are estimable. The easiest to work with, and the form most often employed in social science and in this volume, is the linear form:

(1) $Y = A + B_1 X_1 + B_2 X_2 + \ldots + B_n X_n + E$

Linearity may not be a valid assumption over all ranges of possible observation, but if the relevant range is small, many non-linear forms can be closely approximated by linear estimates.

Particular attention should be paid to E, the so-called "error term," since its composition and distributional properties will influence the nature of the parameter estimates which are made. In any social science research, we are confronted with several problems which usually do not permit us to establish precise relationships among variables, thus resulting in the error term, E. Some of these problems are amenable to control through careful research methods, but it is very unlikely that even the most careful researcher can eliminate E entirely. Consider that

$$(2) \quad E = L + M + N + S$$

where L is the error introduced by using a linear form to approximate a non-linear one. Measurement of most social science variables is far from precise, and therefore, additional error, M, can be expected from measurement inaccuracies. Even where L and M can be successfully eliminated, some random variation in our data always appears, and this "pure noise" is represented by N (Rao and Miller, 1971: 1-4).

We are most often forced to take a sample of observations from the population of statistical interest to us. The randomness of our sampling procedure adds one more source of error to the regression equation, since it is most unlikely that *all* elements in the population would have *exactly* the same properties as the elements in the sample. This source of error is indicated by S.

It is clear that the variation E can be eliminated by careful attention to the sources of L, M, N, and S. Nevertheless, some error will remain in any regression equation, and it is usually not operationally possible to separate out the influences of the components of E. To the extent that E is large, the confidence we have in our equation estimates is weakened. Tests of statistical significance of the parameters estimated in the equations are designed to place some qualifications on our estimates (Johnson, 1963).

Researchers very often debate the need for significance tests. Some maintain that if the regression equation (or any other statistical relationship) is based not upon a sample but upon the entire population under study, statistical tests are not appropriate. Their main point is that when the entire population is analysed, the resulting relationship is not simply an estimate but *is* the relationship itself. However, as we have seen above, sampling error is only one part of the total error to be expected in a regression, and therefore, in spite of having the entire population, we do not have the exact relationship among variables. Remeasurement, respecification of the functional form, and the like would all change the estimated relationship. Since some sources of error are always present, tests of statistical significance remain appropriate in all such analyses.

Let us consider the estimation of a linear regression equation of the form represented by equation 1, but where we are interested in only two independent variables, and:

$$(3) \quad \hat{Y} = a + b_1 X_1 + b_2 X_2$$

where $\hat{Y}$ is our estimate of the true value Y, and a, b_1 and b_2 are estimates of the parameters A, B_1 and B_2.[3] Note that while we know there will be some error, we have no way of estimating its magnitude, and it therefore does not appear in our estimated relationship. It is assumed throughout that e, the error generated by our estimation procedure, is randomly distributed with mean zero. Our estimated relationship (3) answers the question, "What value for Y results, on the average, whenever X_1 and X_2 equal to some specific values, such as X_{1a} and X_{2a}?" The answer, $\hat{Y}a$, is unaffected by the presence of e, since Ya is simply an *average* of all possible Y estimates which could result whenever $X_1 = X_{1a}$ and $X_2 = X_{2a}$, ceteris paribus. The true value of Y could be greater or less than Ya depending upon e.

The so-called "constant term," A in equation (1) and estimated by a, can be interpreted as the average impact on Y of all variables not included in the equation. All relevant independent variables usually cannot be included in the estimation process. To expedite our research, we are forced to include only those independent variables we consider most relevant and ignore those we consider trivial.

Coefficients b_1 and b_2 in (3) are estimates of the unknown parameters B_1 and B_2 in (1). B_1 tells us the change induced in Y by a change in X_1 when X_2 is held constant. Similarly with B_2. In effect,

$$B_1 = \frac{\partial Y}{\partial X_1} \quad \text{and } B_2 = \frac{\partial Y}{\partial X_2}$$

One cannot directly compare B_1 in (1) with B_1 found in, say,

$$(4) \quad Y = A' + B'_1 X_1 + B_3' X_3$$

since

$$B'_1 = \frac{\partial Y}{\partial X_1}$$

holding the value of X_3 constant. When comparing equations containing the same dependent variable but different sets of independent variables, we must be cognizant of the "all else" which is equal. Tests for the equivalence of estimates of B_1 and B'_1 may not be valid since they come from essentially dissimilar relationships.

Regression equation estimates are usually accompanied by summary statistics which aid in the interpretation of the results. The most common of these is the Coefficient of Determination, R^2, which measures the relative amount of the variation in the dependent variable "explained" by the independent variables. While equations with a high R^2 (close to 1.0) are generally considered to be better "fits" than those with low R^2s (close to zero), caution is in order. The use of R^2 to compare the relative performance of two competing equations is only legitimate when the equations compared all contain the same dependent variable (Rao and Miller, 1971: 13-18).

A wide variety of tests exist to test the relative significance of all regression parameter estimates. Most "canned" statistical routines produce test statistics automatically, and in all cases their presence helps in our interpretation of the estimates. In fact, it is the use of these statistics which demands the real skill of a statistical analyst. The derivations of these tests and explanation of their use require some length and are adequately developed elsewhere (Wonnacott and Wonnacott, 1969, 1970).

The regression analysis employed in the essays in this volume are designed to aid in either cross-sectional or time series analysis of public policy. The choice as to the appropriateness of cross-sectional as opposed to time series is dependent upon the objectives of the analysis. Whichever is chosen, the researcher must take care that the technique he selects does indeed capture the relationship sought.

Let us illustrate with an example where we have a choice of either time series analysis of some relationship for each of several countries, or cross-sectional analysis of the same countries. To demonstrate simply, only one independent variable and a cross-section of only three countries are considered. Let us call the countries A, B, and C. In Figure 1, we have drawn hpothetical observations on A, B, and C for five time periods labeled A_1, A_2, and so on. The time series regression equations for each country individually are drawn and labelled as $\hat{Y}_A$, $\hat{Y}_B$, and $\hat{Y}_C$. Note that while there is a time trend in each, they are all quite different. Significance tests on the estimated regression coefficients would tell us how different each was from the others.

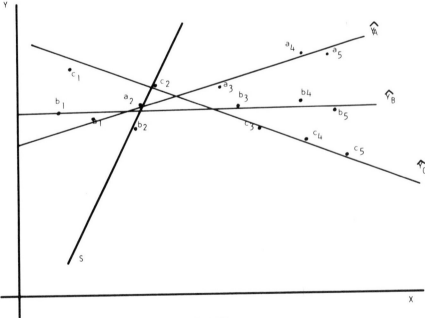

FIGURE I

Suppose, however, we had chosen cross-sectional analysis because of data limitation (which is very often the case). If time period 2 had been selected, the estimated equation S would have resulted, but S has almost nothing in common with the time series results. It tells us only the relative, static relationships between variables X and Y in A, B, and C in time period 2, and is no guide whatever when projections are made into later time periods. Note that in time period 3, the relative positions of countries A and C are reversed, and that in fact, a cross-sectional equation for time period 3 would show a negative slope, whereas in period 2, the slope was positive.[4]

Interpretation of whatever form of analysis is chosen is complicated by problems of multicollinearity, and in the case of time series, autocorrelation. Multicollinearity results from interdependencies among the independent variables. For example, suppose we are attempting to interpret

$$(5) \quad Y = B_1 X_1 + B_2 X_2 + B_3 X_3 + E.$$

Suppose further, however, that X_1 and X_2 are not independent of each other, so that

$$X_1 = f(X_2).$$

Given the single equation (5), we can only interpret B_1 as:

$$B_1 = \frac{\gamma \quad Y}{\gamma \quad X_1},$$

but due to the interdependence between X_1 and X_2,

$$\frac{\gamma \quad Y}{\gamma \quad X_1} = B_1 + B_2 \frac{\gamma \quad X_2}{\gamma \quad X_1},$$

so that we cannot say from equation 5 how much of the influence upon Y is due to X_1 directly, or to X_2 indirectly as it impacts upon X_1. Despite the theoretical independence of the "independent" variables, they are very often in fact interrelated statistically, and therefore, multicollinearity problems creep into our analysis unexpectedly. Methods are available to check for their presence[5] (Rao and Miller, 1971: 46-52), and statistical procedures can be used to adjust for some, though not all, multicollinearity (Nie, Bent, Hull, 1970: 158-61).

Autocorrelation should be suspected in most time series analyses. This occurs where the error terms do not conform to the assumption of independent random variables, but where they are serially correlated, that is, when E for a given time period is some function of E for any previous time periods. When this occurs, predictions made on the basis of the equation will have a needlessly wide variance. Also, our estimates of coefficient variances will be too low and the precise forms of common test statistics (t and F) will no longer be valid (Johnson, 1963: 179). The most commonly used test for the presence of autocorrelation is the Durban-Watson d statistic (Johnston, 1963: 192), and several methods are available to adjust for it (Christ, 1966: 483-85). An application of one of these can be found in the paper by Peters and Hennessey in this volume.

Often we lose sight of the fact that the relationship in which we are interested is part of a much larger system of interrelated events. An "independent" variable, such as X_1 in equation 5, may be a dependent variable in another equation, the solution to which is determined simultaneously with (5). Assumptions can be made about the size and complexity of the system of simultaneous equations of which an equation such as (5) is likely to be a part. Indeed, in most social science research where one equation is estimated and analyzed, it is implicity assumed that there are no other simultaneously determined relationships which are relevant. Researchers constantly (and usually implicitly) make judgments about the trade-off between reality and statistical manageability in their treatment of single equations.

If, in fact, a single equation is to be estimated, and that equation is a part of a system of simultaneous equations, the use of ordinary least squares regression techniques leads to potentially serious underestimates of parameters. Corrections must be made to obtain unbiased estimates. One of these techniques, two-stage least squares, is employed here by Fowler and Lineberry. Other techniques are appropriate under conditions which differ from theirs and these are described along with a general treatment of simultaneous equation systems by Wonnacott and Wonnacott (1970: 149-64; 357-64) and by Christ (1966: 298-346; 432-53).

The papers collected in this volume raise a significantly greater number of methodological and statistical problems than we can deal with here. Our objective has not been to resolve these problems, but rather to familiarize non-statistically oriented readers with the statistical concepts and tools used by the authors in this volume. The brief review here should help these readers make their way through the papers, but in no sense should it be viewed as a substitute for a careful review of the various texts cited above. Indeed, to the degree that our readers are not motivated to seek beyond this essay, we shall in some sense have failed.

NOTES

1. The correlation coefficient is estimated by the procedure shown in Wonnacott and Wonnacott (1969: 286).

2. Tests on correlation coefficients are summarized in Anderson and Zelditch (1968: 277-82).

3. We will not go into the derivation of parameter estimates here as they are somewhat lengthy and readily available in many other places (Johnston, 1963; Draper and Smith, 1966). Basically, they are derived by the minimization of e_i^2 where the e_i are the errors in our estimates.

4. Similar problems are encountered when we change the level of analysis within a given system, i.e., when we do a cross-sectional analysis of, say, a federation as a whole and of the federation members individually. See Przeworski and Teune (1970: Ch. 3).

5. Rao and Miller (1971: 48) warn that it is not sufficient to simply observe the simple correlations between X_1 and X_2 and that further observations are useful.

REFERENCES

ANDERSON, Theodore R. and Morris ZELDITCH, JR. (1968) A Basic Cause in Statistics. 2nd ed. New York: Holt, Rinehart & Winston.
CHRIST, Carl F. (1966) Econometric Models and Methods. New York: John Wiley.
DRAPER, N.R. and H. SMITH (1966) Applied Regression Analysis. New York: John Wiley.
JOHNSTON, J. (1963) Econometric Methods. New York: McGraw-Hill.
NIE, Norman H., Dale H. BENT and C. Hadlai HULL (1970) Statistical Package for the Social Sciences. New York: McGraw-Hill.
PRZEWORSKI, Adam and Henry TEUNE (1970) The Logic of Comparative Social Inquiry. New York: John Wiley.
RAO, Potluri and Roger LeRoy MILLER (1971) Applied Econometrics, Belmont, Calif.: Wadsworth.
WONNACOTT, Thomas H. and Ronald J. WONNACOTT (1969) Introductory Statistics. New York: John Wiley.
––– (1970) Econometrics. New York: John Wiley.

SECTION I

THE DEFENSE WELFARE TRADEOFF

Chapter 1

POLICY CONSEQUENCES OF MILITARY PARTICIPATION IN POLITICS: AN ANALYSIS OF TRADEOFFS IN BRAZILIAN FEDERAL EXPENDITURES

MARGARET DALY HAYES

CACI Inc.
Washington, D.C.

INTRODUCTION

Recent research in allocation policy analysis has demonstrated a fascination with two components of government spending—welfare and defense. The emphasis of the research has been on the negative consequences of military spending for economic growth and social welfare, with particular focus on the modern, industrial nations of North America and Western Europe. The problem of tradeoffs between military spending and economic and social investment is perhaps even more serious in the developing countries. A special study by the United Nations Secretary-General reports that in developing countries military spending increased at a rate of 7% per year during the 1960s.

> When the needs of economic development are so pressing, it is a disturbing thought that these countries have found it necessary to increase military spending so speedily, particularly when their *per capita* income is so low. To the citizen of a developing country . . . even a diversion of a few dollars for military purposes may rob him of one of the necessities of life. [UN, 1971:19]

Moreover, in addition to increased spending for military purposes, it is precisely in the developing states that we see a growing tendency toward direct military

AUTHOR'S NOTE: The research for this study was financed by the United States Department of Health, Education, and Welfare through a Fulbright-Hays Doctoral Dissertation Research Fellowship. The Center for International Studies of the University of Missouri-St. Louis has been most generous in providing support for the preparation of this paper.

rule. Therefore, our concern over the economic and social consequences of militarism in the developing countries will be even greater if the new military governments pursue policies which aggrandize military interests at the expense of the economic and social development of their nations.

From an econometric point of view, some tradeoff occurs whenever resources are devoted to one sector rather than another. However, it is unlikely that any country will reduce allocations to its military sector to zero. Some tradeoff will inevitably occur. Research on the guns-versus-butter problem must go beyond the mere identification of these tradeoffs to focus on the critical issues of (1) the locus and weight of the burden of military allocations on other sectors, and (2) the content of military allocations—how much goes to arms purchases and development. Research to date has not dealt with the problem of content[1] at all. Evidence from studies of arms races (Pryor, 1968) suggests that the level of tradeoff burden depends on political factors. Few scholars have devoted attention to these factors for the developing countries. Research in that context has focused, rather, on the comparison of policy outputs and outcomes of military governments as opposed to civilian governments, and the results have been conflicting, to say the least. Few scholars have attempted to compare policies in the context of exogenous factors such as level and rate of inflation and development or of political stability, which may influence the policy outputs of either type of regime. In an era of long-range programing for economic development, governments of developing countries are confronted with the difficult problem of selecting the best set of policies for the allocation of resources for economic growth while at the same time reconciling these policies to often more immediate demands of economic, social, and political realities.

These remarks should serve as a reminder that we are a long way from understanding the interface of economy and polity. The discussion of substitution effects, particularly by political scientists, should seek to explore that interface in terms of both the social and economic consequences of chosen policies and the political rationale behind the choices.

This article focuses on two basic questions posed in earlier research: (1) Do substitutions occur between military and economic and social spending categories? and (2) Do such substitutions occur more intensely under military than under civilian governments? The subject of research is Brazil, a representative of the developing world. In order to account for both the conflicting hypotheses presented in previous research and for political and economic conditions which exercise important influence on policy decisions in developing systems, the basic questions are modified by a subset of questions: (a) What influence has rapid development and inflation had on the pattern of policy outputs? (b) What has been the influence of the military on civilian policy decisions? and (c) Since much of the argument against military allocations is based on the assumption that the bulk of military expenditures goes toward the purchase of economically and socially unproductive equipment, what is the content of military outlays?

The Brazilian experience of the past twenty years offers a politically active military under both civilian and military governments and an intense focus on national development as a policy goal. At the same time, economic growth has been erratic and inflation-ridden, and political conditions have reflected institutional underdevelopment which has allowed traditional clientelist and status quo maintenance consideration to interfere with the pursuit of development goals. In these respects, the Brazilian experience, while unique in many ways, is not atypical of other developing countries, particularly in Latin America. The findings of the present study should therefore be suggestive of processes which occur elsewhere and of directions which future research may explore.

THE PROBLEM OF TRADEOFFS

EVIDENCE TO DATE

The guns-versus-butter tradeoff implies foregone opportunities, particularly in economic development and social welfare. The problem for the developing countries is stated in the UN report (1971: 29):

> Military expenditures undoubtedly absorb resources which are substantial enough to make a considerable difference both in the level of investment for civil purposes and in the volume of resources which can be devoted to improving man's lot through social and other services.

As noted above, much of the research on this substitution relation has been performed on the developed economies of Europe and North America. In a study of the costs of defense in the U.S. between 1938 and 1969, Bruce Russett concludes that each dollar increase in defense spending resulted in a subtraction of "forty-two cents from personal consumption spending, twenty-nine cents from fixed capital formation, ten cents from exports, five cents from federal government civilan programs and thirteen cents from state and local governments' activities" (Russett, 1970: 141). Unfortunately, Russett's analysis is distorted by the data of the World War II years in which percentage allocations to defense were two to three times larger than in other years. In a reanalysis of the data Hollenhorst and Ault (1971) divide the 1939-1968 series into three war periods plus peacetime. The majority of the significant negative tradeoff relationships occur in the World War II period. Other significant tradeoffs vary across the four periods, and in several instances negative relationships become positive. The authors conclude in answer to Russett's question, "Who Pays for Defense?" that

> in an "intense" war period [World War II], probably everyone pays. In peacetime, however, and in the "lesser" wars of the recent past [Korea, Vietnam], the consumer pays nearly the entire bill while the proportion of GNP consisting of state-local government expenditures and some types of

fixed investment expenditures have, at times, increased along with increases in defense spending [Hollenhorst and Ault, 1971: 762-763].

Russett himself, in a more detailed analysis (1971) which omits the World War II period, finds a substantial reduction in the number of significant substitution relationships.

For a variety of reasons, the U.S. is relatively atypical in both the pattern and content of its defense spending. While this in no way reduces the importance of the concern over possible negative tradeoffs with other program expenditures, it does make the U.S. case inappropriate as a model for cross-national hypothesis testing. Frederick Pryor (1968) performed an analysis similar to the Russett research using data from twelve countries in East and West Europe, plus the U.S. and Canada. In cross-sectional analysis of the fourteen countries in two different years he found no statistically significant substitution relationships (negative regression coefficients) in either year. Using time series data for 1950-1962, he found similar results: "Defense expenditures do not have a statistically significant relationship with non-military budgetary expenditures in any country" (1968: 122). Breaking down the non-military component into GNP aggregates (private consumption, domestic investment, domestic plus foreign investment, and current civilian government expenditures), he found extremely mixed relationships. Only in those countries with relatively high defense budget components were substitution relationships found, and only with current government civilian expenditures, excluding transfers. When transfers were included, no substitution relationships were found for the sample nations.

Eighty percent of world military expenditures is accounted for by six nations, five of which are included in the Pryor sample.[2] The finding that substitution relations occur only in those countries with high defense budgets is therefore striking. With one exception, none of the countries studied by Pryor would be classified as developing, but the UN notes that the military budgets of developing countries are increasing at almost twice the rate of the developed countries (UN, 1971: 19). Is the pattern of tradeoffs in the Third World similar to that of the developed countries? A recent study of the impact of defense on economic growth in a sample of forty-four developing states concluded, much to the author's surprise, that "the evidence simply did not allow one to conclude that any . . . adverse net effect on economic growth had occurred as a result of defense activities" (Benoit, 1973: xix). While Benoit's aggregate measure, economic growth, obscures some of the more critical issues of distribution of economic resources, the conclusion he draws suggests that we must question the assumptions with which we approach the problem of tradeoffs imposed by military allocations.

Most scholars studying the developing states have approached the guns-versus-butter question from a slightly different point of view—the comparison of policy outputs of military and civilian regimes and the consequences of militarism for modernization. Eric Nordlinger (1970: 1131-32) summarizes the "prevailing interpretation":

The likely consequences of military rule are economic growth, the modernization of economic and social structures and a more equitable distribution of scarce economic values and opportunities. As sponsors of these types of change soldiers in mufti are depicted as progressive forces, whose politicization is to be commended if not recommended, rather than being condemned as a surpation of civilian authority.

Nordlinger himself disagrees with this interpretation, arguing that "except under certain conditions (for example, particularly low levels of economic development and political mobilization) soldiers in mufti are not agents of modernization" but rather act in pursuance of their military corporate interests, and to protect "a particular type of political stability" and middle class interests and identities (1970: 1134).[3]

Schmitter (1971c) finds conflicting hypotheses in the literature on the impact of military intervention. (1) The military is dedicated to the preservation of order and maintenance of the social status quo. (2) The military is dedicated to national development goals including "important increments in the role of public authority in areas such as investment, health and education, income redistribution and industrial management." (3) "The military is only one of several groups competing for hegemony over the political system ... and the substance of policy-making is relatively indifferent to military or civilian hegemony" (430-2). Using both cross-sectional (1960) and longitudinal (1950-1968) data on a variety of political and economic indicators for 20 Latin American countries, Schmitter concludes that

indicators of overall system performance (outcomes) are much less predictably affected by regime-type or changes in regime-type than are indicators of direct governmental allocations (outputs) ... but "no regime-type seems to be exclusively responsible for developmental success" in Latin America. ... The military in power definitely tend to spend more on themselves—above all when they are on-again, off-again rulers. ... They seem to spend less on social welfare than ... civilian regimes. ... Civilian regimes definitely spend less on defense (where they are not plagued by frequent interruptions and threats) and more on welfare [492-3].

Both types of regimes have erratic records on public investment, a fact which Schmitter acknowledges is "probably due to vagaries in resource availability more than to internal dynamics ..." (493). Yet another author, examining Latin American data for 1960-1970, finds increased military appropriations more frequently associated with civilian rather than military regimes (Weaver, 1973: 100).

In sum, the evidence on the negative impact of military allocations in either developed or developing states is far less conclusive than Bruce Russett's emphatic "I assume that defense spending has to come at the expense of something else" (Russett, 1970: 133). To the extent that this generalization is correct, or sometimes correct, the evidence clearly suggests that the burden varies from country to country and that political (regime differences) and economic (levels and rates of development and of inflation) factors have important influence on the frequency, the locus (who pays), and the weight (degree of substitution) of the tradeoff burden.

CONCEPTUAL AND METHODOLOGICAL PROBLEMS

One of the reasons why we have such conflicting evidence on the relationships between guns and butter is that research has been performed at a high level of aggregation and across sets of countries which vary widely on the crucial variables—levels of development and types of regime. Working at this level, it is difficult to separate out the effects of individual variables. The economic focus of studies like Pryor's and Benoit's tends to overlook the role of political factors. Moreover, the emphasis on macroeconomic categories (GNP aggregates) places the question of policy choice in an arena which government decision-makers can control only imperfectly. Longitudinal studies rely on summary statistics which obscure sharp yearly variations, a serious problem when dealing with the erratic growth pattern of developing countries. Those studies which do attempt to assess political impacts on policy decisions by examining military-civilian regime-type differences overlook a wide variation of policy orientations within these two categories and, perhaps more importantly, overlook the many other ways (besides overt intervention) in which the military may wield influence (Weaver, 1973: 94-95).

In this analysis, we attempt to resolve some of these conceptual and methodological problems by focusing on a single country. Tradeoffs between military allocations, development-oriented allocations, and more traditional status quo and system maintenance allocations are examined. Data on these policies are derived from a line-by-line recoding of Brazilian federal expenditures (1950-1967) as presented in the General Balance of the Union.[4] By restricting the analysis to tradeoffs between government spending categories, we have only a limited capability to assess the burden of policy decisions for the whole economy, but we do have greater confidence that we are examining the impact of political choices on an arena over which decision-makers have control. The restricted arena also provides a greater opportunity to explore the causes and consequences of yearly variations in outputs, and to deal with differences between regime-types.

Development-oriented policies may cover both human and capital resource development. Within the available data on Brazilian expenditures, allocations to health, education, and welfare—social development allocations—reflect human resource development policies. Allocations to transportation, communication, industry, and agriculture—infrastructure development—reflect capital resource development policies. Allocations to the federal bureaucracy for salaries and administration provide the best indicator of the weight of traditional, clientelistic political relationships on the budget.[5] Military allocations provide a direct measure of the weight of the military sector. Previous analyses (Hayes, 1973a, 1973b) of the Brazilian data have suggested that these four expenditure categories are associated in substitution relationships. They are therefore used in this analysis to explore the pattern of these substitutions in depth. In order to provide mutually exclusive categories for the present study, the bureaucratic expenditures are limited to personnel expenditure for the civilian bureaucracy. Finally, military personnel[6] is separated from the military total in order to analyze the content of military allocations and to compare the behavior of the military and civilian bureaucratic components (see Appendix for detailed description of the contents of each category).

To explore the relationships between these allocation categories a variety of approaches, based on different assumptions as to the nature of the allocation process, are necessary. Previous research has focused primarily on the macroeconomic impact of military spending (Benoit, 1973; Pryor, 1968; Russett, 1969; 1970). Expenditure data were presented in ratio form (spending as percentage of GNP). This ratio variable assumes a zero-sum game in which increases in one category necessarily entail decreases in other categories.

The GNP ratio was selected by the authors in order to overcome the trend effect of serial correlation in their time series. Russett (1971: 30) explains the problem:

> [The data] appear as totals in current dollars, but cannot be used in bivariate regressions in that form. Through a combination of inflation and real productivity increases the total dollar value of the U.S. GNP grew by nearly a factor of ten over the period examined. Since virtually all of the components also increased sharply over the same period, we would have high, and for our purposes, spurious correlations between variables measured in current dollar amounts.

The same combination of inflation and productivity increases caused the Brazilian gross domestic product (GDP) to increase by a factor of over 250 in the shorter 1950-1967 period. Inflation accounted for approximately one-half of that increase. Discounting inflation, central government spending increased somewhat more rapidly than GDP. In the Brazilian data analyzed below, inflationary trend effects have been accounted for by using constant (1965-1967) cruzeiro values[7] for the expenditures, a method which allows the increased government resources to continue to operate in the allocation game.

Rather than a zero-sum game, the Brazilian allocation process is best described as an expanding-sum game. This means that negative shifts in the percentage allocation figures do not necessarily entail negative shifts in the absolute levels of allocation. In an economy and polity characterized by instability, increasing demands for social improvements and increasing need for infrastructure development, distributive solutions may be the only means by which governments can postpone confrontations and keep their tenuous supporting coalitions intact. Such solutions depend on the expanding game context in order to "give more while giving less." Assume, for example, a government with $100 to spend in year 1, and $200 in year 2. If 15% of the budget is allocated to both military and welfare in year 1, each sector gets $15. In year 2 a one-to-one percentage tradeoff occurs and military gets 20% of the total while welfare gets only 10%. Military receives $40, a substantial increase, but welfare gets $20, still an increase over the previous year. Only in percentage terms is welfare slighted. The government has given more to both categories while giving less in percentage terms. No one has "paid" in real terms for the greater amount given to the military. Only when the game fails to expand sufficiently do negative tradeoffs in real terms occur.

Demand also plays a role in the definition of the game context. Expenditures must increase at least proportionately to demand for the zero-sum game effect of negative tradeoffs in real terms not to occur. In the following analysis the expanding-sum game is examined in terms of (1) absolute levels of allocations, and (2) per capita levels, with the latter analysis reflecting growth in demand. The zero-sum game process is examined in terms of (3) allocations as percentage of federal expenditures and (4) allocations as percentage of gross domestic product. It is expected that the tradeoffs between military allocations and other programs will be different under these alternative assumptions.

A second methodological problem is presented by the correlation and regression coefficients utilized by the earlier researchers. These statistics do not adequately reflect the extreme volatility of allocations which may be expected in an unstable economy. At several points in his analysis Pryor observes that substitution relationships vary from country to country and time period to time period. Relationships also vary over time in the U.S. data (Hollenhorst and Ault, 1971).

Our earlier analyses of the Brazilian data have demonstrated that the major allocation categories receive what might be described as episodic attention, that is, a large increment in one year is followed by several years of declining allocations, then another large increment. This pattern is depicted in Figure 1. Allocations increase substantially over time, though the yearly variation is marked. This is particularly true of the personnel, infrastructure, and total expenditure categories. Total expenditures increase in a step-level pattern under each regime. The years of major increments to different categories are frequently staggered across the years of the regime's tenure. This pattern suggests that the combination of limited resources and unlimited demand forces a series of yearly tradeoffs which may balance out even in the very short run. Such shifting tradeoffs may not necessarily reflect the policy preferences of respective governments, but rather the influence of exogenous factors such as economic performance or political forces. To assume that military allocations must come at the expense of something else is misleading in these cases, since the tradeoff is shifted across categories from year to year and may balance out over time. By focusing on the year-to-year pattern of shifting relationships we can discover whether the pattern of substitution falls consistently heavily on one category or sporadically across several categories. Since either case would result in a negative regression coefficient, annual analysis will reveal more about the nature of the tradeoff and the distribution of tradeoff burdens than could be induced from the simple summary statistic.

FIGURE 1

Federal Allocations in Selected Policy Areas
by Regime - 1950-1967

(tens of trillions of 1965-67 Cruzeiros)

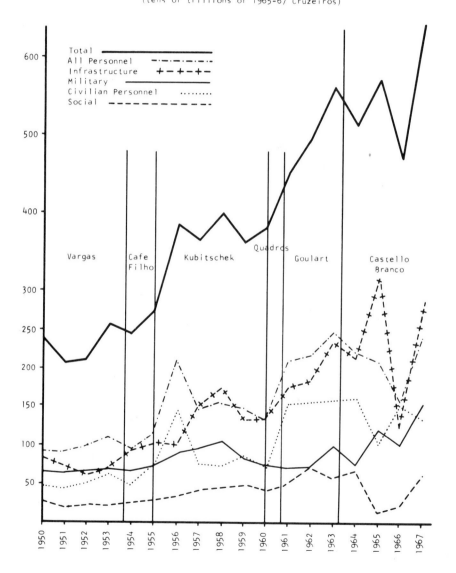

TRADEOFFS IN BRAZIL

THE PATTERN OF ALLOCATIONS—MULTIPLE GAME CONTEXTS

Figure 1 presents the pattern of allocations of Brazilian federal resources to four major expenditure categories—military, infrastructure development, social development, and personnel—from 1950 to 1967. Vertical lines in the graph indicate the different governments in office during the period and these will be compared in the subsequent analysis. The first five governments, Vargas, Café Filho, Kubitschek, Quadros, and Goulart, were elected civilian governments. The last government, that of Castello Branco, was the first of the military regime still in office. Two observations are necessary to clarify the regime breakdown. The expenditure data represent end-of-year (December 31) total expenditures, not budgets. Regime changes would normally occur in January; thus, the new executive would (1) inherit a budget passed by his predecessor administration, but (2) would have the entire year to alter it through authorization of extra-budgetary expenditures, or by substituting or adding according to his own policy preferences. In the graph the regime changes mark the end of the period over which a given government exercised fiscal authority. The occurrence of a suicide (August 1954), a resignation (August 1961), and a coup (March 31, 1964) somewhat beclouds the interpretation of the pattern in those years. The regime change is marked at the point at which it occurred, though the new executive may have had less authority over expenditures than he would have had, had he been in office for the whole year.[8]

Expenditures are presented in terms of level of allocations—an expanding-sum game—in Figure 1. The same data are shown in Figure 2 as percentage allocations (percent of total government expenditures)—a zero-sum game. The difference between the two game contexts is particularly evident in the case of military and infrastructure allocations. In Figure 2, infrastructure traces a pattern of steady growth interrupted by a single extreme deviation (1966, a year of obvious budgetary belt-tightening—note the decrease in total expenditures). In percentage terms, infrastructure allocations maintain a more constant pattern overall, but episodic tradeoffs with other categories are more marked (compare 1954, 1956, 1957, 1958, 1965, 1967). The distorting effect of the zero-sum game percentage computation is more apparent with military allocations. From a high of 33% in 1952, the percentage of government resources to the military declines steadily to 16% in 1962, after which it increases sharply, particularly under the military regime after 1964. However, these percentages are calculated on a sharply expanding total resource base. In absolute terms (Figure 1) military allocations maintain a more constant level under the civilian governments, rising sharply under the military.

It is interesting that the military component should begin to increase after 1962 under the Goulart government, which was ultimately overthrown by the military. Goulart, like other political leaders, required military backing in order

FIGURE 2

Percentage Allocations to Selected Policy Areas
by Regime - 1950-1967

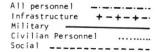

All personnel   — ·—·—·—·—··
Infrastructure   + — + — + —·
Military   ————————
Civilian Personnel ··········
Social   — — — — — — — —

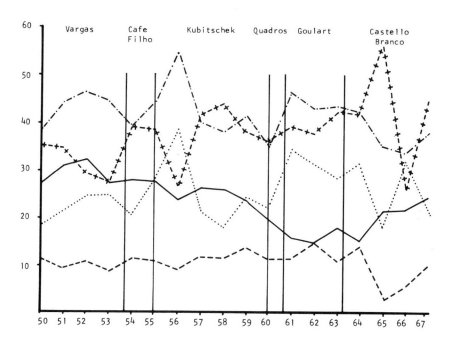

to rule, and he consciously courted officers who shared his political views. Parallel to his populist appeal to urban workers, he appealed to the non-commissioned ranks of the military. These policies were ultimately to work against him as they undermined the highly valued military norm of institutional solidarity (Schneider, 1971; Skidmore, 1967; Stepan, 1971). Nevertheless, the efforts to court the military are reflected, in part, in the expenditure data.

The substantial increase to the military after the 1964 coup would appear to confirm the thesis that military governments tend to prefer spending policies which serve their own interests (Nordlinger, 1970; Schmitter, 1971). The present data set would need to be extended in order to test this hypothesis more thoroughly. A rough approximation of the data used here, using military ministerial total expenditures as percent of total government spending, indicates, however, that the percentage increases to the military reached a high in 1967, declining by 2% per year through 1970. This evidence would tend to contradict the corporate interest hypothesis.

Schmitter's findings that military governments do tend to spend less on social development is supported by the Brazilian data. In the years immediately following the military coup, spending on social development was cut sharply. However, allocations to this category were not substantial under civilian regimes, either. Though expanding slightly in real terms, the percentage of total expenditure is both low and erratic. Viewed either as total amount of money or percent of federal spending, social development programs do not appear to have been high on the agenda of any regime.[9] This indicates something about the preference orderings of governments of rapidly developing countries. Ronald Schneider (1971: 69), commenting on the development goals of one administration notes that

> The policies of the Kubitschek administration [1956-1961] were, in their general outlines, a continuation of those initiated by Vargas, under whom both Kubitschek and Goulart [president, 1961-1963] had served their political apprenticeships. In the domestic field, the policies were directed primarily toward accelerated economic development, with control of the exploitation of natural resources retained in Brazilian hands. *Only secondarily were they concerned with improved social welfare programs for the workers.* [Emphasis added]

The Goulart government, appealing for the support of the urban working classes, attempted to rectify poor social conditions, as indicated by the sharp increase in social allocations in 1962 and 1963. In the process, however, he antagonized conservative and middle-class elements which ultimately lent support to the military coup in 1964.

Comparison of the pattern of allocations to all personnel and civilian personnel (Figure 1) provides another view of the policies pursued by the several regimes. After a sharp increase in 1956, civilian personnel allocations drop sharply, almost back to 1955 levels, while the total personnel allocation figure remains high between 1957 and 1960. The difference is due to the military component which continued to increase under the Kubitschek administration. A similar pattern is seen between 1961 and 1964. In 1961 a major increment was allocated to personnel. The civilian personnel category remains stable at the 1961 level, however, while the total reaches a new peak in 1963. Again, the difference is due to the military personnel component.

The pattern of allocations to the personnel categories is particularly important. Personnel expenditures account for a substantial portion of total government allocations. In the Brazilian context patronage and spoils played a major role in traditional politics and the courting of the federal bureaucracy was an important political activity. The military, with its own bureaucracy and clientele, was an equally active participant in this game. One way of insuring the political support of the civilian and military bureaucracies was by granting large wage increases. These were frequently far in excess of cost-of-living increases (Kahil, 1973).

Because of the zero-sum game effect, tradeoffs are most evident in Figure 2, the graph of percentage allocations. Tradeoffs are particularly marked between infrastructure and civilian personnel and between military and both development categories as indicated by the movement of these categories in opposite directions from year to year. Tradeoffs between military and civilian personnel occur almost annually. Social development and infrastructure development demonstrate marked divergences in 1954-1955 and 1963-1966. Military and the two development programs move in opposite directions, with military declining and development increasing between 1950 and 1962 and military and infrastructure increasing and social development decreasing through 1966.

The differences between the two game contexts, represented graphically in Figures 1 and 2, are demonstrated statistically in Tables 1a to 1c. The correlation of the absolute levels of allocation values, representing the expanding-sum context, are presented in Table 1a. With the exception of three relationships, the intercorrelation of the variables is strong to very strong, and all variables are highly correlated with time, reflecting the growth trend. (The lower social development value is due to the two deviations in 1965 and 1966. When these are omitted, the correlation of the variable and time rises to .93.)

It was argued above that the rapid expansion of both the whole economy and the federal sector had an important influence on the allocation process, defining this as an expanding sum game rather than a zero-sum game. A comparison of the values in Table 1a with those in 1b, in which growth is held constant by regressing the variables on time and correlating the residuals, indicates the degree

TABLE 1A

Correlations of Levels of Allocation

	Total Expenditures	Military	Social Development	Infrastructure Development	Civilian Personnel	Military Personnel
Military	.75*					
Social Development	.62ᐟ	.21				
Infrastructure Development	.91*	.73*	.49*			
Civilian Personnel	.81*	.39*	.66*	.57*		
Military Personnel	.86*	.95*	.31	.83*	.50*	
Year	.95*	.71	.56	.82	.79	.80

*Significant < .05

to which the growth factor was operative. While the absolute values are all positively associated, the residual correlations in 1b demonstrate that only the very strong correlations of 1a reflect non-tradeoff situations. Military spending is negatively related to both social development (though weakly, explaining only 4% of variation) and to civilian personnel (moderately, explaining 24% of variation). Some tradeoffs do occur between these categories. Only civilian personnel is negatively related to infrastructure development. Military and infrastructure spending are positively related. This supports the earlier observation that all regimes have placed a priority on infrastructure development policies.

The pattern in Figure 2 is represented statistically in Table 1c in which each allocation category is computed as percentage of total government expenditures. With the exception of social development and civilian personnel, all relationships are negative. Significant (<.05) substitutions occur with the personnel categories (cf., civilian personnel-military personnel, and civilian personnel-infrastructure development). These correlations confirm that substitution relationships do exist between military and other major allocation categories. However, we need to pay close attention to the pattern of burden of the substitutions. Figures 1 and 2 indicate that military allocations were characterized by a dominant downward trend from 1950 to 1963 and then by an erratic shift upward. Therefore, it may be that military rather than other categories paid the cost of tradeoffs in this period, with the reverse holding true for the 1962-1967 period. Moreover, the correlation matrices indicate that personnel allocations are also involved in substantial and significant substitution relations. In the context of the highly personalist Brazilian political situation, dominated by a traditional and highly clientelistic bureaucracy, these personnel-related substitutions may well be the more interesting in terms of explaining the pattern and cause of tradeoffs.

TABLE 1B

Correlation of Residuals of Allocations

	Military	Social Development	Infrastructure Development	Civilian Personnel
Social Development	-.19			
Infrastructure Development	.44*	.17		
Civilian Personnel	-.48*	.40*	-.30	
Military Personnel	.91*	-.25	.47*	-.43*

*Significant < .05

TABLE 1C

Correlation of Allocations as Proportion
of Total Government Expenditures

	Military	Social Development	Infrastructure Development	Civilian Personnel
Social Development	-.23			
Infrastructure Development	-.29	-.08		
Civilian Personnel	-.48	.12	-.46*	
Military Personnel	.94*	-.28	-.23	-.55*

*Significant < .05

Drawing from the above analyses and other regression analyses not reported here, some conclusions can be ventured as to the general nature of the tradeoffs identified.

(1) The results of the analysis of tradeoffs are clearly influenced by the assumptions made as to the nature of the allocation game. If an expanding-sum game is assumed, increases in total spending over time are sufficiently great to override tradeoffs which occur in percentage terms.

(2) The pattern of growth is quite erratic. No pattern of predictable incrementalism appears. It can be assumed that other factors interfere with the process of steady increase in allocations. These may be economic—as decision-makers attempt to cope with inflation—or political, reflecting attempts to respond to the needs or demands of different constituencies.

(3) Allocations to social development have received less priority than allocations to infrastructure development. In the expanding-sum game they increase minimally in relation to military allocations. They do not increase sufficiently to meet demand, even in the expanding context. A negative substitution occurs between social and military spending if a zero-sum game is assumed. A slightly stronger correlation between social development and previous year military allocations and between changes in allocation levels between these two categories suggests that they may receive emphasis in alternate years.

(4) Infrastructure allocations, particularly those reflecting increased cen-

tral government economic activity, are strongly positively associated with increases in military spending. Only when allocations are analyzed within the limits of the central government resource base do tradeoffs occur between these two categories.

(5) Allocations to civilian personnel are the most severely restricted by increases in military allocations.

(6) Only in the context of a zero-sum game within the federal government resource base do tradeoffs emerge in all categories. This reinforces the notion that the Brazilian allocation process is more appropriately identified as an expanding rather than a zero-sum game.

YEARLY TRADEOFFS: ANALYSIS OF THE FREQUENCY AND WEIGHT OF BURDENS

Because of the extreme volatility of the allocation categories, correlation and regression analysis cannot reflect, except at a very general level, the shifting pattern of tradeoffs clearly seen in Figures 1 and 2. The coefficients presented in Table 1 indicated that the allocation categories do not vary closely together. This makes the coefficients highly unstable. In an analysis of tradeoffs between categories, one or two years of severe deviation can bias regression functions in a negative direction, disguising more general tendencies toward expansion. In discussing the pattern of tradeoffs in a volatile political and economic situation, greater focus is needed on the short-term periodic shifts of emphasis between allocation categories. These may reflect shifts in policy preferences, or the play of political and economic tensions and constraints upon policy-makers, or both. The shifting pattern and its causes may be better understood through analysis of yearly and short-run cumulative patterns of increases, decreases, and tradeoffs.

In order to provide an alternative to the regression coefficient for measuring the relative weight of the substitution in individual years and over time, I have devised a measure of the proportion of the absolute change in categories which can be attributed to identified tradeoffs. The measure assumes an expanding-sum game. If two categories increase from one year to the next, it can be assumed that no tradeoffs have occurred between them. If both decrease, it can be assumed that some third category received greater resources and that the tradeoff occurred between that category and the two categories being examined, rather than between them. In these two cases, tradeoffs are not computed.

Tradeoffs are identified by the movement of two categories in opposite directions. The category to which allocations are decreased is the one which is "burdened" by the substitution. The measure is designed to reflect the "weight" of burden based on the percentage of change which can be attributed to the tradeoff between the two categories. The measure is calculated by the following formula:

$$\text{Burden} = 1 - \frac{\text{absolute difference in observed change}}{\text{sum of absolute observed change}}$$

The formula itself does not identify the direction of burden. This is identified by the negative change from one year to the next in one of the two categories. The negative sign is therefore not needed in the formula and the smaller absolute value is subtracted from the larger in the numerator. The final value measures the burden as the proportion of total change involved in substitution between the two categories. Values range between 0 and 1.00.

As an example, suppose that military expenditures increase $30 over the previous year while social development decreases by $20 in the same period. The formula is computed:

$$\left[1 - \frac{30 - 20}{30 + 20}\right] = \left[1 - \frac{10}{50}\right] = \left[1 - .20\right] = .80$$

Eighty percent of the total change in social development and military allocations is accounted for by the tradeoff between the two categories, and social development is the burdened category. The measure can be calculated for one, two, or more years. Using it, individual governments and regimes can be compared with respect to the way in which they distribute the burden of tradeoffs.

The results of the analysis of the distribution of tradeoff burdens using this measure are presented in Tables 2a and 2b. The matrix of major program variables provides six combinations in which tradeoffs may occur. Thus military is paired with social development, infrastructure development, and civilian personnel; social development is paired with infrastructure development and civilian personnel, and infrastructure is paired with civilian personnel. In addition, the personnel component of military, an indicator of the content of military allocations, is compared with civilian bureaucracy allocations. In Table 2a burdens are measured on an annual basis. Table 2b measures burdens on a cumulative two-year moving average base. The data presented in this latter table show whether or not the pattern of shifting allocations evens out the burden imposed on the individual categories in the annual calculation. Each table includes a computation of the average weight of burden between each pair of categories. These figures indicate which category pairs are most severely involved in tradeoff relationships.

Tradeoffs occur almost annually. Table 2a indicates that only in 1962 does no tradeoff occur at all. In 1955, the only tradeoff is between civilian and military personnel and the weight of that substitution is negligible. From Figure 1 we see that 1955 and 1962 were both years of expansion of the allocation game as represented by increments to total expenditures. Other years of expansion do involve tradeoffs, however, indicating that even in the expanding game some sectors pay the price of the expansion of others. Tradeoffs are least frequent between 1960 and 1963, the years of the Quadros and Goulart governments and the only period not characterized by the jagged pattern of expansion and contraction of total federal spending. That period was also one of severe inflation, against which Brazilian policy-makers had decided not to apply

TABLE 2A

Analysis of Tradeoffs: Percentage Burden Accounted for by Tradeoffs (Annual Base)

	Military-Social Development	Military-Infrastructure Development	Military-Civilian Personnel	Infrastructure-Social Development	Civilian Personnel-Social Development	Civilian Personnel-Infrastructure Development	Civilian-Military Personnel
1950-51	16	10	26	—	—	—	78*
1951-52	—	41	—	49*	—	86	2
1952-53	12	—	58	4	—	87*	68*
1953-54	76*	24*	—	—	59*	69*	—
1954-55	—	—	—	—	—	—	.54
1955-56	—	30	—	74*	—	8	—
1956-57	—	—	24	—	21*	83*	15*
1957-58	—	—	78	—	69*	39*	61*
1958-59	25*	—	73*	16*	—	51	83
1959-60	—	73*	—	76	—	51*	—
1960-61	66*	19*	10*	—	—	—	5
1961-62	—	—	—	—	—	—	—
1962-63	70	—	—	41	44	—	—
1963-64	93*	—	33*	66*	—	15	13
1964-65	77	—	76	69	—	69*	77*
1965-66	66*	—	67*	11*	—	37	50
1966-67	—	—	42	—	59*	17*	76*
Total Number of Tradeoffs	9	6	10	9	5	12	12
Average Weight of Tradeoffs	.2949	.1167	.2883	.2392	.1489	.3619	.3113

*Indicates first-named category is burdened in tradeoff.

monetary controls (Kahil, 1973; Skidmore, 1967). The other periods were characterized by vacillation between policies intended to stimulate growth and those designed to contain inflation. This indecision is reflected in the sawtooth pattern of total expenditures in Figure 1 and is responsible in part for the frequency of tradeoffs found in the annual data.

The data in Table 2a indicate that the burden of tradeoffs falls quite inconsistently. Even in years of successive tradeoffs, the burden is shifted back and forth between categories. This is true even in the period of most frequent and most severe tradeoffs, that of the military regime of 1964-67. The overall pattern would appear to represent a policy of socialization of burden.[10] That is, rather than subtracting resources from a single category to provide them to other areas, the additional funds are obtained by extracting them from several sectors and distributing both the costs and pay-offs across the categories and over time. Each sector thus pays the price of some tradeoff, but has an expectation of being "favored" in the next round. Such a policy would be consistent with the bargaining practices imposed by the heterogeneous coalitions which traditionally have formed governments in the Brazilian experience (Anderson, 1967; Kenworthy, 1970; Skidmore, 1967).

Civilian personnel is the category most frequently involved in tradeoffs. The pairs civilian personnel-infrastructure development and civilian personnel-military personnel are each involved in tradeoffs in 12 of 17 years. Military and civilian personnel are involved in tradeoffs in 10 of 17 years. Social development follows with substitutions occurring between infrastructure development and military in 9 years. Military and infrastructure are the least frequently related in substitutions, with only 6 of 17 years involving tradeoffs for the pair.

Tradeoffs are much less frequent when calculated over a two-year base. Civilian personnel is again the most frequently paired in substitutions in Table 2b. In 8 years out of a possible 16, tradeoffs occur with infrastructure and in 7 of 16 they occur with military personnel and military. Substitutions also occur between military and social development (8 of 16 years) and military and infrastructure (7 of 16). Social development appears to be, overall, the least frequently involved in tradeoffs in the two-year calculations.

Tradeoffs are both most frequent and most severe when compared on the annual basis. The average weight of the tradeoff burden, presented at the foot of each column of the tables, provides an indication of the overall severity of the observed substitutions. In five of the seven comparisons the average value of tradeoffs, or average severity of burden, is greatest in the simultaneous comparisons. The civilian personnel-social development and military-infrastructure development averages indicate the least severe simultaneous burdens. These each increase in the two-year average computation. For the other categories, the two-year average results in the less severe average burden. These figures support the argument made earlier that, given the staggered pattern of increments to categories imposed by limited resources, there is a tendency for the tradeoff burden to balance out over time. The data suggest that the time period in which

TABLE 2B

Analysis of Tradeoffs: Percentage Burden Accounted for by Tradeoff (Two-Year Moving Average Base)

	Military-Social Development	Military-Infrastructure Development	Military-Civilian Personnel	Infrastructure-Social Development	Civilian Personnel-Social Development	Civilian Personnel-Infrastructure Development	Civilian-Military Personnel
1950-52	82%	25	—	—	75	22	—
1951-53	—	56	—	79*	—	78	—
1952-54	.27*	5*	8	—	43*	74*	53
1953-55	—	—	—	—	—	—	—
1954-56	—	—	—	—	—	—	—
1955-57	—	—	—	—	—	—	—
1956-58	—	—	40	—	26*	99*	40*
1957-59	59*	—	70*	55*	—	66	91
1958-60	—	—	14*	—	87	12	18
1959-61	28*	42*	29*	—	—	—	16
1960-62	9*	4*	2*	—	—	—	—
1961-63	—	—	—	—	—	—	—
1962-64	25	—	—	14	55	—	43
1963-65	72	—	63	69	—	79*	—
1964-66	41	22	96	—	—	—	70*
1965-67	—	95	—	84*	—	91	—
Total Number of Tradeoffs	8	7	8	5	5	8	7
Average Weight of Tradeoffs	.2145	.1561	.2016	.1888	.1794	.3272	.2067

*Indicates first-named category is burdened in tradeoff.

such shifts of burden occur is indeed quite short, involving only a two-year time span.

POLICY PREFERENCES AND TRADEOFFS OF REGIMES

The irregular patterns of policy outputs observed in the discussion up to this point can only be understood in the context of two contrapuntal forces—one political, the other economic—which exercised increasing influence over the policy arena. Rapid economic change after World War II made increasing demands on the government for well-informed and authoritative decisions. Meanwhile, the political system—the result of a long succession of tenuous compromises between the traditional conservative oligarchy and emerging middle class elements—was geared more to maintenance of the status quo and either "distributive-cooptive-" or "non-" decision-making. While new forces jockeyed for new positions of power and influence, the heterogeneous incumbent coalition proved either reluctant to change the existing power structure, or lacked the imagination to change it. In short, it was inefficient. As its inefficiency became more apparent, particularly through inability to deal with economic problems, the legitimacy of the system was called increasingly into question.

Getúlio Vargas was the most important architect of the contemporary period, for it was he who forged the successful coalition of military, urban working class, and middle class and government bureaucracy which presided over Brazil between 1946 and 1964. His tenure in office, both as dictator of the Estado Novo (1937-1945) and as president (1951-1954), was firmly based on the political support provided by these sectors. During his presidency he set in motion some of the powerful forces which contributed to the economic growth and the increasing political instability of subsequent years. He adopted an increasingly friendly attitude toward urban workers. At the same time, he stimulated industrialization through creation of national development banks and sponsorship of state-owned basic industries and comprehensive economic recuperation plans. Vargas' suicide in August 1954 occurred at a moment of extreme political and economic crisis which threatened to destroy the coalition. The interim Café Filho government adopted a conservative political and economic stance, hoping to weather the storm.

The next president, Juscelino Kubitschek (1956-1960) represented the right side of the political spectrum within the Vargas coalition. Backed politically by conservative rural interests and courting business and government constituents, he emphasized rapid industrialization—"50 years progress in 5"—and increased government participation in the economy. Following the brief presidency of Jânio Quadros, who resigned in August 1961 after less than eight months in office, João Goulart assumed the presidency (1961-1964). Goulart represented the left of the coalition's political spectrum. As Vargas' protege in the early 1950s, his policies as labor minister had contributed to the crisis which led to the 1954 suicide. As Vargas' heir apparent, he was elected vice-president under both Kubitschek and Quadros. His most vocal support came from the urban working classes through the increasingly radical labor syndicates.

Throughout the 1950-1964 period the Vargas coalition remained intact as an electoral force, but internal cracks began to appear. Kubitschek sponsored an increasing centralization and technocratization in an attempt to mold a decision-making structure dependent on himself rather than on the old coalition, but he antagonized the bureaucratic establishment in the process (Lafer, 1970). Goulart's rhetoric was characterized by greater emphasis on social issues and the redistribution of the benefits of economic development to the lower classes, and he provided free rein to radical elements in the labor and education ministries as he attempted to mobilize support for his issues (Erickson, 1970; Schmitter, 1971; Skidmore, 1967). Jânio Quadros was the only president elected without support of the Vargas machine and his successful campaign was a vociferous attack on the corruption of the system which the machine controlled.

Various reasons have been given for the military coup of 1964. Some scholars regard it as an effort to reassert the conservative wing of the Vargas coalition, strengthening the alliance of military, middle-class businessmen and technocrats against the labor wing (Erickson, 1970; Schmitter, 1971a, 1971b). Others regard the military government as a new configuration, a praetorian response to the corruption, economic chaos, and political radicalization of the coalition's politics (Schneider, 1971; Stepan, 1971; O'Donnell, 1973). In any case, the military regime has reduced the scope and intensity of political bargaining by the various sectors of the old coalition and has concentrated attention on the development of the economy.

This brief discussion of recent Brazilian history has demonstrated that each regime emphasized a different ordering of policy preferences in its efforts to mobilize support within different sectors of the national political spectrum and within and without the traditional coalition. Are these shifting emphases observable in the pattern of policy outputs of the different regimes, or were they only rhetoric? Do different regimes, and particularly the military and civilian regimes, ·differ in their policy emphases? Do tradeoffs occur more intensely under the military than under the civilian governments, particularly between military and development-oriented categories? Does the military pursue policies with respect to itself which differ from the military policies of civilian governments?

Tables 3a to 3c provide data for the discussion of these questions. In 3a the average percentage of expenditures devoted to each category by each regime is presented. Table 3b presents the total and average annual increment which each regime provided to each category. The measure of tradeoffs between the categories under each regime is given in 3c. For convenience, the interim Café Filho government is included with the Vargas government and the Quadros and Goulart presidencies are combined.

Table 3a confirms the earlier contention that all regimes have given priority to national development with prime emphasis on infrastructure development.

TABLE 3A

Average Percentage of Expenditures to Major Allocation Categories by Regime

	Military	Social Development	Infrastructure Development	Civilian Personnel	Military Personnel
Vargas	.30	.10	.34	.23	.20
Kubitschek	.25	.11	.37	.24	.18
Quadros-Goulart	.17	.12	.40	.31	.13
Castello Branco	.22	.09	.42	.22	.16

The largest portion of each regime's average expenditures were devoted to that category. Moreover, the commitment of resources to infrastructure development grew not only incrementally (parallel to growth of federal spending overall), but also absolutely. Each successive regime devoted a greater percentage of its total resources to infrastructure development, with an increase from 34% under Vargas to 42% under Castello Branco.

Allocations to social development increased steadily in absolute emphasis under the civilian governments, but are severely penalized under the military.[11] Even under civilian governments, however, social spending did not command an impressive portion of government resources. The Goulart government, which would have been anticipated to spend considerably more on social items, did not provide a substantial increment over the previous administration's level.

Under the civilian governments, increased allocations to social and infrastructure development occurred at the expense of the military. An overall decrease of 13% occurs between the Vargas and Quadros-Goulart regimes. From Figure 2 we know that Vargas devoted a particularly high percentage of his resources to the military. The relative share of monies going to the military declined steadily after a 1952 high. The military government managed to recoup some of that loss by 1967, but rough calculations extending the data through 1970 indicate that the military percentage between 1964 and 1970 would be slightly lower than the 22% figure given in the table. Military personnel also declined in percentage terms under the civilian governments, though not as substantially as total military expenditure.

Allocations to civilian personnel increased substantially under civilian governments, and particularly during the three-year Quadros-Goulart period. Interestingly, in spite of the very sizable increment to civilian personnel in 1956, the overall average for the Kubitschek government is only slightly higher than the average civilian personnel allocation of the previous government. Average allocations to the civilian bureaucracy reached their lowest point under the military government, due to the drastic cuts in 1965 and 1967. The movement of this category again reflects the nature of political bargaining in Brazil. Civilian regimes were more dependent on patronage for support. The military, independent of the political in-fighting of the old coalition, could afford to ignore demands of the bureaucracy. From Figure 1, it appears that one of the first activities of each new regime was to raise bureaucratic salaries. In this way political campaign debts were paid off. Since the incumbent president could not succeed himself, once his debts were paid he could shift allocations from the bureaucracy to other sectors, allowing demands for new increases to accumulate for the next regime. The result of this practice was the series of severe tradeoffs for civilian personnel allocations which was seen in Tables 2a and 2b.

In an expanding game context these percentage shifts need not entail decreases or tradeoffs in real terms. Table 3b indicates that most categories received increments under all regimes and that the only deviations from this pattern occur in the personnel categories. The Vargas-Café Filho regime was the most conservative in its policy of expanding government spending, as indicated in the final column of the table. The greatest increases occurred under Kubitschek and Quadros-Goulart, with the military again conservative until 1967. Some of the tradeoffs which occur under the military government must be attributed to the strict measures applied to control the inflation caused by the rapid expansion between 1956 and 1963.

The data again indicate that infrastructure development was a priority policy area under all regimes. The three civilian governments all provided the largest increments to infrastructure development. Under the military regime this category received second priority, after increases to the military itself. Social expenditures received second priority under Vargas and Kubitschek, though the gap between the average increment to social programs and that to infrastructure widens in the latter administration. Social development received its largest real increment under the Quadros-Goulart government, but compared with the average increment provided to other sectors by that regime, it appears to have had the lowest priority.

Quadros-Goulart provided the most substantial increases to the personnel categories. This pattern can be understood in the context of the very unstable coalition supporting Goulart. The greater allocations may be attributed to his need to court support among the established political forces (see Nascimento, 1966, on the political bargaining which accompanied the wage law of 1963; also, Kahil, 1973; Skidmore, 1967). Under Kubitschek and Castello Branco, there occurred a net subtraction of resources to the bureaucracy. This pattern is surprising in the case of Kubitschek who was frequently cited for promoting bureaucratic corruption and patronage pay-offs (Graham, 1968; Skidmore, 1967). Castello Branco embarked on an extensive program of administrative reform, and, because of the military's unique power position, was in a better position to impose sanctions on the bureaucratic establishment. Each regime was also careful to provide increases to military personnel. These increase in size with each successive administration, paralleling the increasing tension within the military over the political direction which the country was taking (Schneider, 1971; Skidmore, 1967; Stepan, 1971).

The military government did indeed favor allocations to itself over other

TABLE 3B

Total Increase to Allocation Categories and Average Annual Increase by Regime
[Values in tens of trillions of constant (1965-1967) cruzeiros]

	Military	Social Development	Infrastructure Development	Civilian Personnel	Military Personnel	Total Expenditures
Vargas	+107,72 (21.14)	+180,70 (36.14)	+201,34 (40.27)	90,92 (18.18)	16,18 (3.20)	341,44
Kubitschek	+29,78 (5.96)	+135,98 (27.20)	+326,45 (65.29)	-18,89 (-3.78)	+114,83 (22.97)	1073,62
Quadros-Goulart	+234,49 (78.16)	+171,22 (57.07)	+991,38 (330.46)	847,68 (282.56)	+300,51 (100.71)	1800,11
Castello Branco	+586,54 (146.63)	+44,83 (11.21)	468,04 (117.01)	-249,72 (-62.43)	191,42 (47.85)	804,18

policy areas, and especially at the expense of the civilian bureaucracy. Schmitter's conclusion that military regimes devote more to defense when in power on an "on-again-off-again" basis (Schmitter, 1971: 493) should be recalled in interpreting this pattern. In the first years after taking power, the architects of the coup were not yet entirely committed to long-term military rule (Stepan, 1971). They were, however, interested in recouping prestige and material losses which they had suffered under the recent civilian governments.

Overall, the evidence in Table 3b suggests that regimes did attempt to provide, at least minimally, for all of their program constituents. Table 3c indicates that at the regime level, the tendency for a socialization of burden, seen in Tables 2a and 2b is even more evident. Of a possible 28 comparisons (7 categories times 4 regimes), tradeoffs occur in only 4. Two—between civilian personnel and social development, and civilian personnel and military—occur under Kubitschek and are the result of the 1956 increase to personnel. The other two involve the same categories and occur under the Castello Branco regime. The simultaneous and moving average comparisons in Tables 2a and 2b also reflected the tendency for tradeoffs to be more severe under the military government. This is not surprising, since the critical economic situation required severe measures. Moreover, the military, ruling with extraordinary powers, was more able to impose sanctions without reaping the political consequences which plagued the democratic governments.

An interesting piece of information can be gained from the comparison of the average allocations to military personnel and to the military. Under the Vargas and Castello Branco governments total military received substantially more than did military personnel. This indicates that a greater portion of military expenditures was devoted to purchases of equipment and construction. Under Kubitschek and Quadros-Goulart the client category—military personnel—received greater attention. The greater expenditure for equipment on the part of the military government is directly relevant to one of the major issues raised in this paper: Do military governments pursue policies designed to aggrandize military corporate interests at the expense of national social and economic interests? Based on the evidence presented in Tables 3a and 3b, the answer with respect to economic development and investment in the economic infrastructure is No. It is clear, however, that social development had a low priority and was cut substantially in percentage terms.

Civilian regimes tended to allocate resources away from the military to other programs, but they reduced military personnel allocations less than they reduced total military allocations. The personnel share of military expenditures ranged from 62% (1955) to 87%. This last figure occurs in 1963 under the Goulart government at a time when the higher echelon military was rapidly coalescing against the government and the President was courting the support of enlisted personnel (Nascimento, 1966; Skidmore, 1967; Stepan, 1971). Under the military government, while total military allocations increased, the personnel portion dropped to 68% (1967). The military government therefore apparently

TABLE 3C

Analysis of Tradeoffs: Percentage of Burden Accounted for by Tradeoff (Regime Base)

	Military-Social Development	Military-Infrastructure Development	Military-Civilian Personnel	Infrastructure-Social Development	Civilian Personnel-Social Development	Civilian Personnel-Infrastructure Development	Civilian-Military Personnel
Vargas 1950-55	—	—	—	—	—	—	—
Kubitschek 1956-60	—	—	78	—	25*	—	—
Quadros-Goulart 1961-63	—	—	—	—	—	—	—
Castello Branco 1964-67	—	—	60	—	30*	—	—

*Indicates first-named category is burdened in tradeoff.

spent more on hardware and construction, items directly relevant to the military's institutional prestige and corporate interest. It is expenditures of this type—the guns of military expenditures—which are relevant in the discussion of foregone opportunities in civil investment and social improvements. While the manpower costs to the whole economy may be substantial in terms of skilled labor lost to trade and industry (see Benoit, 1973: 101-112 on this problem in a comparative context, and Stepan, 1971, Ch. 1 for application to Brazil), the wage, pension, and special privilege structure of the Brazilian military allows military personnel to maintain standards of living at least equivalent to and probably better than (especially in the case of officers) those of their working-class and middle-class civilian counterparts. Overall, the content of military allocations, given the high percentage of resources devoted to personnel, does not give cause for undue alarm over increasing military expenditures in Brazil, at least in the terms expressed by the U.N. Secretary General, which focused on the unbeneficial aspects of weapons purchases and arms races.

CONCLUSION

In this analysis we have probed the relationships between military spending and spending in other sectors of social, economic, and political importance for the developing country. We began with a research tradition which assumed that military spending was "bad" but which did not convincingly demonstrate this with empirical evidence. In adapting the research tradition, based largely on the post-industrial, major power experience of Europe and the United States, to an industrializing, minor power context, we have had to reconsider several of the basic concepts, assumptions, and operationalizations concerning the nature of the political and economic game, the role of the military as an actor in that game, and the likely applications and consequences of military allocations in the developing world.

Theoretical generalizations cannot be made and hypotheses cannot be accepted or rejected on the basis of evidence from a single case. The findings of this study should therefore be seen as tentative and as a base on which future comparisons, in other contexts, can be built. The accumulated evidence may then allow us authoritatively to answer the questions, "Does military spending have negative consequences for economic and social investment?" and, "Does the presence of a military government exacerbate that negative relationship?"

The evidence presented here from the Brazilian experience indicates that, for that case, the answer to both these questions is a qualified "no." We found that substitutions between military allocations and allocations to other sectors do occur frequently, but that the burden of these substitutions are distributed across all categories at one time or another. As a result, substitutions are not severe. Overall, increased military spending accompanied substantial increases in spending for infrastructure development and aspects of this associated with greater central government activity (for example, industrial investment and direct government investment). On the other hand, increased military spending had some negative effect on social spending, but this was mild because social investment was not a major priority of any of the regimes examined. It was found that military allocations was the category least frequently burdened in tradeoffs, but that when tradeoffs did occur, the burden for the military was often severe.

Tradeoffs occurred frequently and were very severe under the military regime of Castello Branco, but again, they were distributed across all categories. Moreover, tradeoffs occurred with equal frequency and severity under the Kubitschek administration, a civilian government. We cannot conclude on this evidence that the military government in Brazil was more inclined to reallocate resources in directions unfavorable to national social and economic development.

Both rapid development and inflationary expansion played important roles in the allocation game, defining it as an expanding sum game over time. This allowed governments to distribute minimal increments to all categories at the same time as they concentrated major increases to the critical area of infrastructure development. The expanding game would have permitted even greater attention to economic and social development if political considerations had not periodically required a substantial reallocation of development funds into the civilian and military personnel categories. The military government was more able to impose sanctions on the civilian personnel category, but civilian governments could ignore neither, since they depended on both bureaucracies for electoral support, and in many cases were directly dependent on the military hierarchy to guarantee their tenure in office. After appropriate pay-offs were made to their respective clienteles, and if we consider their different policies with respect to inflation (civilian governments were content to work with inflation, whereas the military government was committed to control it), military and civilian governments do not appear to have differed substantially in policy preferences. It was noted especially that the military did not differ greatly from civilian governments on the content of military expenditures. Both regime types allocated the majority of military funds to personnel. The content of military expenditures were therefore found not to be inimical to civilian national development interests.

These findings for the Brazilian case should not be surprising. A broad literature provides evidence that the developing country military is a much more political actor than its post-industrial counterpart. As a result, the military is more likely to be involved in national decision-making and to be subject to the sanctions, or tradeoffs, imposed by shifts in a generally unstable political landscape. Moreover, because of the different role of the military in the developing country context, and because of generally scarcer resources, it is unlikely that large portions of military budgetary allocations will be devoted to overtly "defense"-oriented applications as is the case for the industrialized state. Rather, military allocations are likely to be applied to ends which reinforce the political position of the armed services. Yet a third consideration suggested in the literature on the military in the developing context is that military corporate interests and civilian national goals are not as divergent in the developing state as they may be in the post-industrial state. Given the middle-class origins and strong instrumental and technocratic orientation to problem-solving of the developing-country military, military corporate interest may be increasingly defined in terms of national economic development and industrialization—terms identical to those of many of the military's civilian counterparts. We should not forget that the Brazilian military intervention of 1964 was not without its civilian supporters.

If military and civilian regimes do not differ extensively in their economic goals and policy outputs, it does not mean that they do not differ politically, and particularly in terms of policies toward political expression. Between 1950 and 1964 the Brazilian political situation was one of praetorian populism and "politics" contributed heavily to economic chaos. The military coup of 1964 ushered in an era of authoritarianism with an unquestionable negative impact on political freedoms, but an equally unquestionable positive impact on economic growth. The evidence presented has suggested that military and civilian regimes may be quite similar on the issue of growth and this similarity is reflected in their spending policies. Where they may differ radically is on the issue of politics, and this is not reflected in the data presented here.

NOTES

1. Most researchers have used aggregate total expenditures by armed forces ministeries as their measure of defense spending, ignoring the fact that most of these monies, except in the cases of the major powers or countries at war, go to salaries, maintenance of military facilities, and health, education, and housing services for personnel. Frequently, military budgets include allocations for construction of roads, airfields and waterways for civilian use. In these cases it is incorrect to infer that military allocations contribute to arms races or channel funds into socially unproductive functions.

2. The six are United States, Soviet Union, People's Republic of China, France, United Kingdom, Federal Republic of Germany. China is excluded from the Pryor study.

3. José Nun (1967) maintains that Latin American middle classes have an affinity for working within a framework of oligarchic hegemony and that the armed forces, themselves the product of the middle class and one of the few important institutions controlled by that class, have assumed the responsibility of protecting the middle class against the threat of the popular sectors.

4. This series (Balanços Gerais da União, published by Brazil, Ministerio da Fazenda, Contadoria Geral da República) is the finance ministry's annual report of federal receipts and expenditures. It is intended by law to cover both direct federal government (administracão directa) income and expenditures and that of the independent federal authorities administracão indirecta), though the latter are conspicuous in their absence. Volume 2 of the Balanco presents an extremely complex breakdown of expenditure items ranging from paper clips to fodder (this item was the subject of often hilarious debate in the Brazilian Congress), outlays for the aircraft carrier Minas Gerais, and transfers to government revolving funds and investment banks. The more trivial the expenditure category, the more detailed the item-by-item breakdown.

The recording of this data from 1950 to 1967 has reduced about one million line items to some 18,000 machine readable data cards which record year, ministry, total authorization (*crédito*), actual allocation (*despesa paga*), and unpaid commitments (*restos a pagar*) in addition to indicating supplementary credits. A series of codes indicates the functional category of the expenditure (e.g., military, education, health, social security, administration, transportation, agriculture) with subcategories for personnel (salaries), administration (bureaucratic expenses), program investment (literacy, hospital maintenance, highway, rail investment, debt reduction, and so on). Also indicated is whether monies are intended for federal application or are transferred to states or other authorities. The codes are in three parts to facilitate breakdown of categories, and in this preliminary analysis, which focuses on trends in major expenditure categories, only a portion of the available codes has been utilized.

With a single exception my recoded totals come within a few thousand cruzeiros of the official totals in the Balanços. The exception, 1966, is a puzzle, for the published figures do not agree with each other. The volume 2 Análise da Despesa indicates total expenditure for 1966 as Cr$4,580,495 thousands, current, while the summary tables in volume 1 record expenditures of Cr$6,138,559 thousands current. My totals equal those of the Análise.

5. Salaries to federal civilian and military employees account for between 30% and 40% of total federal expenditures. If transfers to inactive and pensioned public servants are added to this, the burden of the bureaucracy ranges between 40% and 50% of total expenditures. This is a serious constraint on government ability to use federal funds to promote development. In the case of Brazil it is more serious because bureaucratic employment was used extensively as a source of patronage. Jaguaribe (1968) has argued the importance of both the civil service and military as client groups of the executive, and he stresses the dependency relation which existed between them—based on the need for jobs on the one hand and the need for political support on the other. Demands for wage increases from these client groups became an increasing political liability, in the later years of the period studied here.

6. In coding the data on which the present study is based I found few budget lines which indicated major allocations for military materiel. The bulk of this comes to Brazil from the U.S. in the form of outright grants and long-term loans (payment of these latter is made through the finance ministry, but are coded as military expenditures in the present data set). Between 60% and 87% of yearly military expenditures was earmarked for personnel, active and retired. An additional substantial sum is used to maintain housing, educational, and health facilities for armed services personnel. If administrative expenses are added to this, little is left to support major purchases of equipment, or research and development of weapons. Because of the very substantial portion of military expenditures devoted to salaries and pensions, and because of the political import and interaction between military and civilian personnel allocations, I have focused on the personnel component as an indicator of the "non-defense" nature of Brazilian military expenditures.

7. The constant cruzeiro values are calculated on the basis of change in the wholesale price index as reported in *Conjuntura Econômica* (Rio: Fundacáo Getúlio Vargas, vol. 23, no. 12, 1969).

8. Because of uncertainty over the amount of revenue which would ultimately be available in any year, most expenditures were actually realized in the last half of the year. In addition, large supplementary expenditures were frequently authorized in the last days of the fiscal year. This is particularly true of salary supplements. Therefore we can be fairly confident that the three presidents who assumed office in mid-year had considerable discretion over the money spent in their first year.

9. The data used here represent only federal government expenditures. Certain programs, notably education, are financed largely at the state (secondary education) and local (primary education) levels and are therefore underrepresented in the data. Large health and welfare programs are maintained by the federal social security institutes and the activities of

these independent federal authorities (*autarquias*) are not included in the federal budget or the Balance. Social programs would undoubtedly fare better in the analysis if the activities of the authorities and state and local governments were included in the data set.

10. The concept of socialization is borrowed from Celso Furtado (1968) who uses the term "socialization of losses" to describe the policies adopted during the depression of the 1930s to protect the coffee sector from the collapse of the world market. The intent and effect of government policy was that "the bulk of losses could . . . be transferred to the community as a whole" (205).

11. Figure 1 indicates that a substantial increase to this category occurred in 1967. The present data set would have to be extended in order to determine whether this marked a beginning of a new emphasis on social spending.

APPENDIX

Contents of Variable Categories

Military—all allocations to armed services except civilian air transport development, maintenance of civilian air fields, and transfers to civilian airlines (all allocated through the air force); Higher War College (Escola Superior da Guerra); Chiefs of Staff (Estado Maior das Forcas Armadas)

Social Development—
   Health
   Education
   Welfare (social security, child and maternal welfare stipends)
   excludes purely administrative ministerial expenditures.

Infrastructure Development—
   Public works—transportation—air, rail, highway, river, and maritime; communication—postal and telecommunications; water resources development and irrigation

   Industrial Development—mining, coal, steel, and oil industry development; automotive industry; energy—hydroelectric and nuclear

   Agriculture development—agriculture extension; research; rural credit; marketing and warehousing

   Government investment—regional development including transfers to regional development authorities; transfers to state and local governments of funds earmarked for social and infrastructure development; transfers to development banks

Civilian personnel—salaries, pension, and stipends

Military personnel—salaries, pensions and stipends, including funds for civilian employees of the armed services (these cannot be separated from military salaries for the entire data series and comprise a relatively modest proportion of total personnel allocations made by the military ministries)

SECTION II

THE SEARCH FOR THEORY

A. Theories of Process and Environment

Chapter 2

COMPARING APPROACHES TO THE STUDY
OF FINANCIAL RESOURCE ALLOCATION

JAMES N. DANZIGER

School of Social Sciences
University of California, Irvine

INTRODUCTION

Interest in the performance of government—in what comes out of political processes—has always been a central concern of political scientists. Such "public policy research" has increased markedly in recent years. This paper takes financial resource allocations by governments as the dependent variable, as what is to be explained. Like most public policy research, it is "comparative" in the sense that there is more than one unit of analysis. The paper is comparative in two additional ways. The research applies and evaluates more than one explanatory approach to the same set of dependent variables. And finally, in the traditional comparative government sense, the units of analysis are from a non-American context.

The dependent variable. Public policy research has often identified the allocation of resources as that which is to be explained. This derives from the definition of a political system as the institutions and processes which authoritatively allocate public values. Among the diverse value-outputs of government, allocations have often been operationalized as financial measures. Many governmental goods and services are, at some point, translated into amounts of money.

AUTHOR'S NOTE: This research was undertaken while the author was supported by a Foreign Area Fellowship (Western Europe), administered by the Social Science Research Council. The author gratefully acknowledges their financial support. Computing facilities for early data analysis, were provided at Stanford University and, were provided by Essex University, with assistance from James Alt and Jean Blondel. The research owes much to many county borough councillors and officers, whose cooperation and patience were extraordinary. Thanks are particularly due to Heinz Eulau, who provided insightful commentary on the analysis.

These measures have imperfect correspondence to quality of service provision (Sharkansky, 1967a); but they are a uniform, relatively valid measure across many services of the commitment to provide (Davies, 1968: 43). Hence a set of resource allocations, primarily ones measured as amounts of expenditure, are the dependent variables in this study.

Explanatory approaches. Two explanatory approaches are employed: the "demographic approach" (phrase from Wilson, 1968: introduction) and the "organizational process approach" (phrase from Allison, 1971: 67-100). Each will be elaborated below. Briefly, the demographic approach holds that the inter-unit variation in an allocation measure can be explained, in statistical terms, by the variations in important economic, social and/or political indicators for the units of analysis. The organizational process approach, however, explains resource allocations as the history-dependent product of certain regularized problem-solving routines by the government unit. The notion of "approach," used to characterize the two modes of analysis, is similar to Merton's concept of "general orientation." There is a set of empirical generalizations that possesses a common focus and identifies sets of interrelated variables (Merton, 1957: 142). But there are neither covering laws specifying general laws nor a structural correspondence between components and actual phenomena (Mayer, 1972: 25-26).

Units of analysis. This paper analyzes resource allocations in the county boroughs of England and Wales. County boroughs are the "all purpose" local authorities for all large urban communities (outside Greater London). They are extremely interesting and appropriate units of analysis for a number of reasons: (1) they provide a full range of services to their citizens, including education, highways, housing, local health services, personal social services, parks, town planning and development, fire service, and the like; (2) for most services, there is no overlap of responsibility with special districts or boards; (3) they control their own local property tax, "the rate"; (4) they have the same governmental structure, with a partisan Council elected by wards and a large professional staff; (5) they are the meaningful sub-national governmental unit for their citizens; (6) they are relatively autonomous (from the central government and its departments).[1] In examining the demographic approach, data are gathered for all county boroughs which existed from 1960-70 (N = 77); for the organizational process approach, intensive study was made of four county boroughs: Brighton, Dudley, Southend, and West Bromwich. This selection was based on various demographic characteristics by which Brighton and Southend on the one hand, and Dudley and West Bromwich on the other are relatively matched sets that are relatively dissimilar to each other.[2]

The form of this paper is to examine the demographic approach and then the organizational process approach. For each approach, the methodology and assumptions are explicated briefly. The approach is conceptualized and operationalized in the county borough context. The findings are summarized and then evaluated, both in terms of public policy implications and of methodological considerations. The final section is a general comparison of the two approaches as modes of examining resource allocations.

THE DEMOGRAPHIC APPROACH

The demographic approach has dominated the research on financial resource allocation during the last decade. Based on a relatively simple input-output conceptualization, it holds that the analysis of governmental outputs must locate the political system in the environment within which it operates. The method entails selecting a reasonable number of units of analysis—of comparable government systems. Indicators of policy output are compiled for all units, and a set of indicators which characterizes the political system and its environment is developed.

THE THEORY

The basic methodology is to apply statistical techniques of correlation and regression to these sets of variables. The policy output measures, the dependent variables, are "explained" to the extent that they are systematically related to political or environmental system variables. The explanation is a statistical one—it measures the percentage of inter-case variation in the dependent variable that is predicted by variation in the independent variable. Other statistical manipulations can combine or control for the effect of other variables.

There has been an immense outpouring of social science research employing the demographic approach.[3] But a few basically valid generalizations can be made. The research has primarily been based on American states or municipalities. Until recently, most studies have concluded that social and economic characteristics have much stronger associations with output measures than the political variables do.

Such conclusions, disturbing to political scientists, have provoked a range of responses. Some scholars accept the approach and its methodology, but argue for different measures of the independent variables. In particular, it has been asserted that the political system variables should be processual rather than structural (Pulsipher and Weatherby, 1968; Clark, 1969). Others have developed more refined dependent variables (Fry and Winters, 1970) or amalgamated these variables into factor packages in order to salvage a political component in the explanation (Hofferbert and Sharkansky, 1969). A broader stream of criticism has attacked the methodology of the demographic approach. It has challenged the use of correlation rather than regression coefficients in discriminating among causal models. The problems of multi-collinearity among independent variables and of a cross-sectional data base have been shown (Blalock, 1964; Cnudde and McCrone, 1969). The broadest criticism has argued persuasively that the approach lacks any theory of linkages which explicates the relationships between policy outputs, environmental variables, and political system variables (Jacob and Lipsky, 1968; Rakoff and Schaffer, 1970).

CONCEPTUALIZATION

This application does not avoid most of these criticisms; but it does seem a reasoned and valid examination of the demographic approach in its own terms.

TABLE 1A

Measures of Resources Allocated

Caretaker Services

Highways	expenditure per population[a] on highways, street cleaning and lighting
Sewerage	expenditure per population[a] on sewerage and sewage systems
Refuse	expenditure per population[a] on refuse collection and disposal
Police	expenditure per population[b] on police services
Fire	expenditure per population[b] on fire services
Σ Caretaker	expenditure per population[b] on five services above
Pol Pop/Off	Police provision: population per uniformed officer
Fire Pop/Off	Fire service provision: population per uniformed fireman

Promoter Services

Planning	expenditure per population[a] on town and country planning

Amenities Services

Libraries	expenditure per population[b] on the library service
Parks	expenditure per population[b] on the parks service
Hous-Rent	Rent income as a proportion of the Housing Revenue Account
Hous-Built	Units of Council housing built, 1945-65 as a proportion of total households in the county borough

Personal Social Services

Local Health Srv	expenditure per population[b] on all local health services (includes: home nursing; health visiting; midwifery; domestic helps; mental health services; care for mothers and young children; etc.)
Children's Srv	expenditure per population[b] on the children's service (includes: children in local authority homes and private homes; approved schools; remand homes; etc.)
Welfare Srv	expenditure per population[b] on the welfare services (includes: residential homes for the aged; meals-on-wheels; care for the blind and handicapped; etc.)
Srv for Elderly	expenditure per population[b] on services for the elderly (includes: welfare services; domestic helps; home nursing)

Education Services

Prim Ed	expenditure per population[b] on primary education
Sec Ed	expenditure per population[b] on secondary education
Further Ed	expenditure per population[b] on further education (includes: colleges of technology and art; adult education; financial aid to students)
Cost/Prim Pup	expenditure per primary school pupil
Cost/Prim Pup	expenditure per secondary school pupil
Prim Pup/Teach	primary schools—pupil-teacher ratio
Sec Pup/Teach	secondary schools—pupil-teacher ratio
Σ Education	expenditure per population[b] on total education services

Total Net Exp   total net expenditure per population[a]

TABLE 1B

Parameter Statistics for Measures of Resources Allocated (1968-1969)

	Mean	Standard Deviation	Coefficient of Variation
Highways	82.4 s.	17.5	.21
Sewerage	33.75s.	15.8	.47
Refuse	28.2 s.	5.8	.21
Police	95.1 s.	15.9	.17
Fire	£ 1,326.1	310.4	.23
Σ Caretaker	265.7 s.	33.3	.13
PolPop/Off[c]	521.6	58.6	.11
FirePop/Off[d]	1,585.1	380.8	.24
Planning	12.65s.	9.3	.74
Libraries	£ 836.4	198.1	.24
Parks[e]	23.2 s.	5.5	.24
Hous-Rent	76.4 %	8.15	.10
Hous-Built	17.1 %	5.6	.33
Local Health Srv	£ 2,798.4	471.7	.17
Children's Srv	£ 1,002.7	281.9	.28
Welfare Srv	£ 1,478.2	377.1	.26
Σ Srv for Elderly	£ 2,152.7	455.6	.21
PrimEd	£ 8,215.4	977.9	.12
SecEd	£ 10,080.0	1,148.8	.11
Further Ed	£ 5,666.3	827.5	.15
Cost/PrimPup	£ 80.2	5.2	.06
Cost/SecPup	£ 156.5	11.6	.08
PrimPup/Teach	29.3	1.4	.05
SecPup/Teach	18.3	.9	.05
Σ Education	£ 30,429.2	2,783.7	.09
Total Net Exp	1,183.4 s.	97.2	.08

a. Data measured as total rates levied per head, including all rate and general grant-born expenditure.

b. Data measured as total net expenditure per 1000, including all rate and general grant-born expenditure.

c. Values for 1964-65
d. Values for 1960-61
e. Values for 1964-65

SOURCES: All expenditure per population data is taken from the yearly statistics compiled by the Institute of Municipal Treasurers and Accountants. These include: Children's Service Statistics; Education Service Statistics; Fire Service Statistics; Housing Statistics; Library Service Statistics; Local Health Service Statistics; Police Service Statistics; Welfare Service Statistics. All from the Institute of Municipal Treasurers and Accountants (London: Lowes, Ltd., yearly).

Table 1 displays the dependent variables, most of which are measures of expenditure per head on services provided by the county borough. The allocation measures are normally distributed and have an interesting amount of variation, as reflected in the levels on the coefficient of variation (a ratio of the mean on the standard deviation).[4]

Most demographic approach analyses are presented in more or less causal language. This results in references to socioeconomic characteristics like level of urbanization or median education as "inputs" which "produce" policy outputs.[5] Such conceptualizations are difficult to support. It seems more appropriate to view the socioeconomic and political indicators as measures representing environments. Within these environments, policy outputs are produced. Conceptually, these environments can be understood as *constraints*—as forces that might limit and shape the nature of outputs.

It is suggested that three types of variables represent these constraints. These types have been called "resources," "need," and "disposition" variables.[6] (1) Resources. These measures tap the economic characteristics and the wealth of the county borough. (2) Need. Certain constraints on allocations can be inferred either from the characteristics of the physical environment or from the nature of the borough's population. (3) Disposition. These measures represent characteristics of the political system, particularly the inclination of the county borough toward governmental provision of goods and services. Table 2 displays the indicators utilized to operationalize the concepts of resources, need, and disposition.

It was expected (primarily on the basis of Moser and Scott, 1961) that these independent variables would tend to associate in two contrasting configurations. Correlation analysis confirmed that inter-unit variations on most variables associate systematically. One pattern, which will be termed the configuration of lower resources, greater need, and greater disposition (that is, greater inclination for public provision of goods and services) is characterized by

	higher values on:	lower values on:
Resources:		
	Grant	RV/hd
		Cars
		Wealthy
		Dom/Ind
Need-Personal:		
	SES 2	SES 1
	SES 3	Elderly
	Youth	HighEd
	Pupils	
	LowEd	

TABLE 2

Indicators of Resources, Need and Disposition

Symbol	Measure of:	Operation:	Years
RV/hd	Average Property Wealth	Borough's Total Rateable Value/ Population	60, 64, 68
Grant	Inadequate Local Financial Resources	Total Grant from Central Government/ Population	60, 64, 68
Cares	Affluence	Private Autos in Borough/Population	66
Wealthy	Affluence	Units of Domestic Rateable Valued over £100/Total Units of Domestic Rateable Value	64, 68
Dom/Ind	Domestic versus Industrial-Commercial Nature of Borough	Rateable Value in Domestic Property/ Total Rateable Value	64, 68
	Socio-economic class composition:	% male population over age 15 in Census groups:	
SES 1	—upper and upper middle class	Groups 1, 2, 3, 4, 13: employers, managers, professionals	61, 66
SES 2	—skilled working class	Groups 8, 9, 12, 14: foremen, skilled manual workers, own account workers	61, 66
SES 3	—unskilled laborers	Group 11: unskilled manual workers	61, 66
	Age structure:		
Elderly	—elderly population	% population aged over 65 years	60, 68
Youth	—youth population	% population aged under 15 years	61, 66
Pupils	—school population	Primary plus secondary school pupils/ 1000 pop.	60, 68
	Educational Attainment:	% males aged 25 or over whose terminal education age was:	
Low Ed	—low ed. attainment	under 15 years	61
High Ed	—high ed. attainment	over 20 years or continuing	61
Non-White	Ethnic composition	Number of immigrants with a "New commonwealth country" birthplace/10,000 pop.	66

Symbol	Measure of:	Operation:	Years
Pop	Population	Total Borough Population	60, 64, 68
Density	Density of Population	Population Density per acre	64
MigBal	Net Population Balance	Net Borough population balance due to births, deaths, and migration/ 1000 pop	61 (1 yr.) 65 (5 yr.)
W/inMig	Internal Population Movement	Total Movements of Households within Borough/1000	61 (1 yr.)

	Social conditions:		
Amenities	Household amenities	% households with exclusive use of: cold and hot water taps, fixed bath, and inside water closet	61, 66
Crowd	Crowded living space	% of population in dwellings where the room density is greater than 1.0 persons/room	66

% Labor	Labor Party Strength	% of Council Seats held by the Labor Party—3 year average	57-59 61-63 64-67
Compet	Party competitiveness on Council	$1 \text{ minus} \left(\dfrac{\text{Strongest Pty Seats minus Second Pty Seats}/}{\text{Total Council Seats}} \right)$ 3 year average	57-59 61-63 64-67
VoPart	Voter Participation	% of registered voters casting vote in Council election (contested seats only)	59, 63, 67
Unopp Sts	Competitiveness for Council Seats	% of total Council Seats not contested by two or more candidates	59, 67
Debt/hd	Tendency to incur loan debt to finance projects	Net Outstanding Debt/ population	60, 64, 68
Pub/Priv	Tendency to County Borough versus private activity	% of all housing built in borough 1945-65 that was built by the county borough rather than privately	45-65

COMMENTS:

2. Grant: Includes all government grants except those for housing and agency services. The great proportion of Grant is composed of figures whose amounts are set by national formulas of local resource base relative to assessed need.

5. Dom/Ind: The industrial-commercial proportion also includes a small amount of Crown property.

14. Non-White: "New commonwealth countries" are those other than Canada, Australia and New Zealand. In the main, the remainder are "Third World" people. There was no direct measure of ethnicity prior to the 1971 Census.

17. MigBal: A constant has been added so that all scores are positive. Higher scores signify more favorable balances.

22. Compet: On this measure, an exactly competitive situation between the two strongest parties would have a score of 1.0. Complete non-competition (all seats to one party) would have a score of .00.

26. Pub/Priv: A very small percentage of public housing may be from sources other than the county borough.

SOURCES: Data are taken or derived from a variety of published sources. The data can be found as follows:
Variables 3, 6, 7, 8, 9, 10, 11, 12, 13, 14, 17, 18, 19, 20: The General Register Office (1961 and 1966) Census of England and Wales. London: H.M.S.O.
Variables 1, 4, 5: Ministry of Housing and Local Government (1961, 1964, 1968) Rates and Rateable Values in England and Wales.
Variables 15, 16, 21, 22, 23, 24, 25: The Municipal Yearbook (yearly). London: Longmans.
Variable 26: Ministry of Housing and Local Government (1960, 1965, 1968) Housing Return for England and Wales. London: H.M.S.O.
Variables 2, 11: Institute of Municipal Treasurers and Accountants (yearly) Service Statistics. London: Lowes, Ltd.

		(Ambiguous: Non-White)
Need-Environmental		
		MigBal (unfavorable)
	Density	Amenities
	Crowding	W/inMig
		(Ambiguous: Population)
Disposition		
	% Labor	VoPart
	Debt/hd	UnoppSeats
	Pub/Priv	Competition (less competitive)

On the basis of limited existing evidence, drawn primarily from Alt (1971) and Boaden (1971),[7] certain hypothesized dependent variable-independent variable linkages are specified. If the three types of constraint variables are treated in terms of the ideal-type configurations, it is hypothesized that lower resources, greater need, higher disposition will generally associate with:

(1) higher levels of expenditure per head on total, primary and secondary education;
(2) lower expenditure per pupil and higher pupil-teacher ratios;
(3) lower expenditure per head on most caretaker services;
(4) less intensive provision of the fire and police service;
(5) lower expenditure on the promoter service, planning;
(6) lower expenditure per head on most amenity services (e.g., parks, libraries) but higher expenditure and provision of housing;
(7) lower expenditure per head on welfare services and other services whose primary recipients are the elderly;
(8) higher expenditure per head on the local health services and the children's service;
(9) lower total expenditure per head.

The method of analysis is to test these as null hypotheses. That is, does analysis falsify the notion that there is no systematic linkage between the variables? In the first instance correlation analysis is utilized. Where patterns of relationship are complex, regression analysis is used to estimate the most powerful constraint variables.[8] While tests of *statistical significance* are not necessary (given the whole population as units of analysis), these tests are employed as a rule-of-thumb measure of the real interest, *substantive significance*. Only those associations are reported which are higher than might occur by chance ($r = \pm .22$, at the .05 level of significance).[9]

THE FINDINGS

Table 3 displays the r̄ values for selected measures of resource allocation with the variables of resources, need, and disposition. Prior to examining specific allocation measures, certain general observations about the data are noteworthy.

TABLE 3
Mean Correlation Values for Resource Allocation Measures with Variables of Resources, Disposition, and Need[a]

	RV/hd	Grant	Cars	Wealthy	Dom/Ind	SES 1	SES 2	SES 3	Eld	Youth	Pupils	LowEd	HighEd	Non-White	Pop	Dens	MigBal	W/inMig	Amen	Crowd	%Lab	Comp	VoPart	Debt/hd	Pub/Priv
Highways	22		23			28		-30	30	-40	-33		38	26		-31							28		
Sewerage					-31													-24					-29		
Refuse				24				45				30						29							
Police							-37		24						42	32									
Fire		32	-28												38										
Σ Caretaker	23				-28		44		-30	22	-22		23		-22										
Pol Pop/off[b]					-22																				
Fire Pop/off[c]							-40							-26											
Planning	27	-22					-23						22	30	36									36	
Libraries	29						-26																		
Parks	60	-66	54	36		22			35	-28															
Hous-Rent				53	27	48	26	-44	34	-39	-40	48	40			-30	44	23	47	-52	-61			63	-46
Hous-Built			-32	-40	-42	-50		38	-60	55	49	23				27	-46	-37		47	-40		-27		58
PrimEd[d]					-28	-22			-27		(82)										37			32	
SecEd[d]					-25				-28		(74)										30			37	
FurtherEd				-30	-29	-35		-22	-34	29	25		27	30	36	-26	-32			-28				27	
SpecialEd							31				24		-22	36		28				43		25		35	25
Cost/PrimPupil																									
Cost/SecPupil										-23			25												
PrimPup/Teach																									
SecPup/Teach																									
Σ Ed[d]					-37		-22	-24			(74)		30	30										30	

LocalHealthSrv	-25			-28	-23		-29	23	27	32		34	-34	-33	30	29	31
Children'sSrv	-22	49		-32			-24	22			33	33		-31	31	23	30
WelfareSrv									25								
Σ ServicesElderly																	
Σ NetExp	-22	49	-27	-36	-51	40	27	-36	44	27			-48	-35	44	48	41 33

a. The table displays all correlations for which the mean Pearson product-moment correlation is greater than ± .21.

In most cases, the figure is the mean for two or three r-values. The pairings between independent variables and allocation measures are as follows:

Allocation Measure Year:	Independent Variable Year:
1960-61	same year data, except: 1957-59 (party-political) 1964 (density)
1964-65	same year data, except: 1966 (Five Year Census data, 1961-65) 1963-65 (party-political)
1968-69	same year data, except: 1966 (Five Year Census data, 1961-65) 1965-67 (party-political)

b. Values for 1960-61 and 1964-65 only.

c. Values for 1960-61 only.

d. These education-constraint variables correlations are first-order partials, controlling the effect of the relevant student population.

First, it is both striking and surprising that, with few exceptions, there are a limited number of dependent variable–independent variable associations. For each allocation measure, most of the indicators of resources, need, and disposition do not attain a level of simple correlation greater than chance. Of 676 possible associations, there are only 154 r values higher than ± .22.

Secondly, the magnitudes of significant r̄ values are generally low. Excluding the substantial correlations on the two housing measures, there are only 28 times where any independent variable explains at least 10% of the inter-borough variation in any resource allocation measure.[10]

A third important result is that no single independent variable is highly correlated with a large number of allocation measures. Not one associates significantly with at least half the allocation measures.

Fourth, there is no apparent configuration of associations in the table. There are no systematic patterns of association between a type of independent variable and a type of allocation measure. Unlike most demographic analyses in American contexts, this lack of strong associations is evident for social and economic environment variables, as well as political ones.

The associations between the constraint variables and each specific service cannot be examined in detail here. Rather, the findings for each type of allocation measures are summarized briefly. More thorough analysis is provided for the housing and education measures, which do have strong associations with the independent variables.

The *caretaker service* measures have only scattered and low correlations with the variables of resources, need, and constraint. Highways spending correlates, as hypothesized, with lower personal and environmental need. But it has little association with either resources or disposition measures. Higher spending on refuse collection and disposal has only one interesting correlation, with larger population. It is intriguing that expenditure and intensity of provision on the police and the fire services associate in the opposite direction with the independent variables. Spending and provision increase on the police service with greater population and higher social class; the fire service measures associate with lower population and lower social class groups.[11] This contrast is intriguing but not easily explained. Neither sewerage nor a summary measure of caretaker service spending are substantially associated with the independent variables. Similarly, the *promoter service* of planning has no strong correlations.

The two *amenities* which are indivisible-benefit services, libraries and parks, have no spending-constraint variable correlations. However, the two housing measures do have substantial linkages with constraint measures, in the hypothesized direction. More extensive housing provision and lower rent burden on tenants correlate with indicators of lower resources, greater need, and higher disposition. In order to estimate which constraint variables seem to have the strongest independent relationship with the housing measures, partial correlation and regression analysis were employed. The findings of the latter technique are reported. They are consistent with those from partial correlations.

Housing provision increases with a younger population age structure, and higher disposition (measured as net debt per head and the public/private activity mix[12]), and with the need inferred from migration balance and internal migration (see Appendix). These five variables explain 60% of the inter-unit variation in levels of housing provision.

While the proportion of housing revenue coming from rent is being standardized by central government policies, it remains an interesting measure of redistribution. Rent burden correlates significantly with most independent variables. Regression analysis identifies the lack of local resources reflected in the size of the central grant as the most powerful variable in the regression equation. Other key variables are youthful age structure, the environmental need reflected in high density and low amenities, and the Labor fraction on council. These variables explain 66% of the inter-borough variation in rent burden (see Appendix). Thus each housing allocation measure is powerfully linked to a small set of independent variables. Need and disposition constraints independently affect both extensiveness of housing provision and rent burden, and a resources measure also affects rent burden.

On the *personal social service* allocation measures there is not one $\bar{r}$ value greater than + .35. There are virtually no significant associations for constraint variables with spending on welfare services or on a summary measure of services for the aged. Expenditure on the local health services and the children's service (see Appendix) do have some moderate correlations in the hypothesized direction. Higher expenditure per head is most closely linked to measures of environmental need, such as amenity level and density. These services have a few low-magnitude correlations with low resources and higher disposition. But the constraint variables do not, in general, have substantial associations with outputs on the personal social services. This generalization also holds for intensity of provision measures (as cost per unit of service) on a number of specific personal social services.

The major *education services* are, with housing, the only allocation measures which are strongly linked to the constraint variables. Expenditure on primary, secondary, and total education correlates significantly with most of the measures of resources, need, and disposition. However, a powerful influence is expected for the need indicator representing the size of the client group—the number of pupils. The data confirm this. The spending-client group correlations are .82, .74, and .74 for primary, secondary, and total education expenditure per head. Given these strong linkages, other independent variables are displayed in the table as first-order partials in order to control their collinearity with the pupils measure.

With this control, the remaining education service-independent variable linkages are interesting. For expenditure on both primary and secondary education, the strongest associations are with the disposition measures of Labor fraction on Council and debt per head. Thus on the major education services, as with housing, the Labor Party's commitment to more extensive provision receives empirical support from this data. The level of total education expenditure is not, however, significantly correlated with Labor Party strength when the total number of pupils in the borough is controlled. This measure is, for some reason, most closely associated with the ratio of domestic to industrial-commercial property in the borough.

Unlike the measures for expenditure per head, the cost per pupil and pupil-teacher ratios for primary and secondary education have relatively no significant correlations. In part, this might be explained by the impact of policies from the Ministry of Education and Science. One of the most aggressive central departments (see Griffith, 1966: 522-24), it has promoted target levels of pupil-teacher ratios. There was, by 1968-1969, quite low inter-borough variation in these ratios. These ratios have strong correlations with cost-per-pupil levels. These two pupil-based measures can be viewed as more adequate indicators (than aggregate spending figures) of commitment to provide the education services at a certain level. Thus the strength of the demographic explanation for the major education services seems lower than it initially appears. Consistent with this observation is the fact that expenditure on further education, a more discretionary education service, has only a scattering of low-magnitude correlations with the independent variables.

It is illuminating to examine the allocation measure of *total net expenditure* per head on all rate fund services. This aggregate measure includes both rate- and general grant-financed spending. Generally, one would expect higher spending to correlate with greater need and greater disposition to spend. Table 3 confirms these expectations. Total net expenditure is substantially associated with: (1) the disposition measures of Labor fraction and net debt per head[13]; (2) many need measures, including migration balance, crowding, pupils, and social class; and (3) all resources measures, particularly the domestic/industrial property mix and the size of the government grant.

The strong linkage with resources measures is somewhat unexpected. It is reinforced by regression analysis, which selects four of the five resources measures into the regression equation. The seven-variable equation estimates 80% of the inter-borough variation on total expenditure (see Appendix). Central government grants is the most powerful independent variable. But this resources constraint is balanced by a disposition constraint (net debt per head) which is the second variable in the equation. Using *both* the resources measure and the disposition measure substantially increases the explanatory power (the r^2 rises from 34% to 59%) and the statistical significance (the F-level increases from 36.5 to 49.1) of the analysis. Thus total expenditure per head is not only a function of financial capability but also of the will to spend. Need constraints seem less important than was expected, at least in this mode of analysis.

EVALUATION

The demographic approach assumes that an adequate set of indicators for the economic, social, and political environments can explain much of the inter-uni variation on allocation measures. The basic test of the adequacy of this explanation is the strength of correlations between dependent and independent variables. *The major conclusion of this application is that the demographic approach provides a weak and generally unsatisfactory explanation for the variation in county borough resource allocations.*

The constraints of resources, need and disposition operate in the hypothesized direction on most services. However, for most allocation measures examined, there are only scattered, low-magnitude correlations. With the exception of housing provision and housing rent burden, the patterns of association are inadequate to falsify the null hypotheses that the allocation measure-constraint variable linkages are neither powerful nor systematic. The linkage between expenditure on the basic education services per head and the proportion of pupils is also a partial, if unremarkable, confirmation of the notion that the demographic approach can provide an economic explanation of the level of total net expenditure per head.

On balance, however, the approach must be assessed as inadequate. What can explain this failure, given the viability of the approach in studies of American states and municipalities? One might argue that the measures of the independent variables are unreliable or invalid. While this cannot be disproven, the indicators seem sound on theoretical grounds and are developed from reliable sources.

Some policy analysts have argued, on the basis of American findings, that the economic and social environments will necessarily determine the *levels* of available revenue and, consequently, levels of spending on most services (Fry and Winters, 1970: 511; Clark, 1969: 1173, 1181; Crecine, 1969: 167-68). But the examination of county borough data shows that almost every level-of-allocation measure except the summary measure of expenditure per head is *not* systematically related to levels of environmental development (that is, what we have called resources and need constraints).

It might be that the level of *available revenue* and the general, *areal level of costs* (that is, the areal cost-of-living, wage levels, cost of materials, and so on) are general constraints on the level of governmental allocations. If the inter-unit disparity in available revenue and cost-levels is great (as in an inter-state or inter-city American comparison), it is probable that allocation levels for individual services will vary in a somewhat corresponding manner. That is, a unit with high revenue capacity and high cost-levels is expected, ceteris paribus, to have higher spending levels than a unit low on these constraints. Moreover, certain socioeconomic characteristics which would tend to correlate with revenue capacity and areal cost-levels would also tend to correlate with the allocation measures.

Under these conditions, the demographic variable-allocation level correlations could be viewed as spurious, in causal terms. At least, it is unclear what proportion of inter-unit variation is attributable to cost-levels rather than revenue capacity. Only the latter might be influenced by socioeconomic variables (more specifically, by personal wealth or property wealth measures, to the extent that available resources are dependent on local wealth).

If this argument is valid, a central reason for the failure of the demographic approach in the county borough context is the affect of two levelers—government grants and uniform wage policies. General grants from the central government are distributed by means of a formula based upon local need and local financial resources. While these unearmarked funds do not produce resource equality, they do close substantially the inter-borough disparity in available financial resources. Uniform wage policies are also an important leveler because wage scales for most county borough employees are established at the national level. A relatively uniform national wage structure means that staff-related expenditure becomes a function of local decisions regarding the quantity and quality of staff rather than function of gross areal differences in cost-levels.[14] The impact of this on inter-unit variation in expenditure is evident in the fact that staff-related expenditure accounts for well over half the county borough's spending on many costly services, including education, the personal social services, fire and police, and the like.

Therefore, this analysis is a serious challenge to the central conclusions of most demographic approach studies in the American context. In the British case, the impact of the two levelers seems to reduce substantially the effect of confounding macroeconomic factors on the inter-unit variation in resource allocations. It is probable that resource capability is an important constraint on total allocation levels. But the county borough example suggests that, when certain gross economic forces are less varied, there is a great deal of local variation. At least, there is no simple model of socioeconomic determinism which explains resource allocation decisions. In the county boroughs, the demographic approach has minimal explantory power for most allocation measures.

There are other interesting general observations in these null findings. For example, although the local parties are aligned with rather ideological national parties, there are few strong associations between allocations and the party composition of the Council. The exceptions are important ones—provision and rent burden on housing, spending on primary and secondary education, and total expenditure per head. But most allocation measures, including the particular and general categories on personal social services, cost per pupil figures, planning, and caretaker services have little relationship to party make-up. In fact, allocations are more strongly linked to another disposition measure, debt per head, than to party composition. As in most American studies, the Key hypothesis about the influence of party competitiveness suffers another setback (see Cnudde and McCrone, 1969).

The measures employed to reflect need are clearly imperfect. Need is inferred from aggregate characteristics rather than measured directly. On most divisible-benefit services, the associations of outputs with the available measures of need were low. On indivisible-benefit services, correlations seldom reached the level of significance. On the only services with a direct indicator of the size of the client population—primary and secondary education—there was a strong correlation with expenditure. This suggests that allocations by governments are somewhat responsive to the need for service. Yet even in these cases, nearly 50% of the inter-unit variation is left unexplained by the size of the client group. The correlations of need indicators with both cost-per-pupil and pupil-teacher ratios are further evidence that there is no direct translation of need into expenditure. Local actors continually stressed that they simply did not have reliable indicators of either need or demand upon which to make allocation decisions. The failure of the demographic approach data suggests that the explanation of resource allocations might better be sought in analysis of how resource allocation is accomplished in particular units. The next section examines one approach which takes this perspective.

THE ORGANIZATIONAL PROCESS APPROACH

The organizational process approach is another mode of explaining resource allocations. This approach takes the organization as the object unit of analysis. Budget-making is conceptualized as a recurring problem which the government unit solves by regularized decision routines. According to this approach, the nature of the solution is a function of the problem-solving techniques employed. This contrasts with the perspective of the demographic approach, which held that outputs were explainable without any attention to the internal decision processes of particular units. This approach also contrasts with approaches which take the behavior of individual role-takers as the basic units of analysis. To evaluate the organizational process approach, intensive case analysis was done in four county boroughs.

ASSUMPTIONS

The most important theoretical work for this approach is *A Behavioral Theory of the Firm* by Richard Cyert and James March (1963). Four key concepts underlie their theory of organizational choice and control (116-27):

(1) *Quasi-resolution of conflict,* including goals as independent constraints, acceptable-level decision rules, sequential attention to alternatives;
(2) *Uncertainty avoidance,* involving negotiated environments and reaction to feedback;
(3) *Problemistic search,* which is motivated, simple-minded, and biased;
(4) *Organizational learning* by means of adaptation of goals, attention rules, and search rules.

In general, the Cyert-March theory argues that certain *standard operating procedures* (SOPs) dominate the making and implementation of choices in the short-run. These SOPs include task performance rules, records and reports, information-handling rules, and plans (Cyert and March, 1963: 101-12).

Given the interest in resource allocations, the organizational process approach stimulates a series of questions for analysis:

(1) What are the major goals of budget-making?
(2) How is uncertainty avoided?
(3) What is the nature of the search for information?
(4) What are the crucial standard operating procedures of budget-making?
(5) What is the strategy of search for solutions?
(6) How are acceptable-level decisions characterized?
(7) Is there evidence of organizational learning?

OPERATIONALIZATION

The preferred test of the Cyert-March approach is a computer model. The most thorough application to resource allocations is Crecine's simulation model for municipal budgeting in three large American cities (Crecine, 1969; also see Gerwin 1969). However, in using the organizational process approach in the county boroughs, such an application is not, at this stage, realizable. One basic reason is that there is little empirical data on how budgeting occurs in the county boroughs.

There are two further reasons why a computer model is not possible. These are based on the greater complexity of the budgeting systems in the county boroughs relative to those in Crecine's study. Briefly, the first reason is that county borough budgeting involves interdependent solutions to the problems of level-of-spending and level-of-taxation. In Crecine's municipalities, the level of available revenue is a given for the budget-making model (Crecine, 1969: 68). Secondly, the county borough budget involves a huge increase in the number of allocation decisions which must formally be made. In Crecine's cities, there are about five major expenditure categories (per department) upon which specific allocation figures must be authorized. In some county boroughs, each specific category within each particular service of each spending department must be decided and authorized separately and accurately.[15] Thus in some county boroughs there are over 1500 separate "votes"—allocation decisions—within a single budget. Given these factors, the attempt to develop a computer model is clearly premature.

This paper examines the organizational process approach by means of intensive case analysis of two county boroughs. It draws upon the fuller research design in which four units of analysis were studied (Danziger, 1974). These were selected on the basis of a set of criteria including population, class structure, age structure, geographic location, and party political balance. This paper takes one county borough from each "relatively similar" set: Southend and West Bromwich. Southend is a seaside, business and resort town, with a Conservative-oriented Council, a large middle class, and a high proportion of elderly persons. West Bromwich is a Black Country industrial town, with a Labor-oriented Council, and a young, working-class population.[16] Primary data are open-end interviews with about 35 budget-makers in each county borough and various public and confidential documents.

Case-studies are not a thorough test of the adequacy of the organizational process approach. But the approach does provide a set of theory-based concepts by which the process of resource allocation can be explicated. By use of case-studies, it is possible to assess whether these concepts are illuminating, whether they stimulate useful cross-unit generalizations, whether they are adequate for explicating the allocation process. This paper presents specific findings from two of the four units analyzed in order to suggest certain virtues and inadequacies of the organizational process approach.

In order to make the research manageable, the focal question of the analysis is: how is the problem of budget-creation in Y_n solved? The perspective is cross-sectional rather than longitudinal. It aligns with the perspective of the budgetary decision-makers, whose problem is to create a new budget, given certain important antecedents. There are four primary antecedents which act as constraints in the budgetary process. (1) The previous year's budget. It is a commonplace that the Y_n budget solution is based on the Y_{n-1} pattern of allocations. This paper focuses on the dynamic of change between Y_{n-1} and Y_n in order to avoid an infinite regress explanation. (2) The capital program. New capital projects, which were initiated several years before Y_n, have an impact on current expenditure through new operating costs. While this impact is important, it must be viewed as a constraint in this analysis. (3) Staffing decisions. Since over half of current expenditure is related to staff, decisions on number and grading of staff are significant. Prior to budget creation, a committee authorizes changes in staff numbers and grading. Most upgradings are incorporated into Y_n spending figures; but many key changes, determined during budgeting, concern whether to leave authorized positions (either vacant or new ones) unfilled for all or part of Y_n. (4) Policy decisions. Policy commitments, based on Council decisions, Parliamentary acts, or central department circulars, are difficult to characterize. Briefly, this analysis determined that most policy commitments are policy-serving—that is, they propose alterations or elaborations to existing schemes (see Danziger, 1974: chapter 2). With few exceptions, a policy decision is not a guarantee of resource allocation; rather it is a force which increases the demand to consider funding the scheme and the probability that allocators might fund it.

RESULTS

Description of the Two Budgeting Systems

Initially, the budget-making processes of Southend and West Bromwich are presented in a brief, descriptive mode. Then each budgeting system is examined in terms of the analytic questions posed for the organizational process approach. Of the four county boroughs, Southend's process corresponds most closely to the classic notions of incremental budgeting.[17] Estimates (allocation requests) are prepared by the senior officers in each spending department. In the subsequent three-month period there is a series of reassessments of the department's estimates. There are several important characteristics of these assessments. First, they are undertaken on a line-item basis. Secondly, each line-item is broken down into two parts: (1) expenditure to maintain the same standard of provision; and (2) additional expenditure proposed. In each episode, attention focuses on the second aspect, on that expenditure which is "new." The basic question addressed is: How is this increase justified?

Each episode in Southend is best understood as a structured confrontation between "spenders," who advocate and justify the increase, and "pruners," who locate and effect reductions in the requests. Episodes progress from the level of specialists to the most influential and powerful role-takers. Most key decisions occur in meetings between an Executive Board of Chief Officers and the individual Chief Officer of each spending department. If the Chief Officer is not satisfied with some aspect of his allocation, his appeal is normally resolved by the Council's Policy and Finance Committee.

The procedure in West Bromwich is consciously structured to avoid the Southend-type system of detailed, marginal adjustment. The allocation process in West Bromwich is anchored in a sixteen-category schedule developed by the Finance Department. The schedule classifies all types of expenditure increases in categories which are generalized priority rankings from 1 to 16. Examples are:

1 Precepts and pooled expenditure contributions.
3 Running costs of newly completed assets.
4 Additional demand where Council has no discretion.
7 Increased provision for services operating below an acceptable standard.
11 Provision to implement Council policy which has been agreed "in principle."
14 Other desirable developments.

Each Spending Department submits estimates for Y_n. A single Senior Finance Officer, using information from his accountants and the spending department officers, determines the location of each increase between Y_{n-1} and Y_n in one of the sixteen categories. The figures are treated (unlike Southend) in constant Y_{n-1} prices, in order to "kill" inflation. The Finance Officer then compiles an aggregate schedule which reflects the spending implications of all proposed increases, in Y_n prices. The schedule shows the tax rate for the borough if all departments are granted the increases categorized as # 1, as # 1-2, as # 1-3, and so on. The Chairman of Council's Finance Committee is then able to examine this schedule and, moving from # 1 toward # 16, to determine the rate levy and, as a consequence, the amount of new expenditure granted to each department.

Each Chief Officer is notified of his "ration" of funds for Y_n. He now allocates his resource share, with minimal restrictions. An intriguing aspect of this process is that the Chief Officer can, with authorization from his Committee and agreement from the Finance Department, substitute alternative schemes for those comprising his resource increase in the sixteen-category schedule. Thus the Chief Officer has substantial discretion over the allocation of his ration of funds.[18] Moreover, this procedure contradicts the ostensible rationale for using the schedule to establish priorities.

Explication of the Two Budgeting Systems by Means of Organizational Process Approach Concepts

Despite these evident differences in budget-creation, certain analytic similarities between Southend and West Bromwich are identified by means of organizational process approach concepts.

(1) The *major goals* in each system are the same. The primary goal, viewed as a constraint, is to balance expenditure and revenue. One secondary constraint is to maintain the Y_{n-1} level of provision on every service, as the minimum. Another constraint is never to reduce the tax rate. Above this minimum, any increase in the tax should be within the constraint of political feasibility rather than need.

(2) *Uncertainty is avoided* by comparable techniques. Budgeters negotiate the external environment by insulating themselves from community demands. This is done by a variety of methods, including the articulation of a Burkean view of representation, the classification of many groups and demands as illegitimate, the rationalization of low levels of community support, and the like (see Dearlove, 1970; Gregory, 1969). Also, local officials cultivate friendly relationships with Ministry officials, whose backing and information are valuable resources. The internal environment is negotiated by the routinization of standard operating procedures. Moreover, although the allocation process can be viewed as the struggle among spending units for scarce resources, procedures are systematically structured so that direct inter-departmental conflict never occurs. Advocates of expenditure requests in different departments are insulated from contact with or information about the requests of other departments. This is a part of the general use of confidentiality. Most documents and all meetings during budget-creation are strictly private.

(3) As posited in the Cyert-March theory, *information gathering (search)* is motivated, biased, and simple. Basic expenditure information is generated by accountants motivated by statutory requirements of auditing and by department officers motivated by the role-responsibility of generating requests. Biasing is evident because nearly all information during budgeting comes from two sources: the spending department provides information to promote the maximum expansion of expenditure, and the Finance Department counters with information, grounded in the criterion of economies, concerning minimum costs, the analysis of requested increases, and the general economic constraints facing the borough.[19] Information is simple in the sense that only direct data about the costs of provision and about available resources are gathered and employed.

There is neither the capability to gather complex kinds of data (for example, measures of service need or demand) nor the time to analyze it.

(4) The most important *standard operating procedures* in Southend and West Bromwich are clearly different. The crucial SOPs are evident in the characterization above of the two budgeting systems. In Southend the basic SOP is the chain of task performance rules which establishes the nature and participants in the series of reassessments of the allocation requests. The form of the budget is also central, since allocations are broken into a very large number of specific headings which are perceived as separate sub-problems. In West Bromwich, the crucial SOP is a planning rule—the sixteen-category schedule. There is virtually no challenge to the right of the Senior Finance Officer to identify and classify each increment. Moreover, while the Treasurer oversees these classifications, it does not seem that anyone challenges the *nature* of decisions—that is, why a particular estimate is located in one or another of the somewhat ambiguous categories. It seems that the Chief Officers tradeoff this SOP for another one: their right to determine how their resource share is actually to be allocated.

(5) The *strategy of search for solutions* in the Cyert-March theory posits a sequential consideration of alternatives. Evidence from the two county boroughs is not clear on this point. It is true that the central problem is broken down into a series of sub-problems and that cognitive complexity forces decision-makers to attend to one area of problems at a time. In both systems, attention is focused on expenditure which is either new or an increase in the level of provision. This is most explicit in Southend, where each line-item is analyzed in this fashion, and all existing expenditure is unchallenged. But Southend's solution to the problem of evaluating increases is the product of a swirl of reassessments and bargaining. Available data do not reflect any pattern to the manner in which solutions are generated across departments or line-items. There are simply too many points at which a particular role-taker can substantially influence the solution.

The strategy of search in West Bromwich is clearly structured by the sixteen-category schedule. The size of a department's share of the resource pie is a function of the manner in which requests are classified across the priority scale. The schedule provides the Chairman of Finance Committee with a clear set of alternatives to the level-of-the-tax-rate problem, whose solution determines the configuration of departmental shares. But the allocation decisions within each department are not based on a systematic problem-solving approach. These decisions vary among departments. They are primarily a function of the priorities and perspective of the individual Chief Officer, mixed with the influence of the senior Finance Department officers and the strength of the Council's commitment to particular policy decisions for that spending department.

(6) The nature of *acceptable-level decisions* is implicit in the explication of other concepts. In both county boroughs, the pivotal decision is the level at which the tax rate is to be set for Y_n. This determines available resources for new expenditure. In West Bromwich it also determines the size of each department's allocation. This level-of-the-rate decision is essentially a political one,

made by the leaders in the Majority Group on Council. As one Borough Treasurer observed:

> The real decision-making comes at that point where the Finance Committee Chairman knows, either by political instinct or by consulting his majority colleagues, what the rate increase limit is. The senior and/or influential members of the majority party have a quiet natter and decide what they will accept. . . . Inherent in every town is this testing of the wind by the senior members of the majority party.

After this point, "local rationality" (Cyert and March, 1963: 117-18) prevails, in the sense that each Chief Officer has the potential to dominate allocation decisions within his service jurisdiction.[20] It is clear that a Chief Officer in West Bromwich has far greater discretion than his counterpart in Southend. The latter must bargain on each individual line-item while the former has a relatively free hand to allocate his ration of resources.

(7) In the short period of research, it is difficult to assess whether *learning and adaptation* are occurring. There is little evidence of adaptation in the more stabilized system of Southend. In West Bromwich, it does seem that some actors are learning how to manipulate the new budgeting system. In particular, the more perceptive Chief Officers have realized the payoff from "loading" their requests with items which are likely to have high priority classifications and then substituting other schemes. But most Chief Officers seem unwilling to alter the priorities established by the schedule.

In general, analysis of budget-creation in these and the other two county boroughs made it clear that the four budgeting systems cannot be characterized by a single organizational process model. That is, one could not construct a computer model whose problem-solving format would correspond to the actual processes in the four budgeting systems.[21] The analysis of Southend and West Bromwich is meant to show the substantial differences in the structure of problem-solving. This contention is most strongly supported by the variations in standard operating procedures, particularly the task performance rules. It should be noted that, to some extent, this finding is a function of the decision to explicate the *crucial* SOPs in each county borough and of the decision to characterize each system in a partly analytic, partly configurative fashion.

However, the organizational process approach does guide research and analysis within the structure of a valid and useful set of concepts. It makes sense to conceptualize budget-making in the four county boroughs as a recurrent task which activates regularized problem-solving routines in each system. Analysis of the search routines, SOPs, information processing, and the like of a problem-solving system is a sensitive and illuminating method of explicating budget-creation. While these concepts are not yet linked into a theory (they are linked operationally in the Cyert-March and the Crecine applications), they do seem capable of integration. This approach could achieve Verba's (1967) "disciplined configurative approach," in which relevant factors vary in their configuration but not in their nature. At least, the organizational process approach has much explanatory appeal (Mayer, 1972: 44-46).

POLICY IMPLICATIONS

The analysis reported here suggests certain observations about the nature of resource allocation in county boroughs. One important finding is that the data do not support the notion of "environmental determinism." Most allocations are not systematically related to general demographic characteristics of the units of analysis. The absence of strong associations with outputs is evident for measures of the economic, the social, and the political environments. It is noteworthy that the few substantial linkages are with important allocation variables—provision of housing, expenditure per head on the main education services, and the summary measure of total expenditure per head. But in general, there seem to be individualistic allocation patterns in the various county boroughs.

A related finding is the inadequacy of either need or demand indicators. A recurring theme of Chief Officers and other Spending Department personnel is the lack of policy-oriented information on either the need or demand for particular services. This is particularly salient for divisible-benefit services, those which do have a definable clientele. In the demographic approach analysis, most measures tapping the concept of need were aggregate level characteristics from which individual need has been inferred. In fact, these are the kind of measures Spending Department Officers report they use to estimate need. They explain that they lack the time, funding, or personnel to do the type of research necessary to establish either need or demand.[22]

A third finding, which is supported in the case studies but is most clearly shown in longitudinal analysis, is the history-dependent nature of budgetary allocations. The basic axiom of the budgetary process is that the best predictor of this year's allocation level is last year's allocation level (the "base") (Wildavsky, 1964: 16; Davis et al., 1966: 533). In all four county boroughs, the previous year's allocations are, with rare exceptions, taken as prima facie valid. The procedures focus attention on increases—on explaining their components and justifying them. The procedures in Southend explicitly structure the problem in this mode. The Chief Officer in West Bromwich does have the option to de-emphasize the analysis of increases. However, under the guise of "uncontrollability," (Barber, 1966) which really translates as organizational inertia and political feasibility, every Chief Officer continued to operate in terms of marginal yearly changes.

The findings also support the generalization that *the processes of resource allocation are structured to facilitate the avoidance of responsibility by role-takers.* According to the norms, the elected Council makes policy decisions and allocates resources. But resource allocation decisions are the product of a rather complex chain of delegation of responsibility. Council delegates budgetary decision-making to a Finance Committee. Within this committee, the chairman is normally granted broad discretion to make decisions. But most of the actual decision-making/problem-solving discretion is tacitly transferred to the senior bureaucrats in the Finance and Spending Departments. The role of the Finance Committee Chairman and the leaders of the Majority Group is comparable to Sir William Harcourt's description of the Government Minister: He exists to tell the civil servants what the people will not stand. Thus the elected officials establish broad policy constraints; but they relinquish their responsibility to determine the shape or the nature of resource allocations.

A further aspect of responsibility avoidance is the recourse to financial rather than programmatic decision criteria. Decisions about the selection of programs and the level of support are, according to the norms, determined by their expected impact, by their public and political support, and, in short, by their merit. In fact, decisions about impact and even about the level of support are perceived as either too complex or too problematic. Neither the elected officials nor the Chief Officers are inclined to take responsibility for the difficult value choices intrinsic in the allocation of scarce resources. Consequently, decision-making has gravitated to the financial officers, whose primary decision criteria are *financial*. The situation is aptly described by a senior accountant:

> These schemes are cut back on grounds of financial expedience. If you have a situation where there are two schemes and you can only afford to do one of them, ideally you would do the most pressing from the point of view of amenity. I would not like to say this is necessarily so. Certainly these things are not done without consultation; but it has been our experience that Chief Officers don't want to make these choices. Someone has to come along and arbitrarily say which schemes have to be cut. That person has been the Treasurer. I am sure the Treasurer would agree that he is not the most qualified person to choose among schemes on technical grounds. This is not perfect decision-making—for financial considerations are more important than planning ones. When a chop has to be made, it is made in the final analysis by the Treasurer; and so it is made on financial, if impartial, grounds.

Thus the decisions on financial support are primarily a product of "financial, if impartial" considerations. Chief Officers in systems like that of West Bromwich have the option to set decisively their own priorities. In most cases, they decline this option. The Chief Officer has support for more schemes than he can finance. The Finance Department "suggests" reductions to achieve a certain level of expenditure. The Chief Officer can make substitutions. Rather, he usually accepts the Treasurer's decisions under protest. Responsibility for difficult and unpopular choices is transferred and the Chief Officer is absolved of blame for the roads not taken.

Two other characteristics of budget-making merit brief note. Many studies stress the importance of feedback in guiding further decisions (Cyert and March, 1963: 119-20; Lindblom, 1959; Wildavsky, 1964). There was little evidence that feedback from the community affects resource allocation in the county boroughs. In the first place, few groups or individuals are sufficiently motivated to make concrete demands on budgeters. This stems from a lack of information about allocations generally and about points of effective access. Many of the messages are received and muffled by individual Councillors. Other messages are defined by decision-makers as illegitimate or naive. While decision-makers attend to information from central government and from the local bureaucracy (what Easton calls "withinputs"), response to community feedback is rare.

A second noteworthy characteristic is that the budgetary process is clearly structured to reduce the possibility of conflict. All budgetary deliberations are private and confidential. Documents and information are also private, and the flow of information is controlled so that each role-taker has no more than is necessary to perform his task. Only a few participants, primarily senior Finance Department officers, have sufficient information to consider the broad choices of resource allocations. Conflict is avoided by preventing any direct meeting of "spenders"—each seems to advocate his case in a vacuum. In fact, they express little awareness that they are involved in an (essentially) fixed-sum game. To reinforce this, the confrontations between "spenders" and "pruners" are highly stylized and accentuate bargaining, not competition. The procedures of compartmentalization "sanitize" the making of decisions which, potentially, involve open conflict over values and scarce resources.

In a sense, the drive to "rationalize" the allocation process reflects this desire to treat budget-making as a mechanical problem-solving routine. This view seemed evident in Brighton and Dudley, as well as West Bromwich. The sixteen-category schedule epitomizes the kind of new machinery being developed. The norms have always held that policy questions and priorities should be established prior to budget-making. In reality, this is often the only time when there is a real attempt to compare the value of more home nurses versus recarpeting more roads versus lower pupil-teacher ratios, and so on. The evidence can be interpreted to reflect the elevation of technical criteria. Financial criteria are used to determine the size of resource shares to functional areas and the technocrats allocate the funds among schemes. Thus decisions might or might not be responsive to community demands, to felt needs, etc. But these decisions are clearly the domain of what Lowi (1967) has called "new machines"— relatively irresponsible, technocratic, structures of power.

CONCLUDING REMARKS

Research on resource allocations has seldom provided an explicit examination of multiple approaches in a single context. This paper has considered the adequacy of two of the possible approaches. The demographic approach and the organizational process approach are "explanation sketches." That is, they are probabilistic, identify only a few key variables, and are based on extremely vague covering laws (Mayer, 1972; Hempel, 1965: 238). There are no rigorous or clear-cut critieria for assessing the "adequacy of explanation" for either approach. Subjective appraisals have been made concerning whether an approach meets its own critieria of success, whether it is useful in locating regularities, and whether it identifies key analytic factors.

The substantive interest in the allocation of resources by county borough governments has generated two kinds of questions: (1) how is the existing pattern (or the existing levels) of allocations explained? and (2) how is the creation of a new budget ("the budgetary process") explained? It is evident that, as employed in this paper, the demographic approach is clearly directed to the former question and the organizational process approach to the latter.[23]

The fundamental difference between the approaches is in the type of explanation they present. Using Van Dyke's (1960: 22-33) distinction, the demographic approach is an explanation in terms of *causes*. It specifies certain conditions or events which seem to produce the budgetary *outputs*. The formal test of adequacy is the amount of variation estimated by predictive equations. The organizational process approach is an explanation in terms of *reasons*. An action is explained when it is made intelligible. The focus is normally upon behavior, which is viewed as purposive and rule-following. The goal is to provide Popper's "logic of the situation" for the *process* of budget-making. The yardstick of an adequate explanation is the correspondence between the analytic components (often units of behavior) and the linkages among components, on the one hand, and the actual budgeting process on the other.

Most research on resource allocations has failed to distinguish, in its explanatory modes, between these alternative foci. Most studies are presented as if an explanation of process is necessarily an explanation of output, and vice versa. This would be true to the extent that complete explanation was achieved. There is no such theory. The organizational process approach is intriguing because it does attempt to bridge the conceptual gap between process and outputs. In the county boroughs the key components seem to vary substantially; further research is necessary to establish whether a model like Crecine's can be developed. However the null findings are strong evidence that the demographic approach is inadequate, in its own terms, to explain county borough outputs. An interesting research question is whether the county boroughs are a deviant case for a normally useful approach.

Gilbert Ryle contrasts "competing explanations," which are mutually exclusive, with "alternative explanations," which are complementary and reinforcing. The two approaches examined in this paper are competing ones in terms of the type of explanatory variables they identify. But at this stage of theory-building, they seem to be essentially alternative explanations. They focus on alternative central research questions, they operate at alternative levels of analysis. and they provide alternative kinds of explanations.

NOTES

1. This last observation is not the conventional wisdom among most scholars of English local authorities. It is beyond the purposes of this paper to deal adequately with the

complex question of county borough autonomy. There is, however, a growing empirical literature which suports this notion. See, for example, Danziger (1974): Chapter 2; Dearlove (1973): Chapter 4; Boaden (1971); Boaden and Alford (1968). The undoubted supremacy of Parliament was resolutely asserted in the Local Government Act, 1974. This act has reorganized local government structures in England and Wales, amalgamating the county boroughs into larger, county-wide units.

2. The pairing technique is derived from the notions of "most similar system" and "most dissimilar system" designs (Przeworski and Teune, 1970: 31-39).

3. This enormous body of research often takes either the American states or selected municipalities as the units of analysis. The state-level studies have tended to be more comparable and their findings somewhat more consistent. Examples of the state-level research are Dye (1966) and Sharkansky (1968). Representative of the city-level studies, which have been done by many disciplines within social science, are Brazer (1959, Fisher (1961), and Masotti and Bowen (1965).

4. The formula is: coefficient of variation (C.V.) = $\frac{\mu}{\delta}$. The measure is meant to capture the relative amount of dispersion around the mean in a manner that is standardized across different variables (see Allen, 1968: 86).

5. This language is clearly evident in Thomas Dye's (1966: especially chapter 1) representative conceptualization of the demographic approach.

6. This division of variables is derived from the one used by Boaden (1971). The application of the approach in this paper differs from Boaden's less in conceptualization than in the formation of dependent and independent variables and in the use and interpretation of methodological techniques.

7. The classic, early analysis in this mode is Hicks and Hicks (1943). Alt (1971) and Boaden (1971) are the two main applications of the demographic approach to the county boroughs. Alt takes a sample of about half the county boroughs and uses a small set of simple, partial, and multiple correlation analyses. Aside from the limited group of dependent variables, the main shortcoming is the independent variables. There are only four indicators and no explication of why these were selected. One of these, a competition index, is invalid because it fails to account for the possibility of an important third party representation on the Council. During the period studied, there was a substantial third party on nearly one-third of the Councils and one-sixth of them had clear three-party systems. While this problem pollutes many analyses, Alt's study is a useful first step. Boaden's book-length study is much more disappointing. The analysis shows only the most rudimentary understanding of the methodologies employed. The choices of independent variables in the partial correlation analyses are unsystematic and often puzzling. Dependent variables are taken from only one particular year. Moreover, the independent variables are often strangely operationalized. For example, Boaden's education level measure is taken from the 1951 Census (why not 1961?) and includes only a small percentage of the adult males (those aged 15-25). Analysis of the data and explanations are often ad hoc. The cumulative effect of large numbers of small and not-so-small deficiencies is that Boaden's analysis does not gain one's confidence. In fairness to Boaden, however, his is the first large multivariate analysis of county borough expenditure and his conceptual framework is a useful departure from the Dye model.

8. It must be stressed that the regression equations cited are only *estimations* of the most powerful variables. Given the substantial multicollinearity among the independent variables, the outcomes of such regression analyses are rather volatile. However, careful analysis and data exploration were employed to select the most accurate and reasonable set of variables for each equation. In no case was there an alternative equation with any notable improvement on either the F statistic or the r^2.

9. This assumes a two-tailed significance test for N = 77 cases. This decision is similar to that made by Dye (1966: chapter 1). Moreover, one could argue that while the analysis covers all cases, it is cross-sectional—it is a sample, in time, of the cases.

10. The coefficient of determination, which measures the fraction of explained variance, is the r^2 statistic. An r value must be greater than $\pm .33$ in order to explain 10% of the variation in the dependent variable.

11. During the 1960s, provision of the police service became the responsibility of area-wide jurisdictions for most county boroughs. The county boroughs were levied a yearly charge for service to their citizens. Thus effective control over provision was lost by 1968-1969. The analysis holds, however, for the early 1960s, when most county boroughs still controlled their own police service.

12. This independent variable is a measure of housing activity and thus corresponds, to some extent, with the output measure. The distinction is that the latter is the amount of postwar (1945-1965) public housing that has been built relative to the potential clientele (the number of households) while the independent variable is a cross-sectional (1960-1965) ratio of publicly-built units to total units built. The correlation of the two variables is +.58, although there is no reason to expect that they must necessarily correlate.

13. There is also a growing association with the disposition measure of public/private activity mix. Its r-values increased during the three data points from +.18 to .37 to .43.

14. Teachers' salaries is an illustrative example of the impact of local discretion upon staff-related expenditure. National decisions set wage scales and the Ministry of Education and Science sets guidelines on such factors as desired pupil-teacher ratios. But one finds substantial latitude for choice-making at the local level. Most apparent is the fact that even a small variation in pupil-teacher ratios between boroughs results in differences of 20-30 teachers at the primary school level, given existing enrollments. More subtle is the range of local decisions on hiring and retention policies. For instance, some county boroughs vigorously recruit highly qualified or specially trained teachers in order to enhance the quality of their education staff. Other county boroughs tend to hire those with minimal qualifications and experience. The mix, in a particular county borough, between these two extremes is a function of decisions which are primarily local. The financial impact of such decisions on the quality of staff can be tens of thousands of pounds per year.

15. One of the county boroughs is a clear example of the level to which allocation decisions are broken down in the budget-creation process. Each detail head is separately authorized. The level of specificity is: Service = Local Health Services; Division of Service = Care of Mothers and Young Children; Sub-division of Service = Clinics; Detail Head = Salaries and Wages. Each detail head must be accurate, since only a minimal overspending is allowed without a supplementary authorization procedure.

16. Southend and West Bromwich might be characterized briefly by these selected characteristics:

	Southend	West Bromwich
Population (1968)	165,760	172,650
Population density (1968)	16.2	14.7
Rateable value per head (1 Apr. 1968)	£ 51.4	£ 48.3
Percent of population under age 15	19.7%	23.5%
Percent of population over age 65 (1966)	19.0%	9.6%
Percent of population in professional and managerial class [Census Classes 1, 2, 3, 4, 13 (1966)]	20.7%	8.2%
Percent of population in skilled working class [Census Classes 8, 9, 12, 14 (1966)]	32.5%	49.6%

17. The best general explanations of incremental decision-making remain those of Lindblom (see Lindblom, 1959; Braybrooke and Lindblom, 1963). Important studies of the incremental style for budgetary decision-making are Wildavsky (1964), Barber (1966), and Fenno (1966).

18. The only important constraint other than approval is that schemes must be calcu-

lated at the level of expenditure for a full year. This is meant to prevent the "smuggling in" of schemes in Y_n which overcommit the spending department's resources in Y_{n+1}. Financial actors are suspicious that Chief Officers often attempt this ploy.

19. Cyert and March (1965: 110) observe: ". . . in the long run, the organization learns to provide counter biases for each bias."

20. The Chief Officer must sustain the support or the acquiescence of his Council Spending Committee. Except in the case of an inept Chief Officer or an exceptional Spending Committee Chairman, the Committee normally defers to the Chief Officer's expertise and accepts his decisions. This is particularly true on matters of financial resource allocation (see Danziger, 1974: chapters 8, 9).

21. This point is stressed because those who have applied the model argue that its adequacy depends on the structural correspondence between the model and actual processes (see Crecine, 1969: 143-44).

22. The lack of such measures and the difficulty in creating adequate ones is stressed by Davies (1968: 303-04) in his thorough study of the personal social services in English local authorities.

23. It is, of course, possible to operationalize the demographic approach in a dynamic frame. Several other studies in this volume have taken that analytic perspective. The dependent variables can be taken as either actual values at Y_{n+1} or as change values between Y_n and Y_{n+1}. These can be correlated with either static demographic variables or measures of the change in the demographic variables over the same time frame (or with the allocation variables lagged). This sort of analysis was also performed on the data analyzed in this study. It did not lead to particularly high levels of correlation and the results and conclusions are quite consistent with those in the text. These findings are not reported due to space constraints. It was decided to present the cross-sectional analysis because it has been the dominant form of the demographic approach, not in order to create a "straw man."

APPENDIX

Regression Equations for Selected Measures of Resources Allocated

Housing Provision =

	b	Stnd. Error	Par. F
Elderly	-.759	.165	21.093
Pub/Priv	.115	.034	11.569
MigBal	.063	.019	11.493
Debt/hd	2.954	.928	10.136
W/inMig	-.119	.050	5.588
(constant)	17.094		

Mult. R   =   .775
R^2 =   .600
F   = 20.742 $<$ .01

Housing Rent (1968) =

	b	Stnd. Error	Par. F
Grant	-.044	.007	39.874
Pupils	.157	.047	11.000
Density	-.365	.123	8.777

%Labor	-.114	.044	6.759
Amenities	.200	.085	5.538
(constant)	73.825		

Mult. R = .809
R^2 = .655
F = 26.208 < .01

Children's Service Expenditure (1968-69) =

	b	Stnd. Error	Par. F
Density	18.246	5.741	10.100
Non-White	.650	.228	8.163
Amenities	-8.946	3.277	7.452
(constant)	1250.351		

Mult. R = .566
R^2 = .320
F = 11.132 < .01

Total Expenditure per Head (1968-69) =

	b	Stnd. Error	Par. F
Grant	.689	.069	99.939
Debt/hd	79.497	11.262	49.827
Dom/Ind	-7.401	1.195	38.360
Wealthy	2.847	.717	15.774
Amenities	-2.742	.841	10.635
Cars	6.827	2.696	6.415
Elderly	6.369	2.756	5.342
(constant)	900.034		

Mult. R = .897
R^2 = .804
F = 39.845 < .01

NOTE: The procedure in the selection of independent variables and in the determination of the multiple R^2 (fraction of explained variance), etc., is to utilize a combination of stepwise and simultaneous multiple regression analysis. The inclusion level for independent variables is based on the statistical significance of the regression coefficient (unstandardized) for each variable. The test of significance is an F statistic whose formula is:

$$\left(\frac{b}{\text{standard error of b}} \right)^2.$$

The F is interpreted in the normal fashion from a table for the distribution of F, given the relevant degrees of freedom. For the best discussion of the F statistic, see N. Draper and R. Smith, *Applied Regression Analysis* (New York: Wiley, 1966).

Chapter 3

OBSERVATIONS ON A DISTRIBUTIVE THEORY
OF POLICY-MAKING: TWO AMERICAN
EXPENDITURE PROGRAMS COMPARED

BARRY S. RUNDQUIST
Department of Political Science
University of Illinois
and
JOHN A. FEREJOHN
Department of Political Science
California Institute of Technology

Why government policies take the form they do is a question that has long interested political scientists and is currently the focus of widespread research efforts (Heclo, 1972; Tribe, 1972; and Bauer and Jergen, 1969). There are essentially three basic approaches to this question: the environmental, the structural, and a combination of these two approaches. The first, evidenced in other papers in this volume, attempts to explain government outputs without discussing the structure of government decision-making. Implicit in this approach is the assumption that governmental decision-makers respond directly, whether rationally or like billiard balls, to environmental influences. The second approach would explain outputs only in terms of government decision-making. The implicit assumption in this approach is that decision-makers can produce outputs that differ from those imposed upon them by their environment. The third approach attempts to explain the outputs of government as a function of both government structure and environmental influences. This approach assumes that if decision-making were organized differently, different influences in the government's environment would be able to affect policy decisions, and consequently government policy would take a different form. This paper takes a prevalent theory following from this third approach and examines it in the light of data on two expenditure programs.

AUTHORS' NOTE: The authors gratefully acknowledge the help of David Griffith, Susan Rundquist, and the suggestions of Gerald Strom, Cal Clark, Lester Seligman, and Craig Liske.

THE DISTRIBUTIVE THEORY

The theory is about how the institutional structure of decision-making in Washington relates to the geographic distribution of federal expenditures. Since it only concerns the formation of distributive policies, it will be referred to as the distributive theory.[1] Distributive policies are those that can be subdivided into many parts, each of which can be implemented in different areas of the country and regarding which separate choices can be made by legislative or bureaucratic decision-makers (Lowi, 1964: 690). The distributive theory does not purport to explain other policies which do not meet these requirements.

The basic assumption of the distributive theory is that congressmen are motivated to serve the economic interests of their constituencies.[2] The theory states simply that congressmen are best able to benefit their constituencies if they are members of standing committees with jurisdiction over government activities that affect their constituencies. Three basic hypotheses follow from this theory. Hypothesis 1, the recruitment hypothesis, is that members from constituencies with a pecuniary interest in a particular form of government activity seek membership on a constituency-relevant authorizing committee or appropriations subcommittee. Hypothesis 2, the overrepresentation hypothesis, is that when the districts of committee members are compared with those of other congressmen, the committees will be found to overrepresent constituencies with a stake in their subject matter. Hypothesis 3, the benefit hypothesis, is that relative to those of other congressmen, the constituencies of committee members benefit disproportionately from the distribution of expenditures under their jurisdiction.

Underlying Hypothesis 1 are assumptions about the relationship of congressmen and their constituencies and the structure of decision-making in the House. It is assumed that congressmen generally desire reelection or advancement to statewide office (Schlesinger, 1966); that the achievement of both goals is contingent upon the approval of people who live in the congressman's constituency; and that the approval of constituents rests in part on the congressman's provision for their economic well-being.[3] It is also assumed that in the House, decisions relevant to any particular policy are formulated in a limited number of standing committees (usually one), that members with the most influence over committee decisions are those whose uninterrupted tenure on the committee is longest, that House rules limit the number of standing committees on which one can serve, and therefore, that members can hope to be influential in only a few policy areas. In its pure form, this hypothesis would assume that members rank the economic activities of their constituencies from those to which they must pay the most attention in order to get reelected to those which they can ignore, then become members of the standing committee that will allow them to serve the highest ranked activity.

The overrepresentation hypothesis follows from the reasoning underlying the recruitment hypothesis, but also requires an assumption that nothing interferes with the ability of congressmen seeking to serve a particular interest in their constituencies to obtain membership on the relevant committee. That this latter assumption is somewhat unrealistic in the House context is discussed below.

The benefit hypothesis follows in part from the assumptions underlying Hypotheses 1 and 2, in the sense that members with a constituency-serving incentive would not choose membership on a committee if they did not expect to be able sooner or later to benefit their constituency. However, there is a reason why the districts of committee members would benefit disproportionately even if members from districts with a pecuniary interest in the government activity under the committee's jurisdiction were not overrepresented on the committee (Ferejohn, 1972, and Strom, 1973). This again has to do with the nature of House decision-making on distributive issues. We noted earlier that distributive decisions are made in standing committees and/or agencies and that the congressmen best able to affect agency decisions are on the committee with jurisdiction over the agency (Niskanen, 1971). It is also the case that committee decisions tend to be accepted on the floor of Congress (Fenno, 1966 and 1973). This means that those congressmen who can exercise the most influence over a distributive policy are within the relevant committee rather than outside of it. And this means that committee members who wish to withold their support for an agency's request until it is changed to include consideration for their constituencies will tend to obtain that objective. Indeed, it is easier to add their preferred programs than to mobilize committee members to override their veto of the request, in part because the other members can reasonably expect reciprocal treatment in the future. To the extent that only members of a committee have this ability, members' constituencies should be expected to benefit more than those of nonmembers.

We should emphasize that the benefit hypothesis does *not* require the committee itself to decide on programs that benefit its members' constituencies. Rather, it allows both for such direct constituency-serving behavior and for indirect constituency-serving in which committee members support the program and budget requests of agencies that in turn benefit their constituencies. In either case, the theory contends, the distribution of government activities will be different from what would be produced by Congress as a whole rather than Congress in committee (Rundquist, 1973).

EXTENDING THE DISTRIBUTIVE THEORY

At its present level of generalization the distributive theory is of little use to those who would better understand national-level policy-making in the United States because it fails to take into account the institutional complexity of those processes. Among other things, it fails to stipulate whether it covers appropriations as well as authorizing committees, foreign as well as domestic policies, and states as well as congressional districts. This is a problem because there is no consensus among scholars that the theory pertains to these phenomena. For example, as we explain below, students of the appropriations process would seem to argue that the theory cannot characterize appropriations subcommittees with jurisdiction over distributive programs. In other words, the theory needs to be extended so that it specifies the conditions under which it is valid. In what follows we report on an attempt to extend the theory by ascertaining (1) whether it is valid in both authorizing and appropriating distributive programs, (2) whether its unit is the congressional district or the state, and (3) whether the theory accounts for the formation of both domestic and foreign policies.

APPROPRIATIONS VS. AUTHORIZATIONS

Richard Fenno (1966: 141) has argued that there is a norm on the House Appropriations Committee which excludes members from constituencies with an interest in a subcommittee's subject matter from obtaining membership on that subcommittee. This norm, which can be called the Cannon-Taber norm after the chairman and ranking Republican who allegedly enforced it, was designed to prevent subcommittees from being packed with members favorable to particular programs. Of course, if this norm is operative, the recruitment, overrepresentation, and benefit hypotheses should not be valid for appropriations subcommittees. No such norm is known to have operated on the authorizing committees (Fenno, 1966: 149).

STATES AND DISTRICTS

In previous work on military procurement and on the civil works program of the Army Corps of Engineers, the authors discovered (Ferejohn, 1972, and Rundquist, 1973), largely independently, that there are several institutional and behavioral reasons that may interfere with the operation of our hypotheses at the district level. To illustrate: a Republican member of the Agriculture Committee from an agricultural district in California is defeated by a Democrat. As there are no Democratic vacancies on the Agriculture Committee he is given a seat on Education and Labor. Six years later, a Democratic vacancy occurs on the Agriculture Committee to which California may now lay first claim. If the congressman on Education and Labor does not wish to change committees, the dean of the California delegation may ask a newly elected Democrat from Los Angeles to take the vacant seat on Agriculture rather than forfeiting California's claim to it. The upshot is that the operation of the seniority system and the incentives and opportunities to specialize in committee work may constrain the operation of our recruitment hypothesis.[4] A second reason why states and not districts may be the proper units in the distributive theory is that some congressmen desire political careers outside the House. The next step up the political ladder is nearly always some statewide office (Schlesinger, 1966). For this reason, a new congressman from a rural district may find it advantageous to eschew a seat on Agriculture for one on Banking and Currency. Ambition for higher office may therefore produce situations where representatives go on committees in which their immediate constituencies have little interest.

Both of these processes would seem likely to work in favor of our hypotheses at the state level. That is, the state delegation would seem likely to be concerned with maintaining strong representation on a committee only if the state benefits from the program it oversees. Similarly, congressmen with ambitions to become senator or governor would appear to have incentives to join committees which are concerned with federal policies relevant to their states.

FOREIGN AND DOMESTIC POLICIES

It has been argued (Westerfield, 1966) that foreign policies are decided upon in closed, executive-centered processes quite unlike those typical of domestic policies. If this is true, it would seem that the kinds of congressional influences invisioned in the distributive theory could not occur and, therefore, the theory would not be valid for foreign policy-making. However, it has also been argued (Rosenau, 1967) that "the more [a foreign policy] encompasses a society's resources and relationships, the more will it be drawn into the society's domestic political system [and] the less will it be processed through the society's foreign political system." This would suggest that some kinds of foreign policies may very well be formulated in processes that resemble domestic and perhaps even distributive ones.

We addressed this problem by focusing on the geographic distribution of Corps of Engineers Civil Works expenditures and military procurement expenditures. Both types of expenditures can be classified as distributive. Many different items are procured by the military services and these purchases involve thousands of contractors in all parts of the country. Moreover, military procurement officers can choose between a number of alternative criteria, including political ones, in awarding contracts (Rosenau, 1967). Similarly, many Corps projects are eligible for funding each year, and congressmen and Corps engineers decide which ones will be built. Given their characteristics, Theodore Lowi (1964: 690) argues that both are prototypical distributive policies.

The principal difference between these two areas is that military procurement policy is usually considered an instrument of American foreign policy and Corps of Engineers public works policy is normally tagged as a domestic policy.[5] And, just as scholars disagree on whether foreign policy can be formulated in processes similar to those in which domestic policies are put together, they disagree on whether military procurement policies are formulated in distributive processes. Comparing military procurement policy with military construction policy, which she believes is distributive, Goss (1972) argues as follows:

Decisions about weapons acquisition are closely related to matters that affect the perceptions of foreign governments—especially potential enemies. While it is immaterial to potential enemies whether the Texas airfield site is chosen over the California site (the same Air Force commands them both), it *is* important that our technological capabilities be viewed with the utmost respect. If the Defense Department determines that one contractor can do a better job than another, even at a slightly higher cost, it is difficult for the committee member to recommend that the inferior job be done.

Others, like Rosenau (1967) and Williamson (1967) seem to agree with Lowi (1964) about military procurement—witness Williamson's argument that the weapons acquisition process has not been organized so as to minimize the uncertainty that leads to cost overruns and performance failures because the services, the contractors, and congressmen benefit from the present arrangement.

Our comparison of military procurement and Corps of Engineers Civil Works policies is designed to speak to the question of whether two distributive policies, one foreign and one domestic, are formulated in similar distributive processes. The question of whether districts or states are the proper units in the distributive theory is addressed by asking whether the three distributive hypotheses are valid at either or both levels in both policy areas. Finally, membership on both authorizing and appropriating committees is checked to determine whether or not the hypotheses are valid for the former but not the latter committees.

THE RECRUITMENT, OVERREPRESENTATION, AND BENEFIT HYPOTHESES IN THE CORPS OF ENGINEERS CIVIL WORKS AREA

METHODOLOGICAL CAVEATS

As will become apparent, the data and design of this study do not permit a definitive "test" of the hypotheses in the distributive theory. Rather our analysis should be treated as suggestive of both how the distributive theory relates to the actual politics of our two policy areas and the kinds of research needed to get at this relationship. A major limitation is that ours is a static analysis. This is a problem for two reasons. First, we have to assume that to the extent the distributive theory is valid, its hypotheses will be supported against data on the relationship between committee membership and the distribution of expenditures in a given year. However, it may well be that the theory concerns changes in the distribution of expenditures from year-to-year rather than the distribution in any one year.[6] Second, by focusing on single years, we severely restrict the number of cases we can observe. In a given year, the number of congressmen who can be on a committee is quite limited, whereas the longer the period of years, the more committee members one can examine. This is a problem because when we compare the proportion of a small number of cases with the proportion of a larger number of cases—as each of our hypotheses requires—each member in the smaller group exerts a disproportionate effect on the result. Unfortunately, relatively complete data on the distribution of military procurement expenditures among congressional districts are only available for FY 1960, so in order to address our district-level questions in the military area, we were limited to one year.[7] To get around the distorting effect of the small N's we have utilized the chi-square test to estimate the likelihood that the relationships we find between committee members and larger groups could have occurred by chance. Only findings that have a less than 10% probability of occurring by chance will be interpreted as sufficient to reject the null hypotheses under study.[8]

VARIABLES

The House committees with jurisdiction over the Corps of Engineers Civil Works projects are the Public Works Committee and the Appropriations Subcommittee on Public Works (Murphy, 1974). The distribution of expenditures in the Corps of Engineers construction program is treated in two different ways. First, we consider the size of the construction program in each state and district as a measure (partial) of the degree of interest each unit has in the legislative and appropriations committees. Second, to examine the benefit hypothesis, we utilize the number of new planning or construction starts initiated by the House in each state and district.

The rationale for employing total construction funds for examining the recruitment and overrepresentation hypotheses and new starts for the benefits hypothesis is as follows. The current construction budget is determined by decisions made in the House, Senate, Corps of Engineers, and the Bureau of the Budget over a period of about fifteen years. In any given year, new starts comprise only 5% of the budget. Therefore, it is likely that the total construction budget is an indicator of a state's or district's long-term interest in the Corps program, whereas House-initiated new starts are more sensitive to the current makeup of the committees. The reader is referred to work by one of the authors (Ferejohn, 1974) on this point.

RECRUITMENT

The recruitment hypothesis is that congressmen who are motivated to serve a particular interest in their constituency seek membership on the committee that enables them to do so. In our analysis, we have been unable to determine which constituency interests congressmen seek to serve and whether those who seek it find membership on appropriate committees. Instead, we ask whether districts and states that evidence the largest dollar amounts of certain types of federal expenditures are disproportionately represented on committees with jurisdiction over these expenditures. Since recruitment to a standing committee occurs within political parties (Masters, 1961), each partisan side of the committees must overrepresent districts or states that evidence the largest dollar amounts of

Corps expenditures relative to the body from which their members are recruited. Thus Public Works' Democrats must overrepresent such districts or states relative to all House Democrats, and Public Works Republicans must overrepresent them relative to all House Republicans. Similarly, Public Works Subcommittee Democrats must be overrepresentative relative to other Democrats on Appropriations, and Public Works Subcommittee Republicans overrepresentative relative to other Republicans on Appropriations. In order to achieve the comparison for Public Works Democrats, we ranked all districts represented by Democrats from high to low in terms of the level of Corps expenditures they evidenced, then broke the distribution into quartiles. We postulated that the recruitment hypothesis would be supported for this side of the Public Works Committee if significantly more than 25% of the districts of these members are in the top quartile. Republicans on the Public Works Committee and Democrats and Republicans on the Appropriations Subcommittee were treated analogously.

Table 1 evidences some support (more for Democrats than Republicans) for the recruitment hypothesis on both committees. However, since our chi-square tests indicate that these results have a greater than 10% probability of have occurred by chance, we must conclude that there is no significant district-level support for this hypothesis.

TABLE 1

The Districts of Democrats and Republicans on the
Two Public Works Committees in Each Quartile

| Quartiles[a] | Public Works Committee | | | |
| | Democrats[b] | | Republicans[b] | |
	N	%	N	%
Top Quartile	5	(22)	2	(18)
2nd Quartile	10	(43)	3	(27)
3rd & 4th Quartile	8	(35)	6	(55)
Total	23	(100)	11	(100)
	Subcommittee on Public Works			
Top Quartile	2	(33)	0	--
2nd Quartile	2	(33)	2	(66)
3rd & 4th Quartile	2	(33)	1	(33)
Total	6	(100)	3	(100)

a. The quartiles are based on ranking all of the districts represented by Democrats and Republicans in order of the size of the FY 1967 budget request.

In this and the following tables, the third and fourth quartiles are collapsed because the lower half of the distributions include a number of districts and states that receive no Corps dollars at all.

b. Not significant at the .10 level.

We also find no support for the recruitment hypothesis on the state level. Table 2 shows that only 30% of the Democrats on Public Works represent states that are in the top quartile of those that elect Democrats. Similarly, the table indicates that neither the Democratic nor the Republican sides of the Public Works Subcommittee overrepresent such states relative to their parent groupings on Appropriations. The only support for the hypothesis is for Public Works Republicans and even this result is not significant at the 10% level.

TABLE 2

The States Represented by Democrats and Republicans on the
Two Public Works Committees in Each Quartile

| Quartiles | Public Works Committee | | | |
| | Democrats | | Republicans | |
	N	%	N	%
Top Quartile	6	(30)	5	(50)
2nd Quartile	6	(30)	3	(30)
3rd Quartile	5	(25)	1	(10)
4th Quartile	3	(15)	1	(10)
Total	20	(100)	10	(100)
	Subcommittee on Public Works			
Top Quartile	1	(17)	0	––
2nd Quartile	3	(50)	0	––
3rd Quartile	0	––	2	(67)
4th Quartile	2	(33)	1	(33)
Total	6	(100)	3	(100)

OVERREPRESENTATION

The overrepresentation hypothesis requires that the Public Works Committee and the Appropriations Subcommittee on Public Works overrepresent districts and states that evidence the largest amounts of Corps expenditures relative to all nonmembers. To determine this, we ranked all districts and states (separately) from high to low, broke them into quartiles, and counted the number of committee members' districts or states in the top quartiles. To reject the overrepresentation hypothesis, we would have to find that not significantly more than one-quarter of the districts represented on the two committees with jurisdiction over Corps projects are in the top quartile. Table 3 provides some, but clearly not overwhelming, support for the overrepresentation hypothesis. There is no tendency on either committee for top quartile districts to be overrepresented. However, there is a tendency for both committees to over-

TABLE 3

The Districts Represented by the Members of the
Two Public Works Committees in Each Quartile

Quartiles	Public Works Committee[a]		Public Works Subcommittee[b]	
	N	%	N	%
Top Quartile	8	(24)	2	(22)
2nd Quartile	12	(36)	5	(56)
3rd & 4th Quartiles	14	(41)	2	(22)
Total	34	(101)	9	(100)

a. Not significant at .10 level.
b. Significant at the .10 level.

represent districts in the second quartile. Moreover, 78% of the members of the Appropriations Subcommittee are from districts in the two top quartiles and this finding is significant at the 10% level. However, since it requires that districts evidencing the *highest* levels of Corps expenditures be overrepresented on an appropriate committee, this finding cannot be accepted as supportive of the overrepresentation hypothesis.

We find no significant support for the overrepresentation hypothesis on the state level. Table 4 was constructed by arranging all states in quartiles according to the level of Corps expenditures they received. The table shows a tendency for Public Works to overrepresent states in the top two quartiles, but this tendency is not significant at the 10% level.

TABLE 4

The States Represented by the Members of the
Two Public Works Committees in Each Quartile

Quartiles	Public Works Committee[a]		Public Works Subcommittee[a]	
	N	%	N	%
Top Quartile	7	(29)	1	(11)
2nd Quartile	9	(38)	4	(44)
3rd Quartile	4	(17)	2	(22)
4th Quartile	4	(17)	2	(22)
Total	24	(101)	9	(99)

a. Not significant at .10 level.

BENEFIT

In this section we check whether districts or states represented on the Public Works Committee and/or the Appropriations Subcommittee on Public Works benefit disproportionately from the distribution of Corps expenditures. As we mentioned above, we measure "benefit" in terms of the number of new starts added on to the President's Budget as it passes through the House of Representatives. In FY 1967, the House added a total of 63 new starts to a budget which already contained funding for some three hundred projects. Our question is whether or not districts and/or states represented on the committees with jurisdiction over Corps projects received a disproportionate number of these new starts.

In evaluating the impact of committee membership on House new starts, we attempted to control for the number of new starts that would have gone to a district or state whether or not it was represented on one of the Corps committees. To do this we assumed that the influence of these factors is roughly constant over time and bears a constant relationship to the level of Corps activity in the state in previous years. For example, if Colorado receives a high level of Corps expenditures over a period of years, we would infer that a similar level of new starts in our year is independent of whether or not the state is represented on one of the Corps committees. For the benefit hypothesis to be supported, we must find that committee members' districts or states are given more new starts than is proportional to their budget requests. They are. Table 5 shows that, controlling for the amount initially budgeted for each district and state, the districts and states of members of both the Public Works Committee and the Appropriations Subcommittee average significantly more new starts than those of nonmembers.[9] Thus the benefit hypothesis is supported for both committees at both the district and state level.

Thus our analysis in the Corps projects area yields significant support for the benefit hypothesis for both committees on the district and the state levels, but no significant support at all for the recruitment and overrepresentation hypotheses.

TABLE 5

Regression Results: Construction New Starts on Membership on the Two Public Works Committees and the FY 1967 Budget Request

| | | District-Level Analysis | | |
	Constant	PW Com	PW Sub	Budget
Coefficient:	.115	.152 +	.193 +	.004
F =		5.86	2.67	2.4
		State-Level Analysis		
Coefficient:	-.032	1.15 +	.693 +	.016
F =		57.58	4.25	10.57

THE RECRUITMENT, OVERREPRESENTATION, AND BENEFIT
HYPOTHESES IN THE MILITARY AREA

VARIABLES AND CAVEATS

The House committees with jurisdiction over military procurement policy are the Armed Services Committee and the Appropriations Subcommittee on the Department of Defense (DOD Subcommittee). To test our recruitment and overrepresentation hypotheses for these committees, we obtained data on the distribution of prime military contract awards for manufacturing (pmc's) among congressional districts and states in the 48 continental states in FY 1960.[10]

Like the total construction funds for Corps of Engineers projects used above, our pmc measure summarizes a several-year sequence of federal activity in a geographic area. The payment of pmc's to a contractor ends a series of economic transactions between the Defense Department and localities that began some two and one-half to five years earlier (Greenberg, 1967; Lee, 1970). Each prior action had an impact on employment and capital development in the area, and the final level of pmc's is a rough indicator of all of these impacts. In other words, areas with high levels of pmc's can be assumed to have experienced more such impacts than areas with lower levels of pmc's (Rundquist, 1973: Ch. 3).

The major difficulty with our pmc measure is that some prime contractors redistribute pmc dollars to subcontractors in other areas. To the extent this occurs, the level of pmc's awarded to the original area cannot be assumed to reflect the economic impact of military procurement activity in that area. This is a serious problem because about half of all pmc's awarded in FY 1960 were for activities performed by subcontractors. Whether or not pmc dollars that are passed on to subcontractors have an impact on the area in which the prime contractor is located depends, of course, on the geographic proximity of the prime and subcontractors. Unfortunately, little is known about the distribution of military subcontracts. What information is available (Weidenbaum, 1966) suggests that prime and subcontracts are similarly distributed. Nevertheless, it must be recognized that the level of pmc's in each district or state *includes* dollars that are subcontracted out of the area and *excludes* dollars that are subcontracted into the area.

Another problem with the data used here is that we have been unable to obtain pmc information for 110 congressional districts. These districts were in multi-district metropolitan counties and our pmc data could not be disaggregated below the county level. We have, however, made an effort to estimate whether districts in these multidistrict areas are overrepresented on the military committees. To do so, we assumed that congressmen from *areas* with a high average dollar value of pmc's (that is, the total pmc's in the area divided by the number of districts in the area) would have the same kind of incentive to obtain membership on the military committees as would congressmen from discrete, highly involved districts. This assumption is supported by evidence that metropolitan economies are highly integrated (Bollens and Schmandt, 1965), and by interviews with members of the military committees.[11] Accordingly, we treat the missing 110 districts as 26 multidistrict cases and ask whether our recruitment and overrepresentation hypotheses are valid for both highly involved multidistrict areas *and* highly involved discrete districts.[12]

A second variable operationalized here is "benefit" from the distribution of pmc's. The ideal measure of benefit would distinguish between the level of pmc's that are in an area because of the area's representation on the military committees and the level that would be there whatever position the area's congressman occupies in the House. Identifying such committee-induced constituency benefits is made especially difficult by the fact that military procurement decisions are almost always made by the Services and there is nothing like a *House*-initiated "new start" in this policy area. Proposals for new procurement programs originate in the DOD; congressmen tend to be dependent on the DOD for information on procurement matters, and congressmen almost never decide where the work on procurement projects is to be carried out (Liske and Rundquist, 1974). This latter decision is made early in the procurement cycle by Service personnel.

The influence the military committees exercise over the location of procurement activity stems from the fact that the DOD collectively and the Services individually are prototypical budget-constrained agencies. Unlike most domestic agencies, almost all of the Services' new obligational budget authority each year is subject to review by the Appropriations Committees in Congress (Weidenbaum, 1966). In this situation, agency officials have an incentive to pay special attention to their congressional committees (Niskanen, 1971). Clearly, one way of inducing committees to support their program and budget requests is to award military contracts to the constituencies of committee members.[13] Thus, if the districts or states of committee members benefit from the distibution of pmc's, they are likely to do so as a result of the anticipation by agency officials of what committee members want.

Our problem is how to measure "benefit" in this situation. The solution for this paper has been to estimate "benefits" as the level of pmc's in a state or district that is not accounted for by the state's or district's manufacturing capability. "Manufacturing capability" is measured in terms of the number of manufacturing firms weighted by their size so that large firms are given more weight than small ones (Rundquist, 1973: Ch. 3). Thus, in the defense area, the benefit hypothesis would be supported if the level of pmc dollars per unit of manufacturing capability in the districts and/or states of members of the military committees is greater than that in the districts or states of nonmembers.

RECRUITMENT

The recruitment hypothesis requires that Armed Services Democrats should appear overrepresentative relative to all House Democrats; Armed Services

TABLE 6

The Districts of Democrats and Republicans on the
Armed Services Committee in Each Quartile

| Quartiles | Democrats | | | |
| | Discrete Cases[a] | | All Cases[b] | |
	N	%	N	%
Top	7	(47)	10	(53)
2nd	5	(33)	5	(26)
3rd	2	(13)	3	(16)
4th	1	(7)	1	(5)
Total	15	(100)	19	(100)
	Republicans			
Top	3	(21)[a]	5	(31)[a]
2nd	2	(14)	2	(13)
3rd	4	(29)	4	(25)
4th	5	(36)	5	(31)
Total	14	(100)	16	(100)

a. Not significant at .10 level.

b. Significant at the .05 level.

TABLE 7

The Districts of Democrats and Republicans on the
DOD Subcommittee in Each Quartile

| Quartiles | Democrats | | | |
| | Discrete Cases[a] | | All Cases[a] | |
	N	%	N	%
Top	5	(30)	3	(30)
2nd	0	——	2	(20)
3rd	2	(20)	2	(20)
4th	5	(50)	3	(30)
Total	12	(100)	10	(100)
	Republicans			
Top	0	——	2	(33)
2nd	2	(33)	2	(33)
3rd	2	(33)	1	(17)
4th	2	(33)	1	(17)
Total	6	(99)	6	(100)

a. Not significant at .10 level.

Republicans should appear overrepresentative relative to all House Republicans; DOD Subcommittee Democrats should appear overrepresentative relative to all Democrats on Appropriations, and DOD Subcommittee Republicans should appear overrepresentative relative to all Appropriations Republicans.

Our district-level analysis reveals that the recruitment hypothesis receives significant support for Armed Services Democrats; it is not supported for either Armed Services Republicans or Democrats, nor Republicans on the DOD Subcommittee. Table 6 shows that whether or not the multidistrict cases are counted, about half of the Democrats on Armed Services represent districts that rank in the top quartile of Democratic districts. More than three quarters are in the top two quartiles. The results for the discrete districts are just barely significant at the 10% level; those for the distribution which includes the multidistrict cases are significant at the 5% level. Table 7 reveals no such tendencies.

Our state level analysis indicates no significant support for the recruitment hypothesis for either military committee, though fairly strong tendencies for both sides of the Armed Services Committee. Thus Table 8 shows that 40% of the states represented by Democrats on Armed Services are in the top quartile of Democratic states and 73% are in the top two quartiles. Similarly, half of the states represented by Republicans on that committee are in the top quartile, and 79% are in the top two quartiles, but none of these findings are significant at the 10% level. No such tendencies are evident in Table 8 for the DOD Subcommittee.

TABLE 8

The States of Democrats and Republicans on the
Two Military Committees in Each Quartile[a]

| Quartiles | Armed Services | | | |
| | Democrats[b] | | Republicans[b] | |
	N	%	N	%
Top	6	(40)	7	(50)
2nd	5	(33)	4	(29)
3rd	4	(27)	2	(14)
4th	0	––	1	(7)
Total	15	(100)	14	(100)
	DOD Subcommittee			
Top	3	(33)	1	(17)
2nd	2	(22)	1	(17)
3rd	2	(22)	2	(33)
4th	2	(22)	2	(33)
Total	9	(99)	6	(100)

a. The comparison in this table is of the committee Democrats and Republicans and all other states that elect Democrats and/or Republicans respectively.

b. Not significant at .10 level.

BRUCE B. MASON

To conclude, the only significant support we have found for the recruitment hypothesis in the military area is for Armed Services Democrats on the district level.

OVERREPRESENTATION

To determine whether districts that are highly involved in military contracting are overrepresented on the military committees, we ranked the 325 discrete districts, and the 325 plus the 26 multidistrict cases, from those with the highest to those with the lowest levels of pmc's. Table 9 shows how the districts of members of the Armed Services Committee stand in these rankings. Clearly, the pattern on Armed Services is inconsistent with the overrepresentation hypothesis. In the ranking of 325 discrete districts, only 21% are in the top quartile and 55% represent districts in the top two quartiles. The hypothesis receives even less support from the ranking which includes the multidistrict metropolitan areas.

TABLE 9

The Districts of Members of the Two Military
Committees in Each Quartile

Quartiles	Armed Services			
	Discrete Cases[a]		All Cases[a]	
	N	%	N	%
Top	6	(21)	10	(29)
2nd	10	(35)	8	(23)
3rd	7	(24)	10	(29)
4th	6	(21)	7	(20)
Total	19	(101)	35	(101)
	DOD Subcommittee			
Top	5	(33)	3	(18)
2nd	3	(20)	6	(34)
3rd	4	(27)	3	(18)
4th	3	(20)	5	(29)
Total	15	(100)	17	(99)

a. Not significant at the .10 level.

Does Armed Services overrepresent *states* that are highly involved in military contracting? Table 9 also indicates that of the 22 states represented on Armed Services, 36% of them are in the top quartile and 68% are in the top two quartiles. However,. there is a greater than 10% probability that this finding could occur by chance.

TABLE 10

The States of Members of the Two Military
Committees in Each Quartile

	Armed Services	
Quartiles	N	%
Top	8	(36)
2nd	7	(32)
3rd	5	(23)
4th	2	(9)
Total	22	(100)
	DOD Subcommittee	
Top	7	(47)
2nd	2	(13)
3rd	4	(27)
4th	2	(13)
Total	15	(100)

We find no significant tendency for the DOD Subcommittee to overrepresent highly involved districts or states. See Table 9 and 10.

Our conclusion from this analysis is that neither military committee significantly overrepresents highly involved districts or states.[14]

BENEFIT

To establish whether the districts or states of committee members benefit disproportionately from the distribution of pmc's, we utilized regression analysis. The benefit hypothesis examined here is that districts and/or states represented on the military committees average more pmc dollars per unit of manufacturing capability (DPUC) than do areas without members on these committees.[15] Table 11 reveals our district-level findings on this hypothesis. It indicates that the members of Armed Services do average more DPUC than nonmembers, but that the districts of DOD Subcommittee members average fewer DPUC than those of nonmembers. However, neither of these differences is statistically significant.[16]

Do our committee variables do better in predicting distribution among states? Table 11 also shows no support for the benefit hypothesis on the state level.[17] States represented on Armed Services average fewer DPUC than those of nonmembers; states represented on the DOD Subcommittee average more. However, both differences are insignificant.

In conclusion, our study of the distributive theory in the military area suggests support for the recruitment hypothesis for Armed Services Democrats on the district level. Nothing else worked. Although there are some tendencies in

TABLE 11

Regression Results: Total PMC Awards on Membership on the
Military Committees and Manufacturing Capability

	District-Level Analysis			
	Constant	AS	DOD	Cap
Coefficient:	2642.41556	+ 16333.32043	- 1702.88419	+ 2.28933
F =		0.873	0.001	20.239
R^2 = .07829				
	State-Level Analysis			
Coefficient:	- 23590.32	- 26151.74	+ 81086.72	+ 138.84
F =		0.020	0.173	31.215
R^2 = .50249				

the directions suggested by the theory, there is a greater than 10% chance that these occurred by chance.

DISCUSSION

Our analysis suggests that there are no conditions under which all of the hypotheses of the distriqutive theory are valid. Instead, different hypotheses are valid under different conditions.

First, the only support we find for the benefit hypothesis is in the Corps of Engineers area. Both districts and states represented on the Public Works Committee and on the Appropriations Subcommittee on Public Works benefit disproportionately for House new start decisions. Neither states nor districts represented on the military committees benefit from the distribution of pmc's.

A second finding also distinguishes between the two policy areas: the only significant support for the recruitment hypothesis is for Armed Services Democrats. We find recruitment-effect tendencies for Republicans on this committee, and Democrats and Republicans on the Public Works Committee, but none of these are statistically significant. Also, we find no significant support for the overrepresentation hypothesis on any of the four committees.

This pattern of findings suggests that *something* about the way decisions regarding the distribution of Corps new starts are made results in disproportionate benefits to the districts and states of members of the committees with jurisdiction over Corps expenditures, whereas *something* about the way military procurement decisions are reached prevents districts and states represented on the military committees from benefiting. That the "something" is not related to overrepresentation is clear, for the committees are similar on this score—that is, neither committee is significantly overrepresentative and both committees show insignificant tendencies toward overrepresentation. Moreover, it is not due to recruitment effects because the only significant recruitment effect is for Armed Services Democrats and insignificant tendencies characterize committees in both areas. The "something" may be Congress-based. Perhaps Goss (1972) is right, that congressmen do not tamper with military procurement policy because of its strategic implications. Or perhaps the distribution of benefits is not to committee members' states and districts, but to the constituencies of those who vote with the conservative coalition (Russett, 1970). It may also be agency-based. Perhaps the budget constraint Congress places on the Services is insufficient to produce the adjustments in the distribution of pmc's that would benefit committee members' districts. Whatever the case, the distributive theory is in need of a revision that accounts for the tendency for districts and states represented on the two Corps committees to benefit from Corps expenditures and for those represented on the two military committees not to benefit from the distribution of procurement expenditures.

A second pattern which emerges from this study concerns the authorizing and appropriating committees. The only significant finding for an appropriations subcommittee that is consistent with the distributive theory is that areas represented on the Public Works Subcommittee benefit disproportionately from Corps new starts. No appropriations subcommittee evidences a significant recruitment or overrepresentation effect, and there are no recruitment tendencies on the subcommittees. There are insignificant tendencies for the Public Works Subcommittee to overrepresent highly involved districts and for the DOD Subcommittee to overrepresent highly involved states. However, the reason the subcommittees can tend to overrepresent highly involved areas without manifesting recruitment effects is that the whole Appropriations Committee overrepresents districts highly involved in Corps activities and states highly involved in military procurement relative to others in the House (Rundquist, 1973: Ch. 4). In other words, the subcommittee simply mirrors the pattern on the whole Appropriations Committee.

These findings both support and qualify Fenno's argument about appropriations subcommittees. They support his assertion (Fenno, 1966: 141) that "the chairman and ranking minority member have . . . deliberately appointed individuals to subcommittee memberships where no clientele interest exists." Clearly, a number of members are from states and districts without a constituency stake in the subject matter before their subcommittees. However, this does not mean, as Fenno implies, that states and districts of subcommittee members do not benefit from the expenditures of agencies under their jurisdiction, for those represented on the Public Works Subcommittee do benefit. Moreover, they benefit as much as states and districts represented on the authorizing committee—the Public Works Committee (contra Fenno, 1966: 149).

Our appropriations findings again point to the failure of the three hypotheses in the distributive theory to work together. We find support for the benefit hypothesis where there is no support for the recruitment or overrepresentation hypotheses (for example, the Public Works Subcommittee). Among the insignificant findings, there are overrepresentation effects without recruitment effects (for example, both subcommittees). These findings can only reflect the presence of conditions which intervene between the motivation assumed in the distributive theory (that is, that members seek to serve their constituencies' economic interest via the House committee system) and its manifestation in the kind of data we have gathered.

Our third objective was to determine whether the distributive theory involved states or congressional districts. The above analysis does not permit a clear answer. On the district level, we find support for the recruitment hypothesis for Armed Services Democrats, and the benefit hypothesis for the Public Works Committee and the Public Works Subcommittee. On the state level, we find the benefit hypothesis supported for the Public Works Committee and the Public Works Subcommittee. Similarly, we find insignificant tendencies for various of the hypotheses to be supported on both the district and state level.[18] For now, therefore, we must conclude that the hypotheses of the distributive theory can operate at both the district and states levels.

CONCLUSION

In this paper we have attempted to clarify a theory that is often used to explain national-level policy-making in the United States, and to test it against data for the U.S. House of Representatives. The validity of the theory's three hypotheses were checked against the distribution of Corps of Engineers and military procurement expenditures among states and congressional districts. The hypotheses concerned whether the standing committees that authorize and appropriate for the Corps of Engineers and the Department of Defense tend to overrepresent areas with an interest in these programs relative to all other congressmen and relative to other congressmen in the partisan group from which they were recruited. The third hypothesis was concerned with whether areas represented on these committees benefited disproportionately from the distribution of these types of expenditures. We asked whether these hypotheses are supported for authorizing and appropriating committees, for military procurement and Corps of Engineers projects, and for states and congressional districts.

Our analysis suggests that the distributive theory provides a rather inadequate explanation of policy-making in our two expenditure areas. In no case did we find all three of the hypotheses supported. Instead, we found some conditions under which one hypothesis is supported and other conditions under which another hypothesis is supported. The recruitment hypotheses receive more support for the authorizing than for the appropriating committees. There is no consistent tendency for the hypotheses to be supported on only the district or only the state level.

These findings raise considerable doubt about the validity of the distributive theory in our policy areas. They suggest that parts of the theory are valid under some well-defined circumstances; however, the theory's basic assumption that congressmen seek to serve their constituencies' economies by becoming members of relevant standing committees is not reflected in our data. Instead, we find a complex set of institutional constraints that interfere with straightforward predictions of the theory. Clearly, more research should be done on the nature of these constraints. Still, although the distributive theory is inadequate as an empirical theory of policy-making, our investigation of it leads in the direction of incorporating additional, more realistic hypotheses about institutional constraints on the behavior predicted in the theory. In other words, because it draws attention to the nature of the "input/process" and "process/output" relationships, the theory has value as a tool for policy researchers interested in including the government in their theories about governmental policy-making.

NOTES

1. Various versions of this theory have been argued by Cater (1964), Fritschler (1969), Lowi (1967), Seidman (1970), Redford (1969), and Niskanen (1971).

2. Since this study focuses on the House of Representatives, "congressmen" here and throughout refers to representatives. For treatment of the Senate see Ferejohn (1972) and Strom (1973).

3. There are other advantages of incumbency, of course. For example, incumbents can use the prerequisites of their office to advertise their name and record in their constituency. See Mayhew (1972) for an interesting argument on this point.

4. Elazar (1972), Deckard (1972), and Bullock (1971) present evidence suggesting the importance of cooperation among members of the same state party delegations who are on different standing committees.

5. Arguments that Corps of Engineers projects like the Cross Florida Barge Canal are necessary for the national defense because during wartime oil tankers will be protected from enemy submarines lying off the tip of Florida are, of course, exceptions.

6. The dynamics of the distributive theory will be the subject of a future report.

7. Corps of Engineers construction data for FY 1967 are used because they were readily available from Ferejohn (1972). We have no reason to believe that our findings for the two policy areas could be affected by the difference in years studied.

8. See Gold (1969) for a discussion of using significance tests with nonsample data.

9. The new start expenditure and budget level data used here are from U.S. Congress, House (1967). The committee assignments are from the Congressional Directory (1966).

10. These data were taken from Isard and Ganschow (n.d.) and include $17.1 billion of the total of $21 billion in pmc's awarded in FY 1960. Missing are contracts for nonmanufactured goods, contracts awarded to Hawaii, Alaska, and the District of Columbia, and contracts for less than $10,000 in value. See Rundquist (1973: Ch. 3) for further description of these data.

11. These interviews were conducted in 1972 by one of the authors and Craig Liske.

12. Because of the arbitrariness of this assumption, we carried out the recruitment and overrepresentation analysis in two ways. In the first, we considered only the discrete districts. In the second, we combined the discrete and multidistrict cases. The results of both treatments are reported in Tables 6, 7, and 9.

13. Such adjustments in the distribution of agency activities need not involve communication between the bureaucrats and congressmen involved. Rather, this is a form of what Wildavsky (1964) would call implicit coordination between agencies and committees.

14. This conclusion is similar to that of Mendel Rivers (1969) for the Armed Services Committee:

The idea that the Armed Services Committee members represent the fat-cat districts is simply not true. I had an analysis prepared for fiscal year 1968 prime contracts of $1 million or more by congressional districts. The analysis compared members of the Armed Services Committee with House members as a whole as regards number of prime contracts.

"It showed that we have 10 members on the committee in the top quarter of House Members, 13 in the second quarter, nine in the next to the lowest quarter, and seven members in the lowest quarter. In other words, the membership of the committee almost exactly reflects the membership of the House in terms of the relative number of prime contracts in their districts."

15. Only the 325 districts on which we have discrete data are treated in this analysis. The data on manufacturing capability are from the 1959 Census of Manufacturing and were obtained on a computer tape from the Census Bureau. The committee assignment data are from the Congressional Directory (1958).

16. This equation suggests that knowing districts are represented on the military committees adds almost nothing to the explanation of why pmc's are distributed the way they are. A better predictor is the district's manufacturing capability. But the low whole equation $\bar{R}^2$ suggests that factors outside of this simple model must exercise considerable influence on the distribution of pmc's among congressional districts.

17. The data in the analysis are from the Department of Defense (undated). To estimate state level pmc's for manufactured goods, we subtracted pmc's for military construction from the total level of pmc's for each state. Capability is measured by the value added from manufacturing for each state in 1959 and was taken from the Statistical Abstract of the United States (1963). Committee assignments are again from the Congressional Directory (1958).

18. Specifically, the recruitment hypothesis receives some support for Public Works Democrats on the district level. On the state level, the recruitment hypothesis gets some support for Public Works Republicans and Armed Services Democrats and Republicans. Similarly, the overrepresentation hypothesis gets some state level support for the Public Works Committee, the Armed Services Committee, and the DOD Subcommittee. If these tendencies are confirmed in other research, it can be concluded that at least the recruitment and overrepresentation hypotheses operate more often on the state rather than the district level.

Chapter 4

MILITARY SPENDING IN THE THIRD WORLD:
THE INTERACTIONS OF DOMESTIC AND
INTERNATIONAL FORCES

FARID ABOLFATHI
and
TONG-WHAN PARK

Northwestern University
Evanston, Ill.

INTRODUCTION

The decade of the 1960s was unusual in at least two respects. First, it was a period of unparalleled economic growth for a number of developing countries. Secondly, the primary beneficiaries of this growth were so few that there was little significant change in the socioeconomic conditions of the general population.[1] Among many reasons for this lopsided distribution of benefits, the major factors seem to be unequal distribution of political power, corruption, and excessive military spending.[2] In fact, much of the new capacity, created through massive economic development plans and foreign aid, got channeled into internal and external security forces which functioned as guardians of the status quo or as perpetuators of recurring "tension spots" and interstate wars.

This waste of scarce economic energy on military and internal security activities has apparently hindered programs for education, welfare, and the consumer goods industry (Arkhurst, 1972). These domestic programs are of vital import when a country seeks to free itself of the vicious circle of poverty and social instability. Instead of peaceful growth, the growing pressures of population explosion, urban congestion, and unemployment have led to increased violence and turmoil, to which many regimes responded with increased levels of defense and security expenditures. Rising military spending appears to have been responsible, in turn, for the renewal of tensions between rival nations, which not infrequently exploded into violence.[3]

Furthermore, the implications of this trend are extremely relevant to the

[109]

mounting concern for diminishing resources (particularly energy[4]) in the industrialized world and to the supply of imports from the Third World.[5] Specifically, the future of resource flows from developing countries will largely depend on the stability of these countries and, in the long run, on their social and economic conditions. It is therefore imperative for the Third World nations to reduce defense spending and in its place upgrade their socioeconomic investments. This is why we need to understand the functioning of the international conflict system before we can discuss ways and means of calming down tensions, arms races, and wasteful rivalries involving the Third World countries.[6]

The purpose of this study is, therefore, to identify certain internal and external forces as major determinants of armament expenditures in the Third World. It examines such factors as political instability, resource availability, foreign aid flows, superpower involvement, Cold War tensions, and direct external threats. The study tests a *general* model of military spending for as many as ninety Third World countries for the year 1970. This model is then compared with both the non-Third World and with an "all nation" model. A number of defense expenditure indicators are included for analysis: total defense budget, defense expenditure per capita, defense spending normed by GNP or total government expenditure, as well as the major components of military structure (aircraft, armored vehicles, naval vessels, soldiers, and paramilitary forces). The primary method of analysis is the multiple regression technique.

STUDIES OF ARMAMENTS AND ARMS RACE

The basic mechanisms of arms races have been roughly understood since the ancient times. That is, mutual suspicion and security dilemmas, particularly among rival states, often lead to foreign policy actions and armaments, which have a tendency to lead to further suspicions and, in turn, further armaments.[7] One variant of this process was formalized by Lewis Fry Richardson (1960) and F.W. Lanchester (1916) for arms races and aircraft warfare respectively. Smoker (1967), Wolfson (1968), and Voevodsky (1969) have further modified and crudely tested the original Richardson model. Incorporating the Richardson process models, Milstein and Mitchell (1968) and Choucri and Mitchell (1969) have performed computer simulations for the Vietnam war and the pre-World War I naval race between Germany and Britain.

In terms of validating the Richardson model, however, these studies have not gone very far. The reason for this is that the tests have generally been too crude and have hence proved nothing beyond the fact that the armaments and conflict behavior of some nations have generally been highly correlated over time. This by itself is a relatively trivial finding unless we can also establish some justification for a *causal* link. There have, in fact, been so many anecdotal and historical studies which have pointed to this type of causal action-reaction phenomenon that we think it reasonable not to worry about the existence of correlations between the armaments of rival nations. In other words, because of correlated autonomous growth trends, we expect the armament expenditures of most nations in the world to be highly correlated over time. This makes it almost impossible to distinguish a true arms race, such as the Egyptian-Israeli race, from a spurious one like the armaments of Iran and Brazil which are also highly correlated but not directly connected *causally*. Hence, we need to *determine* the existence of an arms race from descriptive sources, such as area studies and news materials.

Although there have been few studies that have dealt adequately with the causes of armament expenditures in the Third World, there has been no lack of studies of arms *trade* and armament *races*. The London Institute for Strategic Studies (ISS), MIT's Center for International Studies (CIS), and the Stockholm International Peace Research Institute (SIPRI) have published a great many quantitative and qualitative analyses on Third World arms races.[8] But as Ulrich Albrecht (1972: 165-67) pointed out, most of these studies were wanting in any theoretical framework beyond the most fuzzy hypotheses: for example, that the Third World's demand for armaments is in part caused by factors like prestige, security, and aggressive needs of nations, and conversely, that the supply is provided by the industrialized countries' needs to balance their foreign trade, to increase their Cold War security, and to increase their foreign influence. However, there is very little *explicit* theorizing about the linkages that connect these factors to each other and to armament spending. The empirical research involved, with few exceptions, generally never goes beyond crude trend analysis of time series of such dependent variables as army size, major weapon imports and exports, and defense budgets.

Despite the weakness in theorizing, these studies have accumulated relatively good data on the annual defense expenditures, major weapon purchases, and size of armed forces of many Third World nations over much of the last two decades. We can therefore use these data to study some of the trends and constraints in armament expenditures, and identify some of the regional arms races, but we cannot discover the causes or delineate the processes of armament escalation with these data alone. To do this we need a better understanding not only of what causes poor nations to devote substantial amounts of their resources to armaments but also of how the causes and effects of armaments interact.

In addition, there is another group of writers who have written a great deal on the arms flow to the Third World. These writers could be roughly labeled "Soviet aid and arms trade experts."[9] Some of their studies, however, are inculcated with what could be called the U.S. State Department bias, and should therefore be read with caution.[10] These studies generally, but not always, describe Soviet arms flows into the Third World in terms of Soviet and recipients' goals and actions, but largely ignore the interactive aspects of the East-West and Third World rivalries.[11] Nevertheless, these works are often very insightful case studies and are rich data sources on some Soviet-Third World patterns of interactions. Also, they sometimes point out many potentially system-changing events, or turning points,[12] in such patterns of relationships. Our approach in this paper is to use the data and valuable insights of both categories. This, however, will be done in a multidimensional framework, such as that in Singer's (1972) comprehensive analysis of "ties" between weak states and superpowers. But before proceeding to describe our model in detail, we shall briefly describe a few works which have estimated models of arms races for certain Third World countries. Lambelet (1971) has applied the ordinary least squares technique to time-series data to estimate the arms race models of countries involved in the Arab-Israeli conflict. His model, however, does not take into account Cold War tensions which, according to most anecdotal and historical case studies, are responsible for at least some of the Middle Eastern tensions. [13] Furthermore, Lambelet does not examine such factors as internal insecurity and "prestige arms" which can result in increases in armaments even in the absence of external threats of conflict.[14] Finally, as pointed out by Abolfathi (1973), Lambelet is so engrossed with the Arab-Israeli and inter-Arab conflicts that he ignores the possibility of existence of such important conflicts as the Iraqi-Iranian and Turkish-Syrian conflicts.

Mihalka (1973) has estimated models for some Latin American arms races but his models are only for a particular type of weapon—fighter planes. Secondly, they have many of the weaknesses of Lambelet's models. In particular, he does not investigate the armament demands induced by guerrilla activity and other forms of domestic turmoil, which by all accounts are highly salient in armament imports.[15] Thirdly, Mihalka does not consider the resource constraints which limit armament expenditures, particularly in the poorer Third World countries. Finally, his model uses an inconsistent foreign-influence hybrid variable which we believe could have been vastly improved upon with a little further effort.

Abolfathi (1973) has estimated a model for the Iraqi-Iranian conflict in which Cold War tensions, internal instability, resource availability, and foreign aid all play a part in the interstate arms race between the two rival countries. But this model too has some weaknesses. For one thing it ignores the possibility of lagged relationships; secondly, it ignores some important factors, such as changing political relationships between superpowers and rival clients, and changing goals of the clients.

All the above studies, however, have at least one basic thing in common. They all assume that the armaments of one nation generally excite a feeling of suspicion or insecurity in a rival nation. The basis of our study is, of course, such rivalries. For some cases the existence of rivalry is obvious, for example, Middle East or South Asia; for others it may not be so easy to pinpoint the presence of an arms race, for example, Cuba-U.S.A. Where we find no historical evidence that such a rivalry exists, the case is excluded from this preliminary analysis. Furthermore, this study differs from the works cited above on two points. First, its scope goes beyond conventional case studies that involve, at most, a handful of countries. Secondly, the variables included cover a much wider range of substantive domains.

THE MODEL OF MILITARY EXPENDITURE

The basic model of military spending developed and tested in the present study hypothesizes that there are three major clusters of independent variables determining the defense expenditure. These are domestic attributes, dyadic rivalry, and the environmental influences. First, *domestic attributes* refer to the factors considered endogenous to a given country—technology, power capability, internal conflict, and military influence (or involvement) in domestic politics. Many studies have shown that these internal characteristics are the primary determinants of defense spending. In fact, it has been repeatedly demonstrated in cross-sectional studies that the indicators of resource and technology account for a significantly high proportion of variance in defense expenditure (Rummel, 1972).

Secondly, the best-known theoretical accelerator of arms race is *dyadic rivalry*. A rival's defense build-up alone could justify all the "irrational" decisions made by the ruling elite, often against the "general will" of the people. This may be one of the reasons why the technology variable cannot explain fully the disproportionately high level of armament expenditure in the Third World. Also it must be noted that the interactions between the rivals are not entirely conflictual. We have witnessed innumerable cases in which some form of cooperative transactions take place along with arms races. Therefore, both the level and percentage of trade with a rival are included in this study.

Thirdly, the importance of *environmental influences* upon domestic and foreign policy-making is increasing in a geometric scale. As the world shrinks rapidly due to the development in communication technology, as non-renewable resources become more and more scarce, and as the membership in the nuclear club gradually increases over the decades, it is no longer possible to carry out closed-in, two-rival arms races. This is doubly true in the Third World, where big-power involvement leaves little room for independent action (except on rare occasions when a developing country can play one big power against another). Thus major dimensions of environmental influences included in this study are the U.S.-client factors, the USSR-client factors, and the general Cold War tension level. The superpower-client relationships are measured by trade, economic and military aid, military bases and advisors.

These clusters of independent variables are selected from a large body of literature in the field. Ideally it would have been preferable to formulate a complex model of military expenditure specifying causal paths for each independent variable. However, such a task is not attempted in this analysis because there does not appear to be any consensus with regard to the strength and direction of the relationships among the variables in the literature. We have found the relationships presented in the literature to be ad hoc, inconsistent, and rarely based upon systematic empirical analysis. There exist, for example, many different hypotheses dealing with the impact of internal violence upon defense expenditure. These range from a high positive to a high negative relationship. In order to avoid premature specification we present only a model of crude structural linkages in this study. A better-specified model would emerge from further developments in this area of research.

VARIABLES

The variables included in the analysis are listed in Table 1. Their operational definitions and sources are provided in the Appendix. These variables have been carefully selected by factor analyzing several different sets of variables. Data have been collected for over 120 variables spanning the three major domains of independent variables and their subsets. (These domains and their subsets are presented under distinctive headings in Table 1.) Principal component analyses have been performed within each of these subsets. After rotating to a varimax simple structure solution, a marker variable was selected for each factor. When it was difficult to choose a single marker variable, a composite index was constructed by adding the standard scores of the indicators.[16] Regarding the subset of resource and technology, for instance, a factor analysis of fifteen relevant variables produced two orthogonally rotated dimensions. For each factor a single marker variable was selected: GNP and the number of applied science books. A third variable, arms industry, was then added because neither of the two factors extracted could account for this variable. The implication is, of course, that this substantively important concept might have created another factor if we had included a number of arms industry related measures. As revealed by this illustration, factor analysis was employed to *guide* rather than *dictate* our mix of variables.

As far as the convergent validity of our measurements is concerned, a cursory scan across many sources shows that there exists a high profile similarity. Moreover, factor analyses and bivariate correlations of defense indicators demonstrate that the different sources as well as the different indicators of defense are highly correlated.

DATA ANALYSIS

The use of factor analysis in selecting the variables undoubtedly reduced the problems of multicollinearity, missing data, and low degrees of freedom. These problems remained, however. In particular, during the regression analyses we found that either (1) we had severe multicollinearity or (2) low degrees of freedom.

TABLE 1

List of Variables

Independent Variables

(I) **Domestic Attributes**

A. Resource and Technology Indicators:
Gross National Product for 1969
Number of Applied Science Book Titles Produced in 1970
Arms Industry (C. 1970)

B. Internal Violence Indicators:
Ethnic and Linguistic Fractionalization (C. 1965)
Number of Deaths from Domestic Violence (1965-70)
Insurgency (C. 1970)
Number of Military Coups d'etat (1965-71)

(II) **Dyadic Rivalry**

Percent Trade with Rival (1970)
Defense Expenditure of Rival (1970)

(III) **Environmental Influences and Superpower-Client Relations**

A. General Indicators:
Regional Tensions (C. 1970)
Cold War Tensions (or Communist Border, 1970)

B. USSR-Client Indicators:
USSR Military Ties
USSR Economic Aid (1955-65)
Percent Trade with USSR (1970)
Trade Turnover with USSR (1970)

C. U.S.-Client Indicators:
U.S. Military Ties
U.S. Foreign Military Sales (1969)
Percent Trade with U.S. (1970)
Trade Turnover with U.S. (1970)

Dependent Variables

Defense Expenditure (1970)
Defense Expenditure/Total Government Expenditure (1970)
Defense Expenditure/GNP (1970)

In order to cope with these problems we decided to use the exploratory technique of stepwise regression. This procedure allowed us to use the parts of regression analyses that represented statistically meaningful results. Specifically, this meant that we selected only the "steps" up to which no serious degrees of freedom problem existed. It should also be noted that although this procedure does not eliminate multicollinearity, in practice the first several steps often suffer far less from this problem than do the later stages.

The result of some of our stepwise regression analyses are described and shown in more detailed tables in the following pages. The missing data option that was applied in all cases was "pairwise deletion" in the SPSS computer program. This procedure is not an ideal one and sometimes suffers from extreme sensitivity to variables in an equation. But it is a practical procedure for situations in which "listwise deletion" leads to a very low number of cases, as was the case in our analyses. In cases where our equations did not suffer from low degrees of freedom we selected equations which generally included independent variables each of which added at least 1% of variance explained to the dependent variable. This procedure enabled us to include as many important variables as possible. Such a conservative decision, being more inclusive rather than exclusive, was dictated by the exploratory nature of our study. The overall variance explained, or R^2, was generally around 90% and never dropped below 40%. These high explained variances indicate a high degree of predictive power for our equations despite the difficulties in the estimation of individual coefficients. The reason for this is that, although estimation of variable coefficients is sensitive to the presence of multicollinearity, the predictive power of an equation is not.

The mode of analysis employed is cross-sectional. In contrast to time-series analyses, the advantages of cross-sectional studies include (1) generalizability of results to a wide cross-section of cases, (2) maximization of variance in slow changing variables such as GNP, and (3) absence of autocorrelation problem. On the other hand, cross-sectional analysis has the following disadvantages: (1) it tends to suffer much from the absence of "situational" or ecological variables; (2) it is often unable to represent adequately the dynamic interaction processes; and (3) the resulting models become largely a summary type which often cannot include finer details. These properties, however, are matters of degree and, as Caporaso and Duvall (1972) have shown, the logic of both cross-sectional and time-series analyses are the same. The most sensible strategy therefore seems to be to employ both models in the analysis of any given problem. Because of space limitations, here we shall employ only a cross-sectional model of analysis in order to (1) get as general a picture of the determinants of defense expenditure as possible; (2) to obtain maximum variance in our slow changing resource and technology variables; and (3) to avoid autocorrelation. We realize that some of the more dynamic aspects of military rivalry may not be adequately represented by a cross-sectional analysis. But the advantages of this method are strong enough to merit its use.   .

REGRESSION RESULTS

Multiple regression analyses were undertaken for defense expenditure (1970) in raw figures as well as normed by a host of other variables such as GNP, government expenditure, income tax, population, and the number of men in the military as dependent variables. Due to the structural similarity among them, however, only the results from the first two of the normed variables are reported here. The independent variables are all subsets of those listed in Table 1. The original number of cases was 167, but after pairwise deletion of missing cases we were generally left with no more than 60 cases to base our estimates on. Besides estimating regression equations for these 167 cases, we also performed separate analyses for the Third World nations and developed nations using a cut-off point of $500 of GNP per capita. In these cases pairwise deletion often resulted in about 31 and 22 cases, respectively. A discussion of individual regression runs is in order before an overall evaluation is made.

Table 2 reports the results of regression analysis for defense expenditure as the dependent variable. Here all three equations are significant at $p < 0.001$ level (F-test) and the variances explained (R^2) reach the level of 99%. The estimated regression coefficients (standardized) for most of the independent variables are at least twice as large as their standard errors. Among the variable clusters the resource and technology indicators appear in all four equations. It is clear from their high positive coefficients that in all equations resource and technology play the most important role in determining defense expenditure. This confirms the findings from previous cross-national studies (Rummel, 1972).

The examination of individual equations reveals that for the Third World

TABLE 2

Regression Results for Defense Expenditures as the Dependent Variable

Independent Variables	All Nations	Third World	Rich Nations
Gross National Product	0.95*	———	1.04*
Applied Science Book Titles	0.15*	0.17*	———
USSR Economic Aid	———	0.89*	———
USA Foreign Military Sales	-0.22*	———	-0.24*
Number of Cases	53	31	22
R^2	0.99	0.99	0.99
Significant at 0.001 level? (F-test)	yes	yes	yes

NOTE: The regression technique used for this paper was in all cases the "stepwise" procedure. After examining the "steps" we generally selected equations that had no independent variable which explained less than 1% of variance. In cases where the regression ran into degrees of freedom problem, however, we used the regression equation at the step before the problem occurred. The asterisks (*) indicate that estimates are at least twice as large as their standard errors.

countries the level of defense spending can be almost perfectly accounted for by two variables: economic aid from the USSR and the number of applied-science book titles. The strength of the USSR economic aid can be explained by the fact that those countries that receive large amounts of Soviet aid appear to be situated in areas of high interstate or Cold War conflicts (UAR, Syria, North Korea, Cuba). These countries therefore tend to appropriate large sums to their military sectors. The significance of the number of applied-science book titles may be attributed to its association with the scientific aspects of resource and technology of nations.

The reason that there are only two significant coefficients in the Third World equation can be traced to the presence of multicollinearity among the independent variables. First, we have found high positive correlations between the economic aid from the USSR on the one hand and all of the resource and technology indicators on the other. Secondly, there is a high level of collinearity ($r = .93$) between the rival's defense expenditure and the economic aid received from the USSR. Consequently, had it not been for the multicollinearity, the rival's defense expenditure along with GNP and arms industry should have registered in the regression equation. In fact, there is a bivariate correlation of .91 between one's own defense expenditure and that of the rival, which supports the general thrust of the arms race literature. In short, nearly all the variance of the Third World defense expenditure can be explained by almost any subset of only a handful of variables: USSR economic aid, resource and technology indicators, and rival's defense expenditure. This indicates that the level of military expenditure within the Third World does not vary randomly, but is systematically associated with a number of meaningful explanatory variables. Hence, given a prior knowledge of these variables, we can statistically predict the Third World military expenditure with a very high degree of confidence.

The comparison of the regression results for the non-Third World and the all-nation samples shows that both have almost exactly the same structure. That is, 99% of variance of military expenditure in each sample can be explained by resource and technology indicators and foreign military sales from the U.S. The negative coefficient of the latter can be partially explained by the fact that the rich Communist countries imported their armaments largely from the USSR while other rich countries, at least in 1969 (which is our data base for this variable), imported very little arms from the U.S. By the same token, since there were very few Third World countries that actually paid for U.S.-made imports, this variable has not played a prominent part in explaining their defense expenditures.

The examination of bivariate correlations of the non-Third World and the all-nation samples reveals that, as in the case of the Third World sample, there is multicollinearity among some independent variables. Specifically, the absence of some resource and technology indicators and of the rival's defense can be directly attributed to this problem. A further investigation shows that in both samples all these variables are at least moderately correlated with defense expenditure. In both cases, however, the correlations are smaller than those for the Third World. In particular, the bivariate correlation between the defense expenditure of a nation and that of its rival, which was .91 in the case of the Third World, turns out to be much smaller for the samples of "all" and "rich" nations: .41 and .36 respectively. This may imply that the arms races tend to be more intense in the Third World than elsewhere. But it may also mean that, with the important exception of the U.S.-USSR arms race, most of the military rivalries of rich nations are confounded by regional security organization and the "nuclear umbrellas," which are provided by some bilateral treaties, for example, U.S.-Japan.

Regression results of the level of defense expenditure have revealed that it is highly constrained by the measures of resource and technology. At the same time, every dollar spent for military expenditure represents an additional burden on national resources which could be appropriated for non-military purposes. In order to understand the determinants of this burden, we normed the level of defense expenditure by the gross national product. It is widely known that this ratio of defense/GNP has intrinsic importance because of its association with a nation's likelihood to go to war (Newcombe and Wert, 1972). Table 3 shows the regression results when defense/GNP is the dependent variable. Again, all the equations are significant at $p < 0.001$ level (F-test), even though the variances explained range from around 40% for the Third World and all-nation samples to

TABLE 3

Regression Results for Defense/GNP as the Dependent Variable

Independent Variables	All Nations	Third World	Rich Nations
Percent Trade with Rival	-0.20*	———	———
Ethnic and Linguistic Fractionalization	-0.10	———	———
Deaths from Domestic Violence	———	———	0.13
Insurgency	0.17	———	———
Applied Science Book Titles	0.32	———	0.18
Arms Industry	-0.27*	———	0.13
Regional Tensions	-0.13	———	———
USSR Military Ties	-0.28*	———	0.16
Percent Trade with USSR	0.69*	0.64*	———
U.S. Military Ties	———	———	0.78*
Percent Trade with U.S.	———	———	-0.21
Number of cases	53	31	22
R^2	0.40	0.41	0.85
Significant at 0.001 level? (F-test)	yes	yes	yes

NOTE: See Table 2.

85% for the rich nations. This time no single cluster of independent variables appears in all three equations.

For the Third World equation only one independent variable was chosen in stepwise regression, accounting for 41% of the variance in defense/GNP. This independent variable measures a country's trade with the USSR as a percentage of its total trade. The implication is, of course, that the countries which are highly dependent upon the trade with the USSR tend to carry higher defense burdens. This relationship is not easily explainable, however. The past patterns of USSR trade with the Third World appear to support this linkage, but with a reverse direction of causality. For instance, many of the countries that have purchased large amounts of armaments from the Soviet Union had to make payments in goods and hence became dependent on their trade with the USSR. An examination of bivariate correlations demonstrates that the percentage of a nation's trade with its rival is the only variable, other than the percent trade with the USSR, which is at least moderately associated with defense/GNP (r = -.20). This may imply that the trade interdependency between rival countries tends to function as a dampener of a nation's propensity to undergo high defense burdens.

A careful examination of the rich-nation equation shows that only one variable (U.S. military ties) is statistically significant. Yet this may be solely due to the fact that only a few rich nations have received military advisors or aid from the U.S. in 1970 and 1971, thus inflating the correlation. This can also be seen by the disappearance of this variable in the all-nation equation, which combines the samples of the Third World and the rich countries. In contrast, the measure of the percent trade with the USSR remains the strongest predictor in the all-nation equation, which demonstrates that its explanatory power extends beyond the Third World.

In order to look at the variations of governmental priorities on defense we normed defense expenditure by total government expenditure. While Table 3 analyzed defense as a burden on the overall national resources, Table 4 identifies the determinants of the governmental commitment to defense and other military goals, such as deterrence and aggression, or some political goals, such as buying the support of domestic military elites through salary increases and the purchase of modern "prestigious" armaments. Once again all three equations are found significant at $p < 0.001$ level (F-test) and the explained variances of the dependent variables range from 42% to 84%.

The study of individual equations uncovers that for the Third World there are five significant estimated coefficients. The single most important coefficient is that of insurgency, suggesting that the governments which face high levels of internal turmoil tend to allocate a larger portion of their budgets to the military. There are a couple of plausible rival explanations for this. One is that the governments often attempt to reinforce their military forces after the outbreak of an insurgency. On the other hand, a government faced with insurgency usually becomes suspicious of its own military and may try to keep the soldiers

TABLE 4

Regression Results for Defense/Total Governmental Expenditure as the Dependent Variable

Independent Variables	All Nations	Third World	Rich Nations
Ethnic and Linguistic Fractionalization	–––	-0.30*	–––
Insurgency	0.55*	0.72*	0.47*
Military Coups d'etat	–––	–––	-0.33
Gross National Product	0.25*	–––	0.44*
Regional Tensions	0.18*	–––	–––
USSR Economic Aid	–––	0.30*	–––
Percent Trade with USSR	–––	0.34*	–––
U.S. Foreign Military Sales	–––	0.25*	–––
Number of cases	53	31	22
R²	0.42	0.84	0.46
Significant at 0.001 level? (F-test)	yes	yes	yes

NOTE: See Table 2.

happy in their military roles by increasing their monetary rewards and by modernizing their arms. It is worth noting that whereas insurgency has a high positive coefficient, another internal strife indicator (ethnic and linguistic fractionalization) registers a moderate *negative* coefficient. This may imply that the Third World governments do not worry so much about the existing societal cleavages as to appropriate larger sums to the military, whereas they seem to do so in the face of such overt violent conflict as insurgency. In fact, the negative sign of the coefficient might indicate that under such circumstances governmental expenditures are diverted from defense to socioeconomic arenas in order to ease internal social tensions.

The other significant coefficients all belong to superpower-client indicators and are moderate and positive. As before, these variables may be indicators of Cold War involvement, which is associated with higher governmental commitment to military activities. Although the rival's defense expenditure is absent from the Third World equation, bivariate analysis reveals that it has a moderate positive correlation (r = .24) with defense/government expenditure. This suggests that interstate rivalry does play some part in budgetary allocations in the Third World.

The comparison of the equations for the samples of rich and all nations tells us that, as in the case of the Third World, insurgency has the strongest coefficients. However, a further examination indicates that there are only a few rich countries which have experienced insurgency in the recent past. Therefore, the high correlation between defense/government expenditure and insurgency for the rich countries is largely due to the inflating effect of a few outlying cases. Then, the most important explanatory variable for the equation of the rich nations becomes GNP. This may mean that in the rich countries governmental defense allocations have become dependent solely upon levels of national resource and productivity. This makes a striking contrast with the situation in the Third World, where the bivariate correlation between defense/government expenditure and GNP is negligible.

Taking a second look at Tables 2 through 4 we can find several variables that do not appear at all in our nine equations, and a few that only register in one or two equations. In particular, the coefficients of the rivalry variables do not appear significant in more than one equation. Nevertheless, as it was previously pointed out, these and several other variables which lack significant regression coefficients exhibit moderate to high bivariate correlation coefficients with the indicators of defense.

SUMMARY AND CONCLUSION

The results presented in this article are by no means conclusive. They need corroboration from many more cross-sectional and time-series analyses that employ a variety of statistical techniques to circumvent some of the data problems. In due course, these studies may converge toward a model that does not suffer severely from the problems faced in this analysis: multicollinearity, missing data, and poor specification of the model. The problem of multicollinearity is particularly troublesome since it often leads to inefficient estimates, that is, estimates with large standard errors. The estimated structure of such equations would thus become highly unstable. Consequently, as the examination of bivariate correlations has demonstrated, many of the independent variables are absent from the equations largely because other collinear variables have preempted most of their explanatory capability. Hence, we must attach severe qualifications to any substantive interpretation based on our results.

With the above qualifications in mind, we can summarize some of our general regression results as follows. First, the most important cluster of variables in the explanation of military expenditure seems to be that of resource and technology indicators. Secondly, superpower-client relationships represent another important set of independent variables. Thirdly, internal conflict and the social cleavage variables appear to be important determinants of defense/government expenditure. These variables can account for 99% of the variance in military expenditure as well as more than 40% of the variance of the same variable when normed by GNP or total governmental expenditure.

Moreover, the military spending of the Third World can be much more accurately predicted than that of the rich or all nations. This is due to the severe degrees of freedom problem encountered in the case of rich nations as well as the frequent deflation of regression coefficients when combining the Third

World with the rest of the countries. In addition, bivariate analysis has uncovered that the correlation coefficients between the indicators of defense and the rival's defense are always greater for the Third World than for either the rich or all nations. Our most general conclusion therefore is that military spending, particularly in the Third World, is by no means a random behavior. It is highly predictable and only a handful of variables can explain a great deal of its variance.

NOTES

1. See, for example, Grant and Sammartano (1973).
2. See Jacob (1967) and Bill (1972) for the impact of corruption on a developing economy.
3. See SIPRI (1969, 1971 and 1972) and Safran (1969) for the role interactions of armaments and violence; Richardson (1960) and Wainstein (1971) are even more explicit on this point in their analyses of the pre-World-War-I arms race.
4. See, for example, *The New York Times* (April 20, 1973) and the warnings of President Nixon's energy advisor about future energy crises in Akins (1973).
5. The term "Third World" is used in this study to represent the developing countries in general. Its original meaning of the "nations not aligned with either the U.S. or the Soviet Union" seems to have given way to a broader definition describing the "weak states": states which have no significant armament industry, import large amounts of their armaments from industrialized countries, have little wealth (for example, below $500.00 GNP/pop), and export raw materials (Singer, 1972).
6. In the last two decades the average annual defense expenditure of the Third World countries has been about $16 billion, or about 10% of the industrial countries; but because of their low *levels* of GNP this has generally been a severe burden on developing countries. Moreover, the defense expenditure of the Third World has been increasing at a faster rate than their GNP (SIPRI, 1971 and 1972).
7. See, for example, the qualitative analyses of Wainstein (1971), Huntington (1969), Schaar (1967), and Clarke (1972).
8. The United States Arms Control and Disarmament Agency (ACDA) and a few other institutes and agencies have often published reports on armaments. Individual researchers, too, have done some work on this subject. See, for example, Frank (1969) and Carter (1969).
9. See, for example, Hoagland and Temple (1965), Hoagland (1970), Joshua and Gibert (1969), and Ra'anan (1969).
10. Joshua and Gibert (1969: 1-25), for instance, view Soviet aid to Iran and Turkey as "intrusions". This term, however, is only appropriate if one views Iran and Turkey as part of an American sphere, where USSR has not even the legitimate right to give economic aid!
11. Ra'anan (1969), for instance, largely ignores the negative Western response toward Egypt prior to the famous USSR-Egyptian arms deal.
12. For the significance of "turning points" in econometric research, see Choucri (1971).
13. See, for example, SIPRI (1971), Bloomfield and Leiss (1969), Thayer (1972), Hurewitz (1969) and Donovan (1972); case studies and descriptive accounts of instances where Cold War tensions have precipitated local conflicts in the Third World are far too many for this list to be even a representative sample.
14. See Kemp (1969) and Singer (1972) for the role of "prestige" in armaments.
15. Mihalka, however, has been aware of some of these problems and has indicated that he has worked on some of them elsewhere.

16. See Rummel (1970) for a detailed exposition of factor analysis and formation of composite indices.

APPENDIX

VARIABLES

The total number of variables collected since the beginning of the "Third World Armaments Project" numbers over 120 and covers as many as 167 countries. In this paper, however, we have used only 21 of these variables and because of pairwise deletion we had no more than 53 cases to base our equations on. Because of lack of space we shall here give brief descriptions of only the variables used in this study.

1. *Gross National Product, GNP* (1969). Taken from the *Military Balance* published by the London Institute of Strategic Studies. Original source: United Nations.
2. *Number of Applied Science Book Titles* (1970). Indicates all applied science book titles produced in 1970. Source: UN.
3. *Arms Industry* (c. 1965). Indicates the production capability of domestic arms industries and ranks nations from 0 to 7, from no arms industry to capability to design and produce intercontinental ballistic missiles and nuclear weapons. Sources: R.C. Sellers (1969), SIPRI (1971) Dupuy (1970 and 1972), and the *Christian Science Monitor* (1969-1973).
4. *Ethnic and Linguistic Fractionalization* (c. 1965). Taken from Taylor and Hudson (1972).
5. *Number of Deaths from Domestic Violence* (1965-1970). First coded for the 1968-1970 period by Farid Abolfathi and then added to the same variable for 1965-1967 period taken from Taylor and Hudson (1972). Sources: same as in 3.
6. *Insurgency* (c. 1970). Constructed by multiplying "scope" and "intensity" of insurgency which were coded separately in ascending order. The data reflect the 1969-1971 period and is based on "chronologies" and descriptions of sources under "Arms Industry" as well as Institute of Strategic Studies' *Strategic Survey,* 1969-1971.
7. *Number of Military Coups d'etat* (1952-1971). Coded by counting any event that was called a "military coup" by the above sources during 1952-1971 period.
8. *Percent Trade with Rival* (1970). The trade turnover of a nation with its "most important rival" as a percentage of its total trade. The "most important rival" of each nation was chosen as follows. First, after an extensive examination of litera-ture, all rivals of a given nation were listed and the *intensity* of each rivalry was coded on a scale of 0 to 5. Then for each nation the rival with the highest intensity score was selected as the most important rival. Source: UN.
9. *Defense Expenditure of Rival* (1970). Indicates the defense expenditure of the same rival as in 8.
10. *Regional Tension* (c. 1970). Measures the degree of conflict in a given geographical region by looking at the general level of interstate violence in the area. Subjectively coded by first dividing the globe into geographic regions and then giving each region a "tension" score between 0 and 5 and then transferring each regional score to *all* the nations falling within that region. Sources: UN.
11. *Cold War Tensions* (c. 1970). Coded by giving countries that have relatively long border(s) with a Communist country a code of 2; countries that have a short border with a Communist country a code of 1; and Communist countries themselves, a code of 0.
12. *USSR Economic Aid* (1955-1965). The estimated amount of the USSR aid received by a country.

13. *USSR Military Ties.* Constructed by first standardizing and then adding together "USSR Military Aid" (1955-1967) and "number of USSR military bases" (1970).

14. *Percent Trade with USSR* (1970). The trade turnover of each country with USSR as a percentage of its total trade. Source: UN.

15. *Trade Turnover with USSR* (1970). The gross level of trade turnover with USSR. Source: UN.

16. *U.S. Foreign Military Ties.* Constructed by first standardizing and then adding together "U.S. Military Aid" (1970) and "number of U.S. military advisors" (1971).

17. *U.S. Foreign Military Sales* (1969). U.S. *sales* of military equipment to other nations.

18. *Percent Trade with U.S.* (1970) The trade turnover of a nation with U.S. as a percentage of its total trade turnover. Source: UN.

19. *Trade Turnover with U.S.* (1970). The *level* of trade turnover of a nation with U.S. Source: UN.

20. *Defense Expenditure* (1970). The defense expenditure of a nation at 1960 prices and exchange rates. Source: SIPRI.

21. *Defense Expenditure/Total Governmental Expenditure* (1970). Based on UN figures at current prices.

B. Evolutionary Theories

Chapter 5

POLITICAL DEVELOPMENT AND PUBLIC
POLICY IN SWEDEN: 1865-1967

B. G U Y   P E T E R S
Emory University

and

T I M O T H Y   M.   H E N N E S S E Y
Michigan State University

SWEDISH ECONOMIC AND POLITICAL DEVELOPMENT: AN OVERVIEW

Sweden is a truly remarkable case of late but extremely rapid and thorough economic and political development. Indeed, it was not until the late nineteenth and early twentieth century that Sweden exhibited a strong drive to industrial growth, but by 1920 it had been largely transformed into an industrialized system (Heckscher, 1954; Montgomery, 1939). During this brief period Sweden moved from a primarily agricultural economy to one based largely on industry. The Census of 1901 showed that 54.5% of the Swedish population lived on farms or derived their main revenue from the primary sector of the economy. By 1911 this figure had been reduced to 48.3% and by 1921 to 43.6%. Sweden still had a large agricultural work force but the majority of the economy had now shifted to the secondary and tertiary sectors. This process is revealed in Figure 1 below which plots the development of per-capita GNP in Sweden from 1865 to

AUTHORS' NOTE: The authors would like to thank Professor David Ford, Department of Mathematics, Emory University, for his assistance. Professor Hennessey would like to express his gratitude to the Ford Foundation and the Social Science Research Council for support.

1960. Although extremely large increases in GNP were to occur later, one can see a significant period of increase in the period of 1905 to 1920 during which per-capita GNP more than quadrupled.

Paralleling economic growth were fundamental transformations in governmental institutions from an ancient representation system based on four estates to open franchise and a modern parliament. The reform act of 1866 abolished the old representation system and established bicameral representation although property qualifications still remained. A second reform act was passed in 1907-1909 which extended the franchise to all tax-payers. The process of democratization was finally completed in 1918-1921 with the elimination of plural voting, the extension of the vote to women, and the establishment of viable parliamentary institutions.

During this period of parliamentary establishment and the extension of the franchise, institutional mechanisms for processing mass demands for increased government services, notably labor unions and political parties, also grew rapidly. (Lafferty, 1971, Verney, 1957). Hence, three fundamental factors—industrialization, institutionalized parliamentary democracy, and institutionalized mechanisms of mass demand—converged in the period from 1907-1917. This convergence might have led to extraordinary instability had it not been for fortuitous timing and the influence of other events. In particular, the events, of

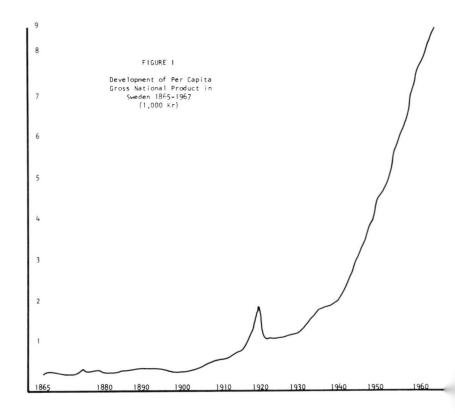

FIGURE I

Development of Per Capita
Gross National Product in
Sweden 1865-1967
(1,000 Kr)

1917-1918 and the third reform act made a peaceful transition possible (Verney, 1957: 206-212). There were a number of mass demonstrations over economic problems stemming from the first world war. This, coupled with the threat of possible revolution following the Russian example, permitted a Liberal-Social Democratic coalition to take office and complete the needed reforms and the conservatives capitulated largely because of the revolutionary threat (Tilton, forthcoming).

But the breakthrough to social democracy as we know it in Sweden today was not completed until 1932 with the victory of the Social Democratic Party. This victory was largely the result of the Depression, a coalition of the Social Democrats with the farmers carried out in the parliamentary context, and the availability of socialist programs to meet societal needs. The Social Democrats have been in office, with some minor coalition parties, ever since. It is from 1932, then, that one can begin to document the construction and operation of the Swedish Welfare State.

This brief overview of the significant forces in Swedish economic and political development is of course far too limited to provide a thorough understanding of the complexities attendant to these changes. However, such a discussion does serve to sensitize the investigator to the types of concepts to be employed in explaining the development of public policy, which is the central purpose of this paper. The task, then, is to construct a series of testable hypotheses, in light of our discussion, which will increase our understanding of the phenomenal growth in Swedish public policy expenditures and services as revealed in Table 1 below.

TABLE 1

Development of Social Programs in Sweden 1865-1967 (Selected Years)

Expenditures (Kr/cap in constant prices)			
	1865	1914	1939	1967
---	---	---	---	---
Total	8.47	39.97	72.16	93.28
Health	.05	2.57	8.73	25.74
Education	1.00	4.82	17.22	38.29
Social Welfare	.18	1.14	16.92	9.47
Labor Benefits	.03	.13	3.03	63.61
Pensions	.03	.63	12.19	60.01
Services				
Doctors/1,000 population	.12	.24	.47	1.18
Students/Population 4-14 yrs.	.67	.72	.77	.99
Pupil-Teacher Ratio	67.30	38.50	24.70	22.30
Pensioners/Population 65+	.03	.04	.96	.99

Our discussion suggests that three sets of factors are central to understanding the development of public policy: economic growth, mass support for political parties, and two key institutional factors—the growth of labor unions and the civil service. The first of these, economic growth, provided the necessary re-source condition for public expenditure but was not, in and of itself, a sufficient explanatory factor. One must also seek measures of mass demand, as well as measures of infrastructural growth in terms of which such demands become salient for policy-makers. The growth of the major social institution in Sweden, the labor unions, has been chosen as the principle indicator of such demands. The civil service was selected because it tends to be the institution closest to the actual design and implementation of social programs.

After a discussion of our major hypotheses—which are grouped under two headings, (1) developmental hypotheses, and (2) cybernetic hypotheses, we shall proceed to test these hypotheses against expenditure data for Sweden in the areas of health, pensions, education, welfare, and labor from 1865-1967 in order to test three sets of relationships: (1) the relationship between developmental factors and expenditures in these public policy areas, (2) the relationship between expenditures for social services and the social "services" actually delivered, and (3) the relationship between expenditures, services, and "societal needs." The empirical indicators for these relationships will be discussed after the construction of our hypotheses. In the section which immediately follows we shall draw on our overview of Swedish economic and political development to specify three stages of development in order to argue for the relative importance of particular development factors in determining public policy expenditures in each stage.

DEVELOPMENTAL HYPOTHESES

STAGE I (1865-1900): THE PREDOMINANCE OF INDUSTRIALIZATION VIS-A-VIS EMBRYONIC POLITICAL AND SOCIAL INSTITUTIONS

Stage I may be characterized as dominated by the processes of industrializa-tion, especially in the later years. The social and political spheres were, by contrast, quite retarded and remained dominated by traditional social elites. Only in the later years of this stage were governmental institutions designed to include the mass citizenry. Even as late as 1900 the franchise had not been extended fully, nor had viable parliamentary institutions been established. Labor unions and modern political parties were still in an embryonic state, although the growth of the former clearly outstripped the latter. Hence, the expression of mass demands for increased governmental services was constrained by a "closed" institutional system. Finally, the civil service was expanding but remained in the hands of established elites. Established elites did attempt to encourage and implement social programs but such programs were largely directed to increasing economic growth via the production of social capital. This is illustrated by the establishment of a national elementary education system in 1842 which was aimed at creating a skilled labor force. This discussion suggests that the major explanatory factors of public policy expenditures in this stage are an increasing gross national product, a growing civil service, unionization, and vote support for particular political parties.

STAGE II (1901-1935): "THE DELICATE BALANCE"–
THE CONVERGENCE OF MASS MOBILIZATION AND THE
GROWTH OF DEMOCRATIC INSTITUTIONAL INFRASTRUCTURE

Stage II consituted the "critical" period of development for the Swedish political system. The process of industrialization begun in Stage I created significant social disequilibria leading to new needs and demands. At the same time, institutions were gradually transformed so as to maximize mass participation, and parliamentary processes were thoroughly democratized. Labor unions and modern political parties grew at a rapid rate. Indeed, it is precisely this industrialization-mobilization-institutionalization convergence which makes Sweden a fascinating case for students of political development.

Here the insights of Karl Deutsch and Samuel Huntington, two prominent developmental theorists, are instructive. Deutsch has emphasized the process of social mobilization as an integral factor in political development, whereas Huntington has argued for the central importance of institutionalization. Both have noted that these two factors are related significantly to public policy, but neither has made the connection sufficiently explicit. Drawing on Deutsch and Huntington's insights we shall suggest some of the connections between these two concepts and public policy in Sweden.

Deutsch's observations reinforce our concerns with isolating developmental stages. He argues that the process of mobilization tends to occur in certain historical situations and stages of economic development, that these situations can be isolated, and that they are relevant for politics. Deutsch defines the concept of social mobilization as

the process in which major clusters of old social, economic and psychological commitments are eroded or broken and people become available for new patterns of socialization and behavior. As Edward Shils has rightly pointed out, the original images of "mobilization" and Mannheim's "Fundamental Democratization" imply two distinct stages of the process: 1) the stage of uprooting or breaking away from old settings, habits and commitments and 2) the induction of the mobilized persons into some relatively stable new patterns of group membership, organization and commitment [1966: 385-6]

Samuel Huntington has argued that "political decay" is likely to occur in political systems in which mass mobilization "over-runs" the process of political institutionalization in the following way:

> Social Frustration leads to demands on the government and the expansion of political participation to enforce these demands. The political backwardness of the country in terms of political institutionalization, moreover, makes it difficult if not impossible for the demands upon the government to be expressed through legitimate channels and to be moderated and aggregated with the political system. Hence, the sharp increase in political participation gives rise to political instability [1968: 55].

For Huntington this sequence can be expressed in three relationships:

(1) $\dfrac{\text{Social Mobilization}}{\text{Economic Development}} = \text{Social Frustration}$

(2) $\dfrac{\text{Social Frustration}}{\text{Mobility Opportunities}} = \text{Political Participation}$

(3) $\dfrac{\text{Political Participation}}{\text{Political Institutionalization}} = \text{Political Instability}$

Given the observations of Deutsch and Huntington, what would appear to be required is some optimal "mix" of institutionalization and mobilization. If this is not accomplished, it is presumed that severe instability will occur. For our purposes, however, a fundamental question still remains. What is the relationship between these two sets of phenomena and the provision of public policies, that is, government behavior designed to meet these new social "needs"? Deutsch (1971: 391) notes the connection between policy and mobilization, although he suggests no specific hypothesis:

> Social mobilization brings about a change in the quality of politics, by changing the range of human needs that impinge upon the political process. As people are uprooted from their physical and intellectual isolation in their immediate localities, from their old habits and traditions, and often from their old patterns of occupation and places of residence, they experience drastic changes in their needs. They may now come to need provisions for housing and employment, for social security against illness and old age, for medical care against the health hazards of their crowded new dwellings and places of work and the risk of accidents with unfamiliar machines. They may need succor against the risks of cyclical or seasonal unemployment, against oppressive charges of rent or interest, and against sharp fluctuations in the prices of the main commodities which they must sell or buy. They need instruction for themselves and education for their children. They need, in short, a wide range and large amounts of new government services. . . . These needs ordinarily cannot be met by

traditional types of government inherited from a precommercial and preindustrial age.

Hence we have "needs" generating demands. Yet how are these demands to be processed? Deutsch (1971: 392) suggests that governmental institutions must be created, particularly the civil service:

A greater scope of governmental services and functions requires ordinarily an increase in the capabilities of government. Usually it requires an increase in the numbers and training of governmental personnel, an increase in governmental offices and institutions, and a significant improvement in administrative organization and efficiency. A rapid process of social mobilization thus tends to generate major pressures for political and administrative reform. Such reforms may include notably both a quantitative expansion of the bureaucracy and its qualitative improvement in the direction of a competent civil service—even though these two objectives at times may clash.

These observations reinforce our selection of mobilization and institutionalization as potential explanatory factors of public policy change during this period. Given the predominance of both mobilization and institutionalization, we hypothesize that the major social mobilization institution, the labor unions, which are the most developed at this time, should have the largest influence on public policy, followed by mass political participation through the vote for parties of the left, followed by GNP, and, lastly, by the civil service. The civil service is not expected to have the powerful effect suggested by Deutsch during this mobilization stage since it was undergoing democratization and expansion. The major public policy directions during this stage were designed by the labor unions and parties, and the bureaucracy tended to take a "back seat" to mass institutional influence. In Stage III, which we will now consider, the civil service is expected to emerge again as a powerful influence on public policy as the Swedish system is transformed into a modern welfare state.

STAGE III (1936-1967):
POST-MOBILIZATION INSTITUTIONALLY DOMINANT WELFARE STATE

During this period the Social Democratic Party came to office and stayed there, largely unchallenged, during the entire period. The party proceeded to establish what is perhaps the most sophisticated welfare state in the West. Mass political participation was no longer of the mobilization variety characteristic of the previous period. Indeed, political competition was virtually non-existent in light of Social Democratic predominance. Enfranchisement had been accomplished, and the labor unions in close alliance with the Social Democrats gradually became part of the established institutional-governmental apparatus. Economic growth remained significant but what dislocations it generated were not met by the government's attempts to adjust social services to meet current needs. Social programs emanated from planning agencies via bargaining with existing institutional groups and were routinely ratified by a parliament controlled by a Social Democratic Party committed to implementing the goals of the welfare state. In short, changing mass preferences were now assumed to be met by "planning and monitoring" bureaucracies, labor unions, and the Social Democratic Party itself. The politics of planning and administration replaced mass mobilization, political participation, and institutional change as the most powerful forces in modern Sweden. This leads us to hypothesize that the civil service and the unions should be the most important factors associated with social expenditures in Stage III, followed by GNP per capita and votes for parties of the left.

In sum, we have assumed that the influence of mass political and social mobilization is curvilinear to expenditures with little association in Stage I, large associations in Stage II, and a diminishing influence in Stage III as institutions are developed and political competition diminishes. Throughout the development continuum, economic growth persists as a necessary condition for public policy expenditures but is diminished somewhat as institutional factors begin to obtain dominant influence over economic growth.

The hypothesized rank-order relationships just discussed are summarized in Table 2 below:

TABLE 2

Hypothesized Rank Order of Relationships of Development Factors
to Five Classes of Policy Expenditures in Three Stages

Rank Order	Stages		
	I	II	III
1	GNP/CAP	Unionization	Civil Service
2	Civil Service	Left-Vote	Unions
3	Unionization	GNP/CAP	GNP/CAP
4	Left-Vote	Civil Service	Left-Vote

CYBERNETIC HYPOTHESES

Karl Deutsch has suggested in his provocative book, *The Nerves of Government* (1963), that the predominant problem of political systems is not "power" but "guidance" through a sophisticated system of information-processing which permits a system to anticipate its needs, design programs to meet these, and then carry them out. His model assumes a system of "feedback"—from "needs" to program design to service delivery to new needs and demands and more "feedback." The political system which is "best" anticipates its needs and "leads" in social program design. In this sense the ideal political system resembles a servo-mechanism driven by "information". We do not think that it is farfetched to suggest that the operation of the Swedish Welfare State since the beginning of Stage III may exhibit a pattern of public policy resembling such a system. Indeed, the Swedish government has made repeated ideological pronouncements which reveal its desire to design social programs which not only meet current needs but anticipate or "lead" future needs. And in many respects Sweden has made remarkable progress in developing innovative social programs designed to do just this.

The idea of treating the Swedish Welfare State as a cybernetic system is, we believe, a fascinating one. However, we are under no illusions regarding the ease of capturing such behavior empirically. Hence, before the specification of our cybernetic hypotheses several observations, qualifications, and caveats are in order. First, the concept of societal "need" is much more difficult to measure than either expenditures or services. Not only are adequate measures difficult to construct and data to test them scarce, but such "needs" tend to change and/or be redefined by citizens and governmental decision-makers. For example, at one point in time reducing infant mortality may be the primary goal of health expenditures and services. But once this problem is under control, *health needs may be redefined* to focus on the maximization of life expectancy or mental health. One of the paradoxes of high levels of development is that needs become increasingly difficult for decision-makers to define and measure the more successful previous programs have been. In this sense, earlier periods of development pose less difficult conceptual and methodological problems than do some later periods.

Moreover, as many social programs in so-called developed systems begin to be defined as "quality of life" problems, expenditures and services in one functional policy area will tend to overlap with other functional areas as bureaucracies become multi-functional. Expenditures for pensions may, for example, come to be related *both* to pension services and to health services as increased life expectancy becomes a goal. *The welfare state then begins to resemble a complex matrix of policy relationships between expenditures, services, and needs across and between several functional areas.* This makes the measurement problem even more severe than in previous periods.

Given these observations and qualifications we suggest the following hypotheses:

(1) If the Swedish Welfare State is operating in rough approximation to a cybernetic system, then *sectoral and per-capita policy expenditures should be more significantly related to services in the welfare period than in the pre-welfare period.*

A. In the welfare state period expenditures should not only be more significantly related to services than in the pre-welfare period, but *these relationships should occur not only between but across functional areas. In the pre-welfare period, what significant relationships do exist between expenditures and services should be confined to functional areas, i.e., health expenditures and health services.*

(2) Given our observations concerning changing social "needs" and the success of the welfare state in solving some of the traditionally defined "needs," we expect that:

A. Sectoral and per-capita *expenditures will be more significantly related to needs in the welfare state period than in the pre-welfare period,* but:

B. *Services will be less strongly associated with "needs" in the welfare period than in the pre-welfare period.*

DATA SOURCES AND VARIABLES

The data used in this analysis are selected from a set of aggregate statistics for Sweden from 1865-1967 prepared by one of the authors. A wide variety of socioeconomic, demographic, and political characteristics of Sweden are included in the data set. Also included are measures of public policy. The latter include expenditure variables, organized by functional area, as well as measures of the services for each of the specified programs. The data are organized on a year-by-year basis yielding 103 observations. The concepts and variables used in the analysis are listed in Table 3.

TESTING THE HYPOTHESES

DEVELOPMENTAL HYPOTHESES

In discussing our findings we shall examine both the magnitude and significance of the correlations. In Stage I we hypothesized that GNP per capita would be related most strongly to expenditures, followed by the growth of the traditional civil service, the labor unions, and finally the left-vote. Stage I of Table 4 shows that GNP per capita and the civil service both have three significant relationships, unionization one, and left-vote none. The relationships for unionization and left-vote follow closely our expectations. The relationships for GNP per capita and the civil service do not support our hypotheses. Indeed, these two development variables are equal with respect to the number of significant relationships and the civil service has the highest magnitude of all those relationships which are significant, namely with pensions. If we compare these two variables for the magnitude of their other significant relationships with

TABLE 3

Variable Listing

Sectoral[a] and Per-Capita[b] Expenditures[c] for:	Services	Needs
Education	*School Rate* = total number of pupils in elementary and secondary schools as a percentage of all children 5-15 years	Number of children 5-15 years of age
Health	Number of physicians/capita	Infant mortality rate
Pensions	*Pension Rate* — total number of old-age pensioners as percentage of population 65 or older	Percentage of population 65 years or older
Welfare	Welfare Rate = Recipients of Public Welfare/Capita	Percentage of work force unemployed
Labor	d	Percentage of work force receiving its income from agricultural employment

a. Percent of non-defense expenditures going to the functional area in that year.

b. Expenditures in functional area divided by total population.

c. Expenditures are deflated using main price level of 1908-13 as base.

d. We have not included a measure of the services rendered for labor benefits. The rather thin line between public and private in things such as accident and sickness insurance makes this quite difficult and we have little confidence in our data.

SOURCES: The data sources are the following: Sveriges officiella statistisk, Sammandrang (Stockholm: Kungliges Boktryckeriet, 1867-1914); Statistiska Central Byran, Statistisk arsbok for Sverige (Stockholm: Kungliges Boktryckeriet, 1914-1970); Statistiska Central Byran, Historisk statistisk for Sverige, 1, 1 (Stockholm: Kungliges Boktryckeriet, 1968); Statistiska Central Byran, Bidrag til Sveriges officiella statistisk: Valstatistisk (Stockholm: Kungliges Boktryckeriet, 1872 to present); Finans department, Riks-stat och intilldess nasta statsreglering vid tager (Stockholm: Kungliges Boktryckeriet, 1866 to present); Erik Lindahl, Einar Dahlgren, and Karin Koch, National Income in Sweden 1861-1930 (Stockholm: P. A. Norstedt och Soner, 1937).

Several important methodological considerations are discussed in the Appendix.

TABLE 4

Relationship of GNP, Left-Vote, Civil Service Rate, and
Unionization to Expenditures for Three Stages

Stage I (1865-1900)

Per-Capita Expenditures

	Education	Welfare	Health	Pension	Labor
GNP/CAP	.42*	.44*	.29	.18	.41*
Left-Vote	.19	.29	.12	.11	.15
Civil Service Rate	.37*	.30	.39*	.61*	.20
Unionization	.24	.51*	.18	.26	.24

Stage II (1901-1935)

	Education	Welfare	Health	Pension	Labor
GNP/CAP	.40*	.38*	.51*	.36*	.22
Left-Vote	.61*	.54*	.79*	.80*	.67*
Civil Service Rate	.36*	.21	.16	.44*	.26
Unionization	.81*	.87*	.63*	.94*	.57*

Stage III (1936-1967)

	Education	Welfare	Health	Pension	Labor
GNP/CAP	.80*	.84*	.56*	.62*	.60*
Left-Vote	.27	.29	.44*	.20*	.36*
Civil Service Rate	.90*	.61*	.67*	.74*	.63*
Unionization	.91*	.19	.58*	.45*	.54*

*Correlation significant at .05.

expenditures, no substantial differences are present—civil service is in the high 30s and GNP per capita in the low 40s.

These findings suggest that we have underestimated the association of the traditional bureaucracy with public policy expenditures. In the areas of education, health, and particularly pensions, the growth of the civil service appears to be an important factor. Hence, although the bureaucracy was dominated by traditional elites these groups significantly influenced public policy in a period dominated by industrial growth. Bureaucratic institutions would then appear to have made important efforts to meet societal needs arising from the social dislocation of industrialization. They did, for example, provide funds for elementary education, restrict hours of work, inspect factories, and grant subsidies to voluntary health and accident insurance organizations. It is also interesting to note the differential influence of the civil service vis-a-vis GNP per capita on particular policy areas. Both were associated with education but GNP per capita was associated with different policy areas than the civil service, namely, welfare and labor. Apparently these policy areas were more directly influenced by industrial growth, while health and pensions were associated with the growth of the governmental bureaucracy. Finally, it is important to observe that unionization had the second largest correlation in Table 4, that is with welfare. Even in this early period the unions were beginning to be associated with social-welfare expenditures.

In Stage II, we hypothesized that unionization would have the highest association with public policy variables, followed closely by left-vote, GNP per capita, and finally civil service. The table shows that both unionization and left-vote had five significant relationships, followed by GNP per capita with four and civil service with two. Our hypothesis with respect to GNP and civil service are supported, as these variables were clearly third and fourth in rank order. However, the associations for unionization and left-vote are essentially tied, whereas our hypotheses suggested a leading position for unions. In three of the policy areas, education, welfare, and pensions, the magnitude of the association is greater for unions; whereas in the areas of health and labor, left-vote has a higher magnitude of association. The differences between the two are greatest for education and welfare, with unionization leading in both cases. One should, however, be cautious in making too much of these differences in magnitude. A more conservative interpretation would suggest that *both* of these factors were dominant factors during this period. What is important to emphasize is that the two insitutions designed to process mass demands during this important developmental stage were associated most strongly with the policy areas, as our stages theory suggested.

For Stage III we hypothesized that civil service would again emerge as most important, followed by unionization, GNP per capita, and left-vote, as planning became the dominant influence in the welfare state and unions took their place as a central institution in designing public policy. The data for Stage III reveal that both civil service and GNP have five significant relationships with the policy areas, followed by unionization with four and left-vote with three. These findings do not completely support our hypothesized rank-orderings. Although civil service is the leader it is followed closely by GNP per capita and *not* unionization as we hypothesized. Left-vote, however, is clearly last, as we hypothesized, although the three significant relationships for that variable are associated with policy areas expected to be particularly salient for parties of the left, given their ideological predispositions.

The unexpected finding of a powerful association of GNP per capita with policy expenditures should have been anticipated when one considers the fact that the Swedish social-welfare state did not, and does not today, rely on wholesale socialization of the industrial sector: only 6% of this sector is government controlled. This permitted GNP to grow largely unimpaired by government control. Part of the resources thus generated could be captured and redistributed via tax schemes. This, in turn, created the necessary conditions for expenditures on public policy. The phenomenal growth in GNP per capita during this period could thus be channelled into social programs.

Moreover, a close examination of the data reveals that unionization does have a large magnitude of association with expenditures. Indeed, with the exception of the welfare category, where the correlation was low and insignificant, the magnitudes are quite close to those for GNP, with unionization actually surpassing GNP per capita in the education area.

Our findings for Stage III reinforce our hypothesis concerning the importance of bureaucratic institutions as important factors in public policy expenditures. GNP was a more important factor than we expected, and this finding suggests a continuing important role for the economic sector vis-a-vis policy expenditures in the Swedish social-welfare state.

If we examine the rank-ordered relationships *across* the stages, several interesting things emerge which also support our developmental argument. In Stage I the process of industrialization via GNP per capita and the traditional civil service are the most significant association with expenditures. This shifts in Stage II to institutional and mass-participation factors; namely, labor unions and left-vote, with economic growth a strong third. In Stage III, the Welfare State, civil service is most significant along with continued economic growth, with unionization a strong third. In sum, over these developmental stages the association between mass-political participation via left-vote *and* expenditures shifts in a pattern suggesting a non-linear relationship: last in Stage I, tied for first in Stage II, and last in Stage III, although stronger in III than I as its institutional infrastructure becomes highly developed. Civil service follows a different pattern, tied for first in Stage I, last in Stage II and very strong in Stage III. Unions follow a less pronounced pattern, moving from a third position in Stage I to a tie for first in Stage II to a strong third position in Stage III. GNP per capita is in many ways the most *stable* factor as related to expenditures, although it is not always the most powerful association at every stage. This is followed by the civil service, which has a significant influence in two out of the three periods.

Unions follow close behind and mass political participation is the least stable association over time.

Finally, we see that the number of significant relationships with our development variables increases across the stages: out of a possible 20, Stage I has 7, Stage II 16, and Stage III 17. The large jump from Stage I to Stage II would seem to substantiate the importance we attached to this period and the slight increases from Stage II to Stage III indicate that developmental variables are reaching a limit of explanation and directs our attention to a test of our cybernetic hypotheses.

TESTING THE CYBERNETIC HYPOTHESIS:

EXPENDITURES TO SOCIAL SERVICES

A. 1865-1914

Our first cybernetic hypothesis concerned the relationship of expenditures to services. Table 5 reports the time-series correlations and levels of these relation-

TABLE 5
(Part I)

Relationship of Sectoral and Per-Capita Expenditures to
Social Services for First Time Period: 1865-1914

A. Sectoral Expenditures					
	Education	Pensions	Welfare	Health	Labor
Social Services					
School Rate	.59*	.08	.24*	.04	-.03
Relief Rate	.01	.20	.13	.22	.15
Pension Rate	-.05	.44*	-.06	.06	-.10
Doctors/Capita	.13	.17	.13	.11	.07

B. Per-Capita Expenditures					
	Education	Pensions	Welfare	Health	Labor
Social Services					
School Rate	.63*	.09	.26*	.09	-.05
Relief Rate	.00	.19	.12	.20	.16
Pension Rate	-.06	.47*	-.02	.09	-.11
Doctors/Capita	.17	.18	.11	.13	.08

(Part II)

Relationship of Sectoral and Per-Capita Expenditures to
Social Services for Second Time Period: 1915-1967

	A. Sectoral Expenditures				
	Education	Pensions	Welfare	Health	Labor
Social Services					
School Rate	.69*	-.04	.11	-.09	.09
Relief Rate	-.08	.16	-.02	.05	.30*
Pension Rate	-.11	.26*	-.06	.49*	.62*
Doctors/Capita	.02	.49*	-.14	.76*	.61*

	B. Per-Capita Expenditures				
	Education	Pensions	Welfare	Health	Labor
Social Services					
School Rate	.74*	-.04	.03	-.07	.11
Relief Rate	-.06	.11	.04	.04	.26*
Pension Rate	-.12	.27*	-.10	.46*	.64*
Doctors/Capita	.00	.54*	-.01	.78*	.71*

*Correlation Coefficient Significant at .05 for Tables 5 and 6.

ships for the two time periods: The pre-welfare 1865-1914 and the welfare period 1915-1967. The first part of Table 5 presents these relationships for the first of these periods.

It will be recalled that we hypothesized that the pre-welfare period should have fewer significant relationships than the welfare period and these should occur between functional expenditure areas and services. In the sectoral area, during the first time period we find only three significant relationships out of a possible 20: education to school rate, pensions to pension rate, and welfare to school rate; all the other relationships are insignificant. In the per-capita area the same relations emerge as significant although at a slightly higher order of magnitude. The first two relationships do, indeed, occur in functional areas, as we hypothesized, although the third does not. Although the relationship of welfare to school rate does not fit our hypothesis it is not a particularly surprising one. Many of the welfare expenditures during this period were designed to provide benefits to households so that children could be released from wage-earning in order to move into schools and *then* into the work force. The first two significant relationships between functional areas were priorities of the traditional bureaucracy, namely, education and pensions, which are clearly related to industrialization and its effects.

B. 1915-1967

As we hypothesized originally, the data show that sectoral and per-capita expenditures to services are more significant in this time period than in the previous period. Eight of the 20 relationships are significant as compared with three in the previous period. The same number of significant relationships occur for both sectoral and per-capita expenditures. Moreover, these relationships occur between the same sets of variables for both classes of expenditures, while the order of magnitude is slightly higher for some of the relationships in the per-capita area.

The second part of our hypothesis which specified an expected "spillover" between expenditures and classes of services also receives support: of the eight significant relationships five are functional relationships and three are not. The significant functional relationships are: education to school rate, pension to pension rate, health to doctors per capita, labor to pension rate, and labor to relief rate. The three "spillovers" are pensions to doctors per capita, health to pension rate and labor to doctors per capita. This convergence of relationships around the health question would seem to be related to our earlier discussion concerning the increasing importance attributed to "quality of life" in the welfare state. We would suggest that "life expectancy" and the problems of old age in general are the underlying dimensions to which this matrix of relationships refer. That is, as the problem of morbidity becomes central, pension programs for the nation's elderly have a geriatric emphasis and this may be why pension programs are related to health expenditures: hence the relationship of pensions to doctors per capita and health to pensions. The labor unions have a strong interest in their memberships' life-expectancy and general life "quality" which stimulates them to demand labor expenditures in relation to doctors per capita.

Welfare expenditures are not significantly related to any services in time period II but are significantly related to education in time period I. This finding highlights the basic differences between the welfare and the pre-welfare period. In the welfare state, welfare expenditures are used by the state as a residual set of expenditures to compensate for the lack of adequate coverage in the other policy areas. They are adjusted periodically to meet marginal failures in the other programs. These expenditures do of course have an impact on particular services at some points in time but not in others. This is the principle reason why no significant associations appear with our service measures.

In sum, we found the cybernetic hypothesis 1 to be largely confirmed. In the welfare period there were a larger number of significant associations of expenditures with services than in period I and the magnitudes were also greater for both per-capita and sectoral expenditures. Moreover, as our hypothesis (1A) suggested, these relationships crossed-over functional program boundaries as the bureaucracies began to take on multiple functions to deal with fundamental problems such as life expectancy.

EXPENDITURES TO NEEDS–SERVICES TO NEEDS

We began our discussion of the second cybernetic hypothesis on a strong cautionary note. The measures we were to employ were of such a crude character as to be suggestive at best. We hypothesized that:

(1) Sectoral and per-capita *expenditures* will be more significantly related to "needs" in the welfare state period than the previous period.
(2) Services will be *less* strongly associated with "needs" in the welfare period than in the previous period.

Table 6 presents the findings for the relationships between expenditures to needs and services to needs for the two time periods. In time period I, 1865-1914, we see that expenditures were related significantly to only education and health needs. (The first is a per-capita expenditure and the second a sectoral expenditure.) The first was of considerable magnitude while the second was relatively weak. When services were related to needs we found three significant relationships out of four: welfare services to welfare needs, health services to health needs, and pension rate to pension needs. The first was relatively weak and the second two were of strong magnitude. Thus, in time period I, expenditures are not strongly associated with "needs," the exception being the cases of education and health. Services, however, have a strong relationship to needs in three out of four cases.

In period II, 1915-1967, we see that expenditures are significantly related to "needs" in four instances: per-capita education expenditures to education needs, per-capita health expenditures to health needs, sectoral health expenditures to health needs, and sectoral expenditures to pension needs. Thus, expenditures and needs are more significantly related in the second time period than in the first, as we hypothesized.

When we examine the relationships of services to needs in the welfare period we find only two significant relationships as compared with three for the first time period. In addition the magnitudes of these two correlations are about the same as for the first time period in the case of welfare services to welfare "needs," and lower in the case of health services to health needs. This finding supports our hypothesis in which we assumed that services would be less significantly related to "needs" in the welfare state as compared to the earlier period. In sum, both our hypotheses would seem to be confirmed by the data in Table 6.

These findings are related to our remarks concerning the problems of constructing adequate measures of "need". A plausible explanation of our weak service to "needs" relationships in the welfare-state period may be located in the circumstance that many of the "needs" we specified have been met by past programs. In the health area Sweden has the best infant mortality record in the world. They have reduced this problem to such an extent that infant deaths

TABLE 6
(Part I)

Relationships of Expenditures and Services to Needs:
Two Time Periods (Correlation Coefficients)

1865-1914				
Expenditures To Needs[a]				
	Education	Welfare	Health	Pensions	Labor
Per Capita	.802*	-.179	-.069	-.069	.227
Sector	-.082	-.122	.275*	.091	.145

Services To Needs[b]			
Education	Welfare	Health	Pensions
-.208	.430*	.727*	.750*

(Part II)

Relationships of Expenditures and Services to Needs:
Two Time Periods (Correlation Coefficients)

1915-1967				
Expenditures To Needs				
	Education	Welfare	Health	Pensions	Labor
Per Capita	-.013	.387*	.608*	.136	.063
Sector	-.098	-.156	.384*	.723*	.027

Services To Needs			
Education	Welfare	Health	Pensions
-.089	.432*	.630*	.087

a. Correlations refer to the following relationships:

EXPENDITURES	NEEDS
Education Expenditures to:	Numbers of children in the population ages 5-15
Welfare Expenditures to:	Percentage of work force unemployed
Health Expenditures to:	Infant mortality rate per 1,000
Pension Expenditures to:	Percentage of population age 65 years or older
Labor Expenditures to:	Percentage of work force receiving its income from non-agricultural employment

TABLE 6 cont'd

- -
b. Correlations refer to the following relationships:

SERVICES	NEEDS
Education—Total number of pupils in elementary and secondary schools as a percentage of all children 5-15	
Welfare—Recipients of public welfare/capita	SAME AS ABOVE
Health—Number of physicians/capita	
Pension—Total number of old age pensioners as percentage of population 65 or older	

occur for reasons which no government can account for. In this sense they have reached their limit. We would perhaps have been better advised to investigate morbidity as a measure of health needs rather than infant mortality. This would have permitted us to examine the problem of governments' attempting to keep the aging section of their population alive. This problem, however, is multidimensional and perhaps unsolvable, for the limits of a solution are constantly expanding (that is, people may be expected to live to x years than to x plus ,n years, and so on).

In the area of pension needs and education we should note that almost all Swedes are now covered by pension programs and almost all children now attend elementary school. Moreover, Sweden until recent years has been close to full-employment and the non-agricultural percentage of the population has expanded immensely with only 3% of the population now engaged in agriculture. Given the accomplishments of the welfare state in bringing about reduction in these particular needs, especially in the postwar period, we should not be too surprised that our relationships for services to needs are as weak as they are. It is interesting to note that this explanation *does not hold for expenditures to needs*. Expenditures for these "need" areas are still justified by administrators attempting to increase their percentage of government allocations, even though programs emphasis may shift. Indeed they are expected to constantly specify new "needs" in order to increase the scale of their operation. Therefore a large part of the expenditures go into maintaining a large bureaucracy to deliver such services. In short, bureaucrats are constantly seeking justifications for increased budgetary allotments to their agency, and they continue to do so using a "needs" argument, albeit the precise definition of these needs will vary over time.

SUMMARY, CONCLUSIONS AND NEW DIRECTIONS

We have argued for the potential theoretical utility of conceptualizing Sweden as a developing polity. We suggested that development concepts and variables might prove to be significantly associated with public policy expendi-

tures at different stages of development, and we constructed several development hypotheses to test these relationships. We also argued that one should
examine not only expenditures but services and needs. This led us to construct
our cybernetic hypotheses.

These hypotheses were tested against longitudinal data for Sweden from 1865
to 1967. Our development hypotheses were largely supported by the data.
Development variables *were* significantly associated with public-policy expenditures over the total time period and our rank-ordered relationships for each
particular stage were also supported, with several notable exceptions. GNP per
capita had a much more significant and stable association with public policy
than we had expected. Also growth of the traditional civil service was more
significantly associated with policy expenditures in Stage I than our hypotheses
indicated. The cybernetic hypotheses also were supported by the data. We found
a number of significant relationships between expenditures and services and
there were more significant relationships in the welfare period than in the
previous period. We also found that relationships between expenditures and
services tended to overlap functional areas as our hypotheses specified, whereas
in the pre-welfare period the significant relationships among these variables were
restricted to functional areas.

When we examined the relationship of expenditures to needs and services to
needs our hypotheses were again confirmed. The relationship of expenditures to
needs was more significant in the welfare period than the previous period, while
services to needs was more significant in the pre-welfare period as compared with
the welfare period.

This latter finding supports our hypothesis but in a somewhat preverse
fashion. The finding suggests that our measures of need were perhaps better
suited for an earlier period of development than the welfare state. Indeed, many
of the needs we specified were probably no longer considered needs in this
particular stage, having been largely solved by previous programs.

Assuming for the moment that more adequate indicators of need could be
constructed, it might, in principle, be possible to use optimalization techniques
to approach the problem. One such method is linear programing which tests for
the optimal use of available resources by the decision-makers. Such a method
maximizes or minimizes a numerical function of those variables subject to
certain constraints. In doing this, it requires the input of three types of
information. The first are the activity vectors. These are the relationships
between the particular commodity and the desired output. For example, in the
classic diet problems the activity vectors were the amount of protein, carbo-
hydrates, fats, and vitamins which would be supplied by one unit of any food.
The second type of input is the price of the commodity per unit. The final input
is a set of inequalities. For example, again in the classic diet problem, the
inequalities were set at the minimal requirements of a human being for protein,
and so on. These three pieces of information could then be used to provide a
desired output at a minimum of cost (Dorfman et al., 1970: 9-24).

In the case of public policy, we would be interested in the optimal allocation of resources among competing governmental purposes. The commodities, instead of being different foods, might be budgetary allocations to different functional areas of government. The activity vectors would be defined by the relationships of those expenditures to service variable (expenditure) with each dependent variable (service). The costs would in this case be benefits. These benefits could be related to changes in certain measures of need for services of a particular type. If we consider, for example, expenditures for labor benefits, a likely indicator of changes in the services provided would be the rate of unemployment. As this fluctuates, so will the need of the government to spend for services to workers via unemployment benefits. Finally the inequalities will be such that the government will spend more in year t than it did in year t-1. This is a fairly accurate description of the ratchet effect which is built into most spending programs (Peacock and Wiseman, 1961). In addition the total change in expenditures should not exceed the total changes in revenue and legal limits of indebtedness. This again is but one possible optimalization analysis. If some means of pricing allocations politically could be developed, such as relating them to demographic trends of the nation weighted by the level of political mobilization of that population grouping, then optimal political models might also be tested.

Regrettably, at this juncture political scientists have not constructed the analytics necessary to employ such a methodology, although they may be able to do so in the near future. In particular we have no adequate notion of political "price" nor the relationship between such a "price" and the demand for political goods. Since many, if not most, of the public policies now generated in modern political systems have the characteristics of public goods, political scientists might be well advised to turn their attention to the literature on such goods being developed by economists and political economists. These scholars have developed a vast body of literature on such goods and one example of their argument might be instructive here.

Public goods theorists argue that in a world of uncertainty and competition it is a characteristic of public goods that consumers of the goods have a incentive to *conceal* their true preferences regarding the provision of the good. This is so owing to the fact that the individual can hope to gain by revealing preferences which lead others to believe that he wants less of a given public good than he in fact really wants. He adopts such a strategy in the hope of being charged a "price" lower than he would in fact be willing to pay. Thus true demand for public goods is always distorted. Moreover, Breton (1966: 462-464) has argued this strategy means:

(1) That it is impossible for governments to know the marginal utility of any given public good to the citizen.
(2) It is also impossible to devise "prices" which would be equal to marginal utilities.
(3) Hence, benefit taxation is also impossible: Governments will always

have to impose non-benefit systems of taxation to pay for public goods.

(4) Of necessity, therefore, the "prices" charged to some individuals will be greater than the marginal utility they derive from the quantity of the public good supplied, while in the case of others it will lower.

(5) Individuals will react to this disequilibrium by attempting to reduce the differences between their desired position and their actual position in two ways: (a) by moving from the jurisdiction or (b) by engaging in political action of a variety of sorts (i.e., voting, joining interest groups, etc.) to influence politicians.

Breton argues that, aside from exit, it is only through the mechanisms of politics that one's true preference for public goods can become known. One can draw the following inference from Breton's argument: *the more political systems such as Sweden's opt for the provision of public goods, the more political activity is required in order that decision-makers can know the true preferences of citizens for such goods. If this is not the case, disequilibrium will increase as the provision of public goods and taxation systems become more error-prone or suboptimal vis-a-vis "true" demands.* In another article Breton and Breton (1969) suggest that social movements will arise under such disequilibrium situations.

This discussion of public goods is related to the interests of this paper in two ways. First, at the beginning of the paper we argued that development theorists should avoid assuming terminal points in the development process. Factors which were important in earlier stages may re-emerge as conditions change. This is relevant for our discussion of Sweden. If one assumes that the modern welfare state is the terminal point of development with political mobilization taking a permanent back seat to planning, then how is one to explain the fact that the leadership of the Social Democratic Party has recently been challenged by the Center Party? The Center Party has attacked the politics of planning advocated by the Social Democrats and has succeeded in gaining a large number of supporters—such a large number, in fact, that Swedish experts predict a victory for the Center Party in the next election. Breton's argument may explain this phenomena. Since the Social Democrats have been dominant for over forty years, political competition has been largely non-existent. The major institutions of mass mobilization, such as the labor unions, have become part of the established government apparatus. At the same time the welfare state has established its preference for the provision of public goods. It may be possible that the system of non-benefit taxation used to finance these goods has led to such social equilibria that these are creating support for the Center Party, leading to increased political competition and new mechanisms of political mobilization. In this sense political mobilization may be replaced by the politics of planning characteristic of the welfare state but only at high political cost for the Social Democrats.

Secondly, this discussion suggests that decision-makers and researchers should resist setting demand and need functions apart from expressed citizens demands. Indeed, public-goods theory argues that without such demand all taxation decisions associated with the provision of public goods will be suboptimal, at least from the citizens' point of view. In short, all we are saying is that the "evaluation" of political systems based on public policy considerations should include mass politics and the institutional mechanisms associated with it, as suggested by public-goods theorists. This should not be especially hard for political scientist to accept.

METHODOLOGICAL APPENDIX

A number of events which are included in the data do not occur on an annual basis, with the most notable example being elections. Two options are available to be able to use this type of data in an analysis which is intended to be on an annual basis. The first is to use the value of the most recent event as the value of the variable in subsequent years. The second option for dealing with the non-annual data, which we have employed here, is to use a linear interpolation of the values from one event to the next. Using the assumption that the dynamics of change over the time between elections or other non-annual events were linear, we calculated a value of the variables for each time period. If our assumption of linearity is correct, then little bias will be introduced by this operation. This is further aided by the presence of relatively frequent elections (at most 3 values had to be calculated) and by a very large number of elections during periods of political stress, e.g. 1907-1920 in Sweden. This provides more closely spaced observations during periods in which it is likely that political variables could be changing at exponential rather than linear rates.

The analysis is based on time-series correlations over the period from 1965-1967 split into time periods based on the hypothesis. There are a number of important considerations in such analysis, principal among these being the question of serial autocorrelation (Johnson: 1972). In any series of data across time, independent and dependent variables may be related not only by function of their true relationships, but may also share some joint relationship with time itself. Thus there frequently are very high intercorrelations of the variables which are not a "true" function of the relationships of the variables. In such a situation, the assumption (usually untested) that the residuals of the regression equation will be randomly distributed will be violated, and there will be a distinct patterning of the residuals across time. In such a situation, it is difficult to tell what portion of the variance explained in any regression equation is a result of systematic relationships with the independent variables (experimental variance) and what portion is a result of the systematic relationship with time (extraneous variance).

In order to correct for the problems of serial autocorrelation it must first be detected, and then the bias may be removed from the equation. There are several standard means of detecting the presence of autocorrelations, but we will rely on the most commonly used of these—the Durbin-Watson statistic (Durbin and Watson, 1950). This statistic is used to test a null hypothesis of no serial autocorrelation, with values below the significance points allowing the rejection of the null hypothesis of no significant positive autocorrelation. Assuming that a significant value of the Durbin-Watson statistic is found, we must then proceed with a process for elimination of the bias. This again can be accomplished through several means, but perhaps the most efficient of these is the iteration technique proposed by Durbin (1960; Grilickes and Rao, 1969). The residuals of the regression are first used to compute a new regression in the form:

$$u_t = q(u_t - 1) + e$$

The resultant regression coefficient q is then used to compute a regression in the form:

$$(Y_t\text{-}qYt\text{-}1) = (X_t\text{-}qXt\text{-}1)+e$$

If the autoregressive structure is of the first order, the above regression should yield a randomly distributed set of residuals. If it is a higher order, then successive iterations can be used to eliminate the patterning of the residuals, and to provide a "true" estimate of the relationships between the variables. We have used this procedure here and the values reported are for the first iteration without significant autocorrelation.

Chapter 6

TWO-PHASE WELFARE POLICIES:
RURAL ELECTRIFICATION IN THE UNITED STATES AND INDIA

S U S A N G. H A D D E N

Oakland University

One answer to the question "Why is a particular policy selected?" is that the benefit/cost ratio of the policy is high. Although this answer may seem to be tautological, it can be very provocative, especially if political costs and benefits are specifically included in the calculations. This study is an attempt to specify the range of costs and benefits that enter into policy decisions by constructing a model of the ways in which costs and benefits of certain types of economic programs change systematically over time. The programs to be considered as examples are the rural electrification programs of the United States and India.

WELFARE AND DEVELOPMENT POLICIES

It seems clear that if a differentiation is to be made between economic and political costs and benefits, the choice for conceptual purposes of policies with specific economic goals will make this task easier. One rather common type of policy employed wherever economic growth or development is sought is the provision of capital in sectors where its lack is creating a bottleneck. Frequently this takes the form of social overhead capital (SOC), which eases supply constraints for large numbers of people and provides the infrastructure for further development in the form of roads, power, and so on.

One outstanding feature of SOC is the fact that it frequently is a collective good—one which is available to all if it is available to any—and that since it is

AUTHOR'S NOTE: The author wishes to thank John McCamant of the University of Denver for his helpful comments on the earlier draft of this paper, and William Morris and W. James Hadden, Jr., of Oakland University for their aid. Research on rural electrification in Rajasthan was sponsored by a Fulbright-Hayes Graduate Overseas Fellowship, 1969-70.

expensive to provide it is often difficult for individuals or small units to receive a large enough return on their investments to justify them. This is partly because many of the benefits accrue to persons outside the small unit, especially in the case of development capital, when the units spends its increased income, thereby increasing the income of others in ripples that spread throughout the economy. However, by enlarging the unit making the expenditure, more and more of these "multiplier effects" that were external to a small unit can be captured and used in internal accounting. Governments very often serve as these large units, capturing some of the external economies through taxation.

Although the effects of these policies do spread throughout large areas of the economy, initial provision of capital accrues to particular groups of individuals. These may be defined geographically, as for roads, or functionally, as in a small business administration program, but in either case specific groups are primary recipients of funds. In many development programs, the target groups are chosen because they are noticeably less well off than other people; economically this may be sound because the marginal revenue per unit of capital should be higher than in more developed sectors. Because the recipients are disadvantaged, however, the programs have a welfare as well as a development component, and thus I have called them "welfare and development" or W+D policies. Depending on the ideological context in which the policy is enacted, W+D policies may have more emphasis placed on the welfare than on the development component, but both impacts are still important.

Many different programs, all of which provide capital of some sort, although not necessarily SOC, fall into the category of W+D policies. Policies in this category include the many programs of the small business administration, the special interest rates on loans to new ghetto businesses, agricultural price supports, and the irrigation schemes of the Southwest. Such policies involve transfers of income, as do other welfare policies, although the sectors involved tend to be defined functionally because of their expected role in economic development rather than ascriptively (as are programs for the poor, elderly, or handicapped). Vocational training programs, Bureau of Indian Affairs activities, and other similar policies are defined in more conventional welfare terms, and they could also fall into the category of W+D policies. In developing countries where ill-health directly detracts from productivity, various health facilities even fall under this rubric.

Let us examine the costs and benefits of W+D policies in somewhat more detail. These can be separated into three parts, economic costs and benefits, political costs and benefits, and costs and benefits that accrue due to interactions between the economic and political sectors. In order to discuss its costs or benefits, it is first necessary to specify the goals a program is intended to achieve. This is especially true in the political sphere, where the multiplicity of actors means that a wide variety of goals is embodied in one program. It is then important to be clear from which actors' viewpoints the benefits and costs are being assessed. In this study, the government as a collection of individuals seeking to remain in power is the major actor (see Ilchman and Uphoff, 1969).

By definition, the economic goal of W+D policies is growth and development. The costs of W+D policies simply include the outlays for the program each year. Direct returns to the policy include the taxes collected on the income generated by it and its multiplier effects as well as any fees paid for the use of the capital directly (such as tolls or interest payments). It is important to note that, over time, the marginal economic benefits should start to decline. This will happen because more and more capital will be invested in the same place, or areas or sectors with less productive potential will gradually be included within the purview of the program as it expands; the marginal revenue of a unit of capital in these areas will be less than that of capital invested earlier.

The political costs and benefits are, of course, more difficult to specify. I have employed the point of view of the government and its goal both individually and collectively of staying in power. Politicians have intermediate goals to this end at two levels: first, in their relationships to their constituencies to minimize dissatisfaction with policies; and, second, in their relationships within the legislature at the time of formulating the policies to minimize personal costs for getting a policy enacted, in order to save as many resources as possible for other important programs. These two goals allow the formulation of some rules of thumb for evaluating political costs and benefits:

(1) The more constituents directly served by a policy, the higher its political benefits.

(2) The more legislators whose constituents will benefit, the lower the exchange costs for any one proponent of the bill.

(3) Politicians discount the future heavily; i.e., costs and benefits accruing too far beyond the next election may nearly be ignored.

It will be remembered that W+D policies tend to achieve their ends by specifying particular groups as recipients; their force as welfare policies especially lies in their use of criteria to define a group of eligible recipients. Policies so defined, however, have three important political costs: first, they may alienate legislators with few or no constituents in the group; second, they frequently contain ideological overtones that exacerbate divisiveness; third and most important, they often create strong dissatisfactions among those voters who realize they cannot be recipients of benefits under the program. This is especially true because taxpayers may interpret such policies as going directly from their own pocketbooks into those of the target group.[1] This leads to a fourth rule for evaluating political costs and benefits:

(4) Policies defined for particular groups are more costly than policies with individual or small unit recipients.

Under these circumstances, we would not expect W+D policies to be chosen often, since they define groups as recipients. Policies that promote economic growth do, however, affect positively large numbers of people and so we would expect to find them enacted as long as they fulfill some minimum equality constraint. Furthermore, if an economic crisis were to arise of such proportions that the very existence of the regime were threatened, then it seems clear that achieving economic growth or stability would become the prime political objective and that "purely political" costs and benefits would be devalued. Since W+D policies represent an efficient use of capital because they invest it where its return is very high, at least some of the political disadvantages of a collectively defined policy will be ignored.

There are other factors which may lower the political costs without initially changing their economic or political benefits. One obvious one is that politicians may stress to those constituents who will not be direct recipients the ramifications of these programs throughout the whole economy, pointing out that they will be indirect beneficiaries. A second is the introduction into W+D policies of provisions to insure their broad application; for example, in federal politics, we might expect to find the states assured of minimum percentages of the allocations or being allowed to distribute the funds among a minimally defined group of recipients. Although this may mitigate the economic efficiency attained in the original W+D proposal, it may be a crucial element in getting the program adopted. Finally, by increasing the funds allocated to the program, more and more of the potential beneficiaries may actually receive benefits, increasing political returns. New categories of beneficiaries may also be specified as the program expands.

If these political strategies are adopted, the political benefits of the policies can be expected to continue to rise. First, if the program has been even moderately successful, the beneficiaries will have gained in wealth, which will lead to a change in the power balance between them and the non-recipients. They will have a stake in continuing the program and additional resources with which to pursue this end. They will very likely have organized an interest group to articulate their position, and in this way they will have access to politicians who will take account of the strong dissatisfactions of the group should a decision be made to discontinue the program. Thus political benefits of continuing are high.[2] Similarly, where the SOC of the program has taken the form of fixed physical capital, demographic changes may alter the number or nature of the beneficiaries, creating a whole new constituency for the program.

Second, many policies are turned over for administration to regulatory or similar agencies. This lowers political costs of exchanges within the legislature by removing policy decisions from that body, and also raises political benefits of continuing the policy by creating a bureaucracy centered upon it.

The interactions between political and economic costs and benefits are complex. The fact that politicians seek larger numbers of beneficiaries while the marginal revenue of units of increased investments declines suggests a partly negative interaction. On the other hand, economic development frequently results in gains for the party in power, which is held responsible for increased sales and incomes. Of course, if development affects primarily one sector, it may turn into a political liability, depending on the numbers and political awareness of non-beneficiaries. In general, however, it is possible to say that increased economic well-being favorably affects politicians seeking re-election.

Figure 1, suggests two stages for W+D policies: phase 1, in which both economic (E) and political (P) benefits are relatively high (assuming the policy is not adopted without the political costs-minimizing strategies outlined above), and phase 2, in which the economic benefit-cost ratio has decreased very noticeably but the political benefit-cost ratio is increasing and is high enough to assure continuation of the policy. Phase 2 presents citizens (and politicians) with a problem: whether or not the political costs of discontinuing a program are so high that continued monetary expenditures are justified despite their low rate of return. We may expect politicians to argue that discontinuation is too costly, especially in light of their short time-horizons. Citizens may not agree, however, and the existence of large numbers of phase 2 policies in a system may fuel movements on both the right and left whose ideologies tend to belittle the social value of "politics."

The pattern of change in W+D policies suggested by this model is illustrated by references to rural electrification (RE) in the United States and in India. In each country, an economic crisis raised the value of economic programs with respect to their political costs. At the same time, however, provisions to ensure the broadest possible scope of the programs were enacted. The United States has already entered phase 2, and its characteristics—few new eligible recipients, greatly decreased economic benefits, entrenched interest groups, broad geographic coverage, and so on—are all visible. India remains in phase 1, but analysis of the policy's provisions suggests that phase 2 will occur.

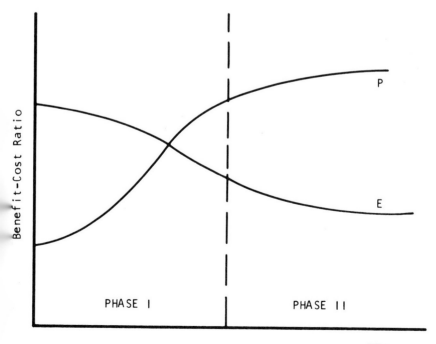

RURAL ELECTRIFICATION AS A W+D POLICY

Before turning to this analysis, it will be useful to show that RE is indeed a W+D policy and to outline the major provisions of the policies in each country. In most countries where it has been adopted, rural electrification has been designed as a W+D policy. Electricity is a form of SOC, seemingly indispensible for economic development. In addition, there is no question that individuals who receive electricity benefit. In rural areas especially, much of the back-breaking labor and monotony of such tasks as pumping water, separating cream, or caring for kerosene lamps—each of which is said to have required a full month of eight-hour days per year on a U.S. family farm in the 1920s (University of Minnesota, 1928: 27)—is alleviated or eliminated by electricity. Indoor sanitation and lighting also help the health and general well-being of the rural population. Finally, electricity aids the entire rural sector, improving its productivity and its quality of life to levels comparable to those in urban areas. It involves a redistribution of status and possibly of real income as well. RE thus fulfills the criteria of a W+D policy, being defined in sectoral or collective terms, providing SOC to individuals, and yielding large gains throughout the economy.

Unfortunately, it is very expensive to provide isolated farms or villages with electricity because of the large amount of poles and wire required and the relatively low demand by agricultural consumers (low load factor). In the United States, where private companies distributed power, only farmers on major roads willing to pay for the poles and wire needed (an investmant of about $2,000) as well as a large monthly minimum charge were able to get electricity for their farms; in 1935 only 10% of America's farms were electrified. In India, although electricity is provided by government bodies called State Electricity Boards (SEBs), the high cost and low returns of RE combined with the unusual scarcity of all resources meant that a similar situation arose: in 1965, only some 5% of India's *villages* (not farms) were electrified.

The RE program in the United States was begun as part of the Emergency Redevelopment Act in 1935; when it became clear that the program could not make use of large numbers of unskilled workers it was reformulated as a separate program and passed in 1936. Under the provisions of the Rural Electrification Act a Rural Electrification Administration (REA) was set up to grant low-interest loans to groups, preferably but not exclusively non-profit cooperatives formed for the purpose of distributing electricity. The REA itself helped farmers to start their coops and to learn how to conduct the business, to wire, and to make the best use of electricity and electric appliances. An additional provision allowed the coops to make low-interest loans to individual members for the purchase of appliances, but of course the individual remained responsible for wiring and deciding which appliances to use. In 1942 the interest rate was fixed at 2% and the program continued indefinitely. In 1949 the RE act was extended to the provision of rural telephone service; by 1954-1959 the character of the program had changed and one-third of all loans to coops were for generating their own power.

In India, the decision to provide electricity in rural areas was taken by the Planning Commission sometime in 1965 in response to a widespread drought. RE was particularly important in this connection since electricity is the most efficient means of lifting underground water to the surface for irrigation, which in turn is required if high-yielding hybrid seeds are to be grown. The long-term potential for use of ground-water irrigation has been estimated at 45 million acres (gross), but this is a very conservative figure (Government of India, 1965: 186). Funds were made available directly to the states (and their respective electricity boards) and also indirectly through loans to the SEB's from consortia of banks and the USAID-funded Rural Electrification Corporation. Since India's peasants tend to live clustered in villages and go out to work the surrounding fields, the unit of electrification used is the village; once his village is electrified, the peasant is responsible for requesting service for his farm. The recently nationalized banks are supposed to try to make loans increasingly available to small farmers so that the SOC provided by the RE program does not go unused.

RURAL ELECTRIFICATION AS A TWO-PHASE WELFARE POLICY

THE CRISES

I have suggested that W+D policies are more likely to be enacted during profound economic crises in which economic policies become the prime political requisite. In both the United States and India such a crisis was occurring at the time the RE program was adopted. These crises put increased value on ideologies of equality and social welfare that in turn altered old patterns of assessing political benefits and costs.

In the United States, the Depression and the concomitant New Deal policies dominated the political environment at the time RE was adopted. The general contraction of demand led to unemployment and still lower purchases and purchasing power. Disposable income declined from $83 billion in 1929 to $74.4 billion in 1930 (Ruggles and Ruggles, 1956: 240). The situation in agriculture was even worse, for in the 1920s, faced with prices for purchased goods that rose much faster than farm prices, many farmers responded with increased production that lowered prices still more. In the general contraction of the money supply after 1929, prices for farm products declined more precipitously than those of the manufactured goods they had to buy—over 50% compared to 32% (Rasmussen and Baker, 1969: 69). Use of expensive fertilizer thus declined and led to rapid leaching of the soil, lower production, and ultimately, the Dust Bowl phenomenon. Many farmers then migrated to cities where they compounded urban unemployment and became much more expensive for society to maintain.

India's problem was different but no less critical. Food production in the latter half of the Second and Third Five-Year Plans (1958-1965) remained almost constant, with the exception of the good year 1964-1965, while population continued to grow. The stagnation in agriculture was a direct result of the planners' persistence in trying to use exhortation rather than capital to raise output. Thus reserves were low and per-capita food consumption already below normal when in 1965-1966 and 1966-1967 a two-year drought lowered food production still further; millions starved and industrial production slowed as a direct consequence of the absence of raw materials. Finally, the planners realized that the agricultural sector contributes directly to economic growth and they instituted a number of village-improvement schemes concentrating on sanitation, education, improved agricultural practices, marketing, and electrification.

In both countries, the presence of the crisis brought into prominence strands of ideology that existed before but were not so much emphasized. India had made a "socialist pattern of society" a formal goal through its incorporation in the preamble to the Constitution. Social welfare, a modicum of equality of income and of opportunity, government control of industries basic to economic development—these were the elements of the "socialist pattern" that was associated with nationalism and the Congress Party. The drought made it clear that the poorest were obtaining few if any of the benefits of the socialist pattern, and increased emphasis was placed on distribution of benefits to underprivileged sectors: agriculture, small shop-owners, and factory workers. The rhetoric of the party conventions following the split in the Congress Party in 1969 captured this mood and ensured a permanent place in India's political lexicon for the "small man" and the "garibi hatao (war on poverty)."

Rhetoric of the "forgotten man" and the New Deal also characterized the political scene in 1930s America. Private enterprise and rugged individualism still had a place, but emphasis was on the need for government to enforce "fairness and justice as they should exist among the various elements in economic life" (Humphrey, 1940: 120 quoting Franklin D. Roosevelt). Threads of old arguments from Jefferson, Jackson, and the Populists were taken up, while other strands from Andrew Carnegie or Adam Smith were woven only into the background.

One sector for which justice was felt to be especially lacking was the agricultural: farmers worked harder for less than almost anyone else, and under less pleasant conditions. New Deal leaders tried to help them to regulate the amount of crops they produced, to preserve the family farm, and to return them to their former relative positions in status and purchasing power. Rural electrification complemented these programs and embodied many of the important goals of the New Deal. First, by providing farmers with a way to get electricity without going to the private power companies, an anti-monopolist blow was struck against the "power trust," still smarting from the passage of the Public Utilities Holding Company Act of 1935 (the Wheeler-Rayburn Act) that prohibited unlimited proliferation of parasitic holding companies supported by the consumers' utility bills. More important, electricity was one sure way to close the gap in style of life that divided the farm from the city and contributed to the ever-declining farm population. While in normal times the flight from the farm offended only the nostalgic image of America, in the Depression it added to the insupportable burden of the unemployed in the cities. Electricity could, and as soon as it was available did, bring to the farmer and his family hot and cold running water, indoor sanitary facilities, irons, radios, dairy and poultry-raising equipment, and, of course, light. Finally, RE was seen as a stimulant to the lagging economy, with Congressmen asserting that every dollar spent on that program could call forth at least one additional dollar of purchases (on wiring and equipment) by the farmer (Congressional Record, 74th Congress).

Although India's basic farm problem was somewhat different from that of the U.S.—poverty resulting from not enough production rather than from almost too much, many of her basic goals were the same. Slowing migration to the city, raising farm income and thereby initiating an ever-spreading circle of purchases, making peasants feel an equal part of the polity and the economy—all these goals were served by RE in India as in the U.S. In addition, RE in India serves the goal of increased food production because it is the cheapest means of raising underground water to the surface for irrigation. This means that improved seeds, fertilizer, and pesticides can provide maximum benefits, and, indeed, RE was developed along with a series of programs designed to increase use of the total package of new agricultural inputs.

Although it would be difficult to prove that the economic crises of the two countries altered the relationship between political and economic values, the above information suggests that this was the case. The large number of economic programs undertaken during the crisis periods and the introduction of new political rhetoric are both signs of the importance of economic growth to legislators. In neither country, however, were lawmakers content merely to adopt radical economic programs, but in accord with rational behavior of more normal times they included provisions in the laws assuring widespread dispersion of benefits and detracting from the collective nature of the RE policies. Before examining these provisions of the laws, however, it will be useful to determine the extent of the economic benefits that could be expected from the two programs, and to show that they fit the proposed model.

ECONOMIC BENEFITS

The major cost of RE to the several Indian governments occurs in the form of a subsidy on each unit (kilowatt hour) of electricity used for irrigation. In order to promote electricity use, a rate of 12.5 NP (Rs. 0.125) was urged by the Center on all State Electricity Boards (SEBs) although their costs vary widely; in Rajasthan the best cost estimates range from 15 to 23 NP per unit generated. In addition, the cost of wires and poles, which generally approach Rs. 110,000 per village, in Rajasthan are borne almost entirely by the state. In 1969-70 about 90 million units were used for agricultural purposes in the state, and 340 villages were electrified. This marks a subsidy of Rs. 44,150,000; this is about three times the amount that the SEB assigns to losses on RE for the year on the basis of operation and maintenance, interest, and depreciation charges (Rajasthan State Electricity Board, 1970-1971).

The monetary returns to this RE program accrue from payments by electricity users, from a 1 NP per unit tax on electricity use, from taxes paid on increased cash income of farmers producing more crops, and from sales taxes on an increased flow of manufactured products and income taxes on the producers of those products. Other non-monetary economic benefits include the availability of more food at reasonable cost, use of higher quality foodstuffs, and, of course, general growth in the economy. In 1971, assuming an overall tax rate on agriculture of about 11%, the Rajasthan government received a total of about Rs. 20,052,750 from its RE program, marking a 26% return on its 1970 investment of Rs. 76,500,000. Table 1 details these calculations.

In the U.S., the subsidy is somewhat more difficult to pinpoint, especially in the earliest period. The need for the subsidy is indicated by the unwillingness of the private companies to try to electrify farms, but other considerations seemed also to be important in that attitude.[3] From 1936 to 1941 money was loaned to cooperatives at an interest rate based on a ten-year average of U.S. Treasury note rates, about 2.8% at the time (NRECA, 1970: 44). The subsidy consists of the difference between this interest rate and the real cost of money, the loss of interest in an initial five-year grace period, and the long amortization period.[4] Sources for the time suggest a commercial interest rate closer to 4%, meaning that the subsidy amounted to some $11 million from 1935-1941. Another observer finds that by 1941 the average yearly deficiency in interest paid was $2.24 million, and, including the administrative costs, the cumulative cost to the government in that year was $16.4 million (Garwood and Tuthill, 1963: 62).

TABLE 1

Benefits of Rural Electrification in Rajasthan

Payments to RSEB (≈ 138,150,000 Units) @Rs. 0.125/unit	Rs. 17,268,750
Taxes on Electricity @Rs. 0.01/unit	1,381,500
Taxes on Farmers' Increased Income 25,500 new wells each irrigate 5 acres double-cropped and increase 600 lb/acre average yield by 50%. (Additional 6000 lb. at Rs. 0.50/lb) Water accounts for 1/2 this additional production and electricity for 2/3 of the additional water available = RS. 1000/well. Extra income due to electricity taxes at 11% rate (includes direct and indirect taxes).	1,402,500
TOTAL	Rs. 20,052,750

Returns come in the same forms as in India: increased taxes paid by farmers, taxes on income generated on the farm equipment and electrical goods industries, and interest and principal payments by cooperatives. Since electricity was put to a much wider variety of uses on U.S. farms than on Indian ones, any computation of returns to electrification is fraught with difficulties. However, three points will attest generally to the ways in which the RE program accomplished its intended effects.

(1) The repayment rate of cooperatives was very good. Total defaults have amounted to less than 1%, and by 1959 $154 million of principal was repaid early (National Rural Electric Cooperative Association, NRECA, 1959: 3). In the earliest period, of course, repayment was slower, but the record was still good.

(2) Many productivity increases seem to be attributable to electricity; a striking example is the effect that heated water in winter has on the fertility of farm animals and the milk production of cows. In addition, although other factors do enter in, electricity helped to lower the man-hours per hundredweight of milk produced from 3.3 in 1925 to 1.7 in 1955, and per hundredweight of chickens produced from 9.4 in 1925 to 6.7 in 1955 (USDA, 1969).

(3) The flow of cash in the rural economy did increase through the purchase of electricity and electrical appliances. From 1935-1951, each of three dealers in a small Virginia town sold over $250,000 worth of appliances to members of the local REA coop (Childs, 1952: 141). A survey for the magazine *Country Gentleman* in 1944 found that farmers planned to spend over $1 billion soon on appliances (Childs, 1952: 81). A survey by the Kansas Committee on Rural Electrification in Agriculture had similar results: a 1955 survey found a future potential investment of about $15 million by the 121,000 families in Kansas REA coops; in 1958, a resurvey ascertained that $34 million had actually been spent on a variety of home and farm appliances (Merrill, 1960: 78). Finally, consumption of electricity by farmers increased over 160% from 1946 to 1950, suggesting further the increased purchase and use of appliances.

Another way of estimating cash flows generated by the program is to obtain estimates of income increases for individual farmers attributable to electricity. While there are wide variations in crops raised, soil conditions, initial investments, and other relevant conditions within both contries, it is clear that individuals do benefit from RE. Table 2 presents data for two farms—one from each country—that suggest the extent to which the installation of electricity is profitable for individual farmers. The U.S. data pertain to a dairy farm, the most highly electrifiable of farm industries, but data can be adduced from other sorts of farms, including small non-specialized farms. For example, analysts of the

TABLE 2

Additional Costs and Benefits of Installing Electricity on a Single Farm

A. India—5-Acre Farm (Wheat)

Costs		Benefits	
Digging Well	Rs. 10,000		
Purchase Pumpset	6,000		
Yearly Payment On Above	4,460	Additional Production (5 additional acres from double-cropping; double production on total 10 acres: 15/md/acre (1200 lb/acre)	
Electricity Charges (Min. Charges, 5 HP Motor)	360	Rs. 40/md	8,900
Installation	500	Saving on labor (for irrigation) 150 man-days	
Additional Seed & Fertilizer	500	@ Rs. 2.5/day	375
	Rs. 5,820		Rs. 9,275

B. United States—Dairy Farm—Original Herd 75
(25 Extra Head Added at Time of Electrification)

Additional Costs		Benefits	
Electricity (Wiring Bill)	$ 225.00	Labor saving 90 hrs/cow/yr @ 35c/hr	
Cooler*	500.00	(75 Cows)	($2,362.50)
Milkers	2,000.00	Extra 500 lb milk/cow/year	
25 Cows (And Feed)	3,000.00	(75 cows) at $5/CWT	$1,875.00
Labor for 25 Cows (73 hrs/cow/yr @ lb .35/hr)	638.75	Extra 4500/lb/ cow/year (25 cows) at $5/CWT	5,625.00
	$6,363.75		$9,862.50

*With a cooler, some of the milk can be sold for $5 a hundred weight as Grade A rather than for $3 a CWT for Grade B.

Red Wing (Minnesota) project of 1924-1927 found that farmers received a 40% return on their investment in the second year if their own labor is capitalized at 35¢ per hour (University of Minnesota, 1928: 26).

These figures all suggest substantial direct and indirect economic benefits for RE programs. The model suggests that these benefits should decline over time—a logical inference as new investment is poured into marginal areas with less potential for development or additional investment or subsidies applied in nearly-saturated areas. India cannot be said to be in a position to be experiencing declining economic benefit-cost ratios yet, as some 85% of her villages remain to be electrified. Indeed, the reputed existence of a black market in blank but signed applications for electricity connections may be taken to indicate that a large market remains untapped.

Analysis suggests that the longer time over which the United States' RE program has been in effect has resulted in declining economic returns:

(1) Increases in average per farm income (from $759 in 1936 to $2400 in 1952, $3049 in 1962, and $5500 in 1972) resulted in lower propensities of farmers to consume, reducing multiplier effects. Some saturation of electrical appliances occurred, and such purchases as took place occurred within an economy so greatly expanded as to be much less responsive to these relatively small expenditures. Finally, at various times in the later period, increased spending hurt rather than helped an inflationary economy.

(2) For the first time in 1954, the interest rate on Treasury notes rose above the 2% maximum specified for the RE program. From that time on, any subsidy for the RE program was increased by the difference between this rate and 2%; this difference has increased steadily (to 2.76% in 1968) as did the amount of loans. One commentator has fixed the 1962 subsidy at .4¢ per kilowatt-hour delivered, a total of over $35 million, and the welfare costs for 1956 at $148 million (Lyon, 1970: 7, 51-2).

(3) Partly due to the effects of electricity itself, individual farmers became more productive and were seeking ever larger farms, buying out small neighbors or selling to still larger agri-business conglomerates. In 1972, 47% of agricultural income went to less than 10% of farmers, who, because of their very size and wealth, tend to be large consumers of electricity and thereby large recipients of subsidized electricity rates (USDA, 1973: 68, 71). (In 1960, the wealthiest 8% received 35% of net agricultural income.)

(4) Finally, there is evidence that the program had reached saturation levels: 95% of the farms were electrified by 1956, and the REA had had to turn to loans for generation (rather than just transmission) in order to maintain need for itself.

Economic benefits of RE are initially high, as the model suggests will happen
in W+D policies; in the United States, where the program has been in effect for
40 years, benefits have definitely declined relative to costs. In order to complete
our analysis of RE programs in terms of the general outlines of the model
illustrated above, political costs and benefits must be examined. Although the
economic crises of the two countries did partially explain the raising of political
benefits relative to costs, legislators in both also adopted other means to increase
P. The next section outlines these tactics.

POLITICAL COSTS AND BENEFITS

One determinant of political costs and benefits that influences many of the
others is a federal structure of government. Federalism puts a premium on
distribution made equal by geographical area. It also brings into political benefit-
cost calculations the consideration of the relationship between the levels of
government, a complication that was not explicitly included in the model. Both
India and the U.S. are federal states, but in the former electricity is named in the
constitution as a concurrent (shared) subject, while in the latter it is not
mentioned. These differences did affect political costs and benefits in the two
countries, but, as we shall see, they did not affect the general pattern of rising
political benefits over time.

The differences in the nature of the federal ties in the republics of the United
States and India have been detailed often. India is usually described as the more
centralized of the two, because of her dominant Congress Party, disciplined
party system and parliamentary form of government, and the control of about
75% of all government revenue by the Central Government. However, in India,
electricity is a concurrent subject and agriculture a state subject, even to the
exclusion of the Center from taxing agricultural income. The Center's lack of
control over agriculture could be an incapacitating problem in a country
oriented to large-scale, long-term planning, but for the fact that the states are
too dependent on the Center for funds. This naturally gives the Center an
important, though far from all-powerful, source of control.

During the second drought year, India's Planning Commission formally decided to implement a number of programs that focused upon the agricultural
sector, including the Intensive Agricultural Area Program and distribution of
seed and fertilizer. Since the several states also wanted economic development,
they were generally pleased to take funds earmarked for these and related
programs; quite naturally they also insisted on exerting their constitutional right
to administer the program and choose its beneficiaries. In many states, rural
notables—generally higher-caste, wealthy rural elites often with strong urban
ties—are one of the dominant political groups, with the result that the programs
designed to aid the agricultural sector actually benefit only the wealthiest part of
that sector. The importance of this group in state politics is reflected by the firm
negative stance the Chief Ministers (in their collective role as the Prime Minister's

Council of Economic Advisors) take on the issue of raising the land revenue or instituting an agricultural income tax, two reforms that would fall most heavily on the rural rich and are much sought by the Center.

Thus, when the planners decided to stress rural electrification as part of their program, they were forced to work through the states to implement their policy. Whether or not RE formed part of a state's concerns, the Center had two important means of control. First, under a law of 1949 each state has a semi-autonomous State Electricity Board (SEB) that has the responsibility for initiating and executing electricity policy. Although the boards' autonomy is limited by the states' power of the purse, they do receive outside funding by borrowing on the open market; more important, the permanent board members have strong ties to the Center. The Secretary, the chief coordinator and policy-maker on the boards, is a member of the Indian Administrative Service rather than of the state services, and his ties are reinforced by annual meetings with the other Secretaries and Central Irrigation and Power Commission personnel. Second, as soon as the RE program was established, the Center found organizations that would loan money to state boards for RE projects; these organizations include representatives of the Center on their own policy-making bodies and approve loans using the criteria for acceptable projects outlined by the Planning Commission.

The rural electrification program that exists is a result of these contradictory pressures within the institutional arrangements. Both the state and the central governments try to exercise influence and both have control of part of the funding for RE. The impetus for the program came from the Center, although in several states efforts had been made earlier, and large-scale RE did not begin until the Center committed large amounts of funds for it. The selection of particular villages for electrification, the rates to be charged, and the technical details belong to the state boards, however, and, in Rajasthan at least, these were subject to political influence. Curiously, no interest group has tried seriously to capture the SEBs; this may be due to the high cost of organizing rural Indians, but part of the explanation must lie in the fact that the state components of the program are strong enough that interested parties simply focus their attentions at points where they can influence a broader range of policies.

At the state level, the policy has followed the pattern of our model. One indication of rising political benefits is certainly the desire to expand the program; all of India's states have increased both their monetary authorizations and their targets in terms of number of villages and wells to be electrified. The central government has responded to demands for more funds for RE by establishing bodies that loan money to states for "compact area plans"—schemes that actually increase the number of people reached by given amounts of funds by providing contiguous areas with electricity.

In addition, political costs of the program have been lowered, at least in the state of Rajasthan, by insistence that the least developed district (an administrative unit next smaller than the state) receive electricity until at least 5% of its villages are electrified before other districts can receive any more funds; in practice, each district gets at least a few projects every year. Legislators make RE the subject of question in the parliamentary Question Hour, and the larger the village, the more likely it is to receive priority for being electrified.

In the United States, the "less centralized" of the two countries, very little role was played by the states directly in the formation or implementation of the program, although the state-based structure of Congress resulted in super-imposing a geographically distributive criterion on the REA. The states' power to grant incorporation and to license and tax public utilities meant that the RE program was not entirely divorced from local power considerations, but the REA consciously decided to discourage statewide association of cooperatives and to foster a national one dealing directly with itself.

Because of the emergency of the Depression, the executive and legislative branches were acting well together, Congress accepting virtually all of the bills presented by Roosevelt as part of his Second New Deal. As with all programs, however, Congress placed its unique stamp on the RE bill. For example, a provision that could only have been conceived in anticipation of the varying needs of representatives from many different states called for the allocation of $40 million for nine years to the RE program; of this, 70% was to be allotted to states in proportion to the number of farms not then receiving central station power, and 30% was to be distributed without regard to this criterion. No state was to get more than $10 million in any one year nor more than 10% of the unrestricted funds.

In 1944 Congress voted to continue the REA program indefinitely. It also expanded the program year by year, from $48 million in 1938 to over $400 million in 1972. More and more recipients enjoyed the benefits of RE, and Congressmen were aware of the rising political rewards to themselves as well. By 1956, 95% of all farms were electrified, and by 1968, over 98%. In 1949 a rural telephone program was added under the REA to bring still another service to happy constituents and remind old electricity consumers that they were still receiving benefits.

In addition to rapidly expanding the REA program in order to increase political benefits (and forestall dissatisfaction of non-recipients), rural electrification in the United States fulfills many of the other dynamic characteristics we expected to find according to the model.

(1) The policy's beneficiaries experienced the desired income gains—from an average annual income per farm of $759 in 1936 to $5500 in 1972—and at the same time became a more articulate and potent political force.

(2) An interest group formed around the program. The National Rural Electric Cooperative Association (NRECA) was established in 1942 and had 393 member coops by January 1943, at the time of its first convention. The NRECA is a strong interest group with close ties both

to Congressional committees and to the REA administration, whose bureaucrats join the coops in raising the political benefits to legislators of maintaining the RE program.

(3) Demographic changes have altered the nature of the REA's constituency: in 1972 only 20% of the purchasers of cooperative electricity were farmers. The suburbanites who have moved into former farm areas and have become beneficiaries of the REA's subsidized interest rates are also a large and articulate political force: it would be very costly to create dissatisfaction among this group of voters.

(4) We have noted above that economic benefits were declining and the program had nearly saturated the available recipients. In light of this, and in order to maintain the political benefits within the legislature of equitable geographical distribution, the provision of 1936 allocating 70% of funds on the basis of need was altered. In 1955 the percentage of REA funds to be distributed to those states with the fewest electrified farms was reduced to 25% in order to avoid concentrating 70% of the enlarged appropriation in a few (mostly western) states.

The above evidence demonstrates that RE in two countries has followed the pattern predicted by the model. Ordinarily, the observer must simply infer from the continuation of a policy that the political costs of abolishing it were insupportably high. However, in the case of RE an actual attempt to end the program resulted in changes that indicate the value placed on the program by Congress. The following section details that attempt.

A TEST OF POLITICAL BENEFITS

Effective January 1, 1973, the Nixon Administration ordered the REA in compliance with the Rural Development Act to make its loans with money earned from sales of government-insured securities to private investors rather than from tax revenues and to raise the interest rate on its loans to 5%. This was expected to save the government up to $279 million in the half of the fiscal year remaining, based on the Congressional appropriation of $565 million for electricity and an additional $145 million for the related rural telephone program. The NRECA immediately asked for reconsideration of this decision, stating that most rural electric coops could not have been formed without the low-interest loans and that many would be "wiped out" under the new system. The REA also lobbied quietly for a retraction of this decision, and Senator Hubert Humphrey, a drafter of the Rural Development Act, stated that the act was intended to provide supplementary funding for the RE program, not replacement thereof.

In a news conference on January 31, President Nixon responded to his critics. He noted that 80% of the REA's money once went to rural development and getting electricity to farmers, but that by 1972 80% of the money loaned at 2%

went to "country clubs and dilettantes, for example, and others who can afford living in the country." However, on February 21 the Senate voted 69 to 20 to order the USDA to revive the 2% interest program and to spend the $455 million that remained from already appropriated funds. Twenty Republicans joined 49 Democrats in an indication of the program's non-ideological distributive character.

On May 11 President Nixon signed P.L. 93-92, a compromise agreed upon by the Administration and the Congress. It provides for insured and guaranteed loans, most of which be at 5% interest, but also includes provision for 2% loans to especially isolated or poor areas. The act also authorizes the guarantee of RE and telephone loans made by other lenders (specifically the Rural Telephone Bank and the National Rural Utilities Cooperative Finance Corporation). In return for an overall 5% rate and increased emphasis on private lending agencies as well as the Administrator having discretion (rather than having this provided for in the law) in granting 2% loans to coops with special financial hardships, the government conceded the continuation of the program, assured the next three years will be funded at not less than the 1974 level, and assured that not less than $80 million for electricity and $25 million for telephones will be available at the 2% rate.

The fight over the REA was characterized by some reporters as a skirmish in the battle over Presidential powers, and undoubtedly this issue affected the outcome to some degree. However, it is clear that many of the pressures on the Administration came because of the specific issue—rural electrification—rather than on general principles. For example, the only northern Democratic senator who voted against restoration of the REA program came from Connecticut, a state with no REA-funded coops.

The events of 1973 clearly illustrate that political benefits of RE were still high enough to warrant a struggle by Congress to retain them. However, the bulk of the evidence cited above suggests that rural electrification does follow the general model for W+D policies, with initially high economic benefits declining over time while political benefits increase from the point at which they were high enough to warrant acceptance of the policy.

A NOTE ON THE BENEFICIARIES OF W+D POLICIES

Once a W+D policy is formulated, an important question arises, namely, how to choose among the many potential beneficiaries in the face of an income restraint. In the U.S., for example, a total of six million farms were elegible for REA loans, yet each year there was a maximum of $40 million to be distributed. In Rajasthan, about one fiftieth of the eligible *villages* can receive electricity in any given year.

Despite the fact that criteria embodied in the RE policies do not explicitly include this effect, in both countries there appears to be a tendency for the wealthier farmers to benefit first. There are a number of reasons for this. The U.S. coops required a $5 fee to join (many organizers took smaller sums and promises to pay later) plus about $175 for wiring, another $50 for indoor fixtures, an average monthly bill of about $6, and the cost of electric farm equipment—a pump for $10.50, a cream separator for $91.70, a feed grinder for $51.40, and so on (University of Minnesota, 1928: 4, 15; USDA, 1946). Although these costs were repaid and the appliances could be bought on low-interest loans through the coops under Section 5 of the REA Act, the initial outlay had to be available. Similarly, in India a connection fee is charged ranging from Rs. 300 to Rs. 800 depending on the size of the motor to be used, various administrative fees must be paid, and the cost of a pump and drilling a well borne. Furthermore, in both countries the subsidy for RE is larger to the wealthier farmers insofar as they consume more of the cheap electricity.

This tendency of the wealthier of the eligible recipients to benefit first is probably an inevitable part of the provision of SOC, unless other programs are provided to counter the tendency. It is very likely also a characteristic of distributive policies generally, since access to the political process is frequently related to wealth. However, economic development gains in two ways what is lost to equality. First, the relatively wealthier are able to make larger initial purchases of complementary equipment, creating more multiplier effects immediately. Second, these consumers can adopt new practices quickly and thus serve to demonstrate their utility to others at no cost; although possibly less important in the U.S., the power of this "demonstration effect" in generating demand for rural electrification in India has been great. Additionally, in India, where government policy is directed at least in part towards the achievement of a large *marketed* surplus (to provide low-cost grain to urban dwellers) as opposed to having much of the new grain consumed on the farms, the wealthier farmers are better able to consume a smaller percentage and thus to market nearly all their entire crop.

In the U.S., because of the size of the program, almost all farmers did eventually get electricity, although some of the very poorest, the American Indians, are just beginning to receive help in organizing cooperatives. In India right now, the principal beneficiaries of the RE program are still the relatively wealthy farmers, especially the "local notables" and absentee industrialist owners. Nationalization of the fourteen major banks in July 1969 was intended to help make loans available for wells and wiring to small farmers; early successes in this area seem to have been negated as more and more of the local notables have sought these loans and have been able to dominate their distribution. However, as electricity becomes available in increasing numbers of villages, its benefits will begin also to reach more smaller farmers.

It is considerations such as these that will help to determine the rapidity with which the political benefit-cost ratio of Figure 1, can rise. It will depend on the number and influence of the initial beneficiaries, the degree of understanding of their deprivation by the non-beneficiaries, their political mobilization, and so on.

Politicians with short time horizons will naturally prefer programs with characteristics that suggest the political benefit-cost ratio will rise rapidly. It is part of our continuing task as political scientists to discover ways of determining these characteristics.

SUMMARY AND SUGGESTIONS FOR FURTHER RESEARCH

Welfare and development policies promote economic development by providing capital to groups of disadvantaged people. Politicians attempt to raise the political benefit-cost ratios (P) of these policies by extending their applications in various ways, most of which lead to increases in the size of the program over time. This in turn leads to a decline in the economic benefit-cost ratio (E). On the basis of the model, two phases for W+D policies can be distinguished, one in which both P and E are relatively high, and a later one in which P is very high but E is very low. Evidence from the rural electrification programs of India and the United States conforms very closely to the model.

Several further refinements of the model would be very helpful. First, it appears that E would first rise and then fall—rather than consistently, if slowly, falling from the outset. Thus, some increase in the size of the program would still find areas in which investment would be highly productive, and this increased size would also raise the multiplier effects with a concomitant rise in E (and also in P, because of the large number of beneficiaries). India is clearly still at this point. Construction of a model that fits this requirement would greatly aid in bringing the model closer to reality, and it would be interesting to see what additional characteristics it might possess.

This suggests the second area for further work: specifying coefficients. The more closely coefficients or the relations among them can be determined, the clearer will be our idea of the exact paths P and E will follow. A third area involves the idea of a critical level of P necessary for policies to be initiated; specification of coefficients can help to show whether these critical levels and, if so, how they depend on P's other characteristics. Also, coefficients must be allowed to vary within the model to incorporate such changes as the energy crisis that affects both P and E for rural electrification.

Finally, we will want to consider the normative choices implied by a model such as this. Although the point of view of politicians has been adopted in this model, clearly the citizens' desires are of more paramount importance. Implicit in the idea of phase 1 and phase 2 is some concept of the relative values to be put on different sorts of social goods such as political and economic costs and benefits. How willing we are to allow high P to saddle us with low E depends in part upon our knowledge of these two variables. It is for this reason, more than any other, that political scientists must persist in building and refining models such as that presented here.

NOTES

1. This formulation bears strong resemblance to the discussion of the costs to a government in coercion and alienation of Lowi's (1964) "redistributive" policies, which are also defined in terms of collectives. Programs with individual recipients may be compared to his "distributive" policies, although there are some differences between the two.

2. Obviously interest groups can exist before the initiation of a policy; this has the effect of raising the political stakes, both costs and benefits. If an opposing interest group exists, costs are higher; if a favorable one, benefits are higher. If neither exists, as suggested here, the politician acts as an entrepreneur which aids his reputation among his constituents and raises the political benefits of a program.

Another important aspect of political costs and benefits is information. If constituents don't know about a policy, it creates neither costs nor benefits. Another reason for establishing regulatory agencies is to keep knowledge about a policy confined to those most interested, and interest groups by serving as disseminators of information raise the political stakes in yet another way.

3. The companies appear simply not to have wanted to electrify farms. The following statement in a letter from industry leaders to the first REA Administrator (Knapp, 1973: 355) bears witness to this attitude: "The problem of actively promoting rural electrification has received serious consideration of utility companies for many years. As a result, there are very few farms requiring electricity not now served.

4. Twenty-five years originally, raised to 35 years in 1944. Another subsidy lay in the fact that most loans require the repayment of interest before principal while REA loans permits simultaneous payment of both, lowering interest charges substantially.

Chapter 7

EDUCATION AND DEFENSE EXPENDITURES
IN LATIN AMERICA: 1948-1968

BARRY AMES
and
ED GOFF

Washington University, St. Louis

If students of Latin American politics were to inventory verified propositions regarding the performance of Latin American regimes, the resulting list might not exceed zero.[1] Such labels as "Christian Democracy," "military junta," and "traditional oligarchy" have been confidently applied to the regimes of the region, but little systematic cross-national research ties either whole regime types or particular regime characteristics to any aspect of regime performance. This paper treats one such aspect, that of monetary allocations for education and defense, and attempts to estimate the importance of economic and political factors in the 1948-1968 period.[2] In particular, four substantive questions are considered:

(1) What is the relationship between changes in spending for defense and changes in spending for education?
(2) What is the effect of prior defense and education expenditures on current defense and education expenditures?
(3) How well can changes in defense and education spending be explained with a model utilizing only "economic" variables?

AUTHORS' NOTE: This paper is part of a project exploring the relationships between the attributes of regimes and their policy outputs. Support for the research has been received from the University of New Mexico and Washington University, St. Louis. Besides helpful criticisms made by participants in the Conference on Comparative Public Policy, we would like to thank John Bailey, Sue Farrington, Glen Fishbine, E. K. Fuge, Sam Jones, Don Korman, Craig Pollock, Jim Powers, and Tom Pynn for help in many tedious jobs associated with data-based research.

(4) Does the addition of cross-nationally equivalent "political" variables substantially improve our explanations?

This paper does not replicate the American state policy studies by arguing for the predominance of either political or economic influences on allocation patterns. Our purpose is simpler: to establish the importance of economic constraints upon allocations and to show the utility and promise of expenditure analysis in a developing region.

A WORKING MODEL OF THE ALLOCATION PROCESS

We began with an optimal model of the expenditure process, but encountered crucial problems of operationalization and measurement.[3] Of necessity we are forced to retreat to a working model which leaves out crucial variables, which itself contains serious measurement difficulties, but which may constitute a first step toward a more accurate conception of allocation processes. In the absence of data measuring policy-makers' perceptions of such elements of the model as resources and bargaining power, we substitute independent judgments. The model then includes measures of economic resources, the electoral and extra-legal strength of the left, and the political involvement of the military. In addition, residuals from the multiple regression equations testing the above variables will be analyzed in a search for clues as to the effects of regime preferences.

FINANCIAL RESOURCES

Policy makers in different regimes may use different economic indicators as measures of yearly resource changes, but they are all trying to predict their revenue base. Since changes in these indicators are generally highly related to changes in the Gross Domestic Product, use of GDP as the sole indicator should yield results deviating little from an ideal multi-indicator approach. In addition, yearly changes in total expenditures have been included in the analysis on the grounds that resources must first be translated into increases in total expenditures before they can be split into program categories.

THE POLITICAL ENVIRONMENT

In Latin America it makes more sense to talk of "lefts" rather than a single monolithic "left." The most important left groupings are blue-collar workers and students. The former express their demands through various kinds of strikes and demonstrations and through electoral activity. Students are too few to wield influence electorally and must often utilize extra-legal tactics.

Once an executive has taken office, the electoral power of the left is channeled through the legislature. The party system must be open to leftist parties, but if no party makes a deliberate appeal for blue-collar votes or has a blue-collar electoral base substantially larger than other parties, then the left has no electoral strength at all.

The monographic literature on Latin American politics makes possible the identification of parties with blue-collar orientations. The percentage of vote these parties received in legislative elections (or, in some cases, their percentage of legislative seats) is our measure of the left's "legislative strength."

What happens when the legislative strength of the left is high is difficult to predict. Increases in the left's share of the vote may not be translatable into greater influence on governmental outputs, because such increases may polarize the society and lead to the development of counter-balancing anti-left groups. Even if more votes mean more influence, leftist parties might not really represent their constituencies, hardly an uncommon situation. If they are representative, their demands may go far beyond social-development spending. Perhaps the most salient demand of leftist parties is for the maintenance of blue-collar workers' share of national income. Wage-maintenance efforts may actually decrease the level of funds available for developmental spending. And finally, strong legislative lefts may feel constrained to vote for large defense budgets as a bribe to the soldiers to prevent coups.

The complexities of the vote-allocation linkage prevent simple predictions of the "more left voting associates with more education and less defense spending" sort. Given the variety of plausible outcomes, the data will have to inform future theory-building.

The relationship between violence and allocations is equally complex. Governments can meet demands with three kinds of responses: substantive, symbolic, or de-participant. The last category includes attempts to lower the level of demand-making both by repression and by cooptation. In practice, of course, governments use all three. For example, Ames (1973) has shown that in the late 1960s student violence in Brazil was met by police repression, attempts to coopt students by inviting "leaders" to participate in powerless decision-making bodies, and substantial increases in allocations to universities. Evidence is lacking, however, to support a conclusion that violence in Latin America generally increases allocations. In addition, powerful arguments can be made supporting other linkages. For example, violence may be a tactic of those facing unsatisfactory allocations but possessing no other political resources. If the costs of repression are low, regimes may easily ignore outbursts of violence, and violence may appear inversely related to allocations. More complex non-linear models are also plausible, and in a later section a quadratic model will be fitted to the data.

Compilations of violent events in Latin America are commonly based on reports from non-Latin American newspapers. As a result, the compilations are biased toward better reporting of more developed countries and urban areas. Unfortunately, these compilations are the only materials measuring violent events currently available. We first took three kinds of violent events (general strikes, riots, and anti-government demonstrations) from Banks (1971) and summed them for each regime. Then we took the categories labeled "protests," "riots," "armed attacks," and "deaths" from the World Handbook of Political and Social Indicators (Taylor and Hudson, 1972) and used these as individual measures to investigate the effects of different kinds of violent activities.

Differences in the percentage of the population attending universities are sharp across the region, and these differences affect both the ability of students to mount violent protests and the costs of repression against them. In order to control for these scale differences, the percentage of the population attending universities was entered with the measures of violence.

MILITARY INVOLVEMENT

The ability of the armed forces to compel responses from the policy elite stems from their involvement in the political process. Military involvement was coded along a four-point scale:

(1) Civilian rule; military used for external defense only.
(2) Military subordinate to and used by government for internal purposes.
(3) Civilian rule; military is a major participant in the policy process.
(4) Military government.

Two other measures, Robert Putnam's (1967) four-point scale and Martin Needler's (1968) five-point scale, approximate this one in construction, deviating only occasionally.

Does greater political involvement lead the military to spend less on social development and more on itself? As Schmitter (1971a) suggests, the obvious may be too simple: civilians may feel constrained to bribe the soldiers to keep them out of power, and besides, the military budget, fattened as it is on U.S. aid and often committed to heavy capital expenditures, may be relatively immune to short-term political changes. Initially we seek evidence of linear relationships between military involvement and spending, but parabolic functions of the type suggested by Schmitter will also be examined.

EXPENDITURES

The dependent variables in this analysis are yearly and "regime" national government expenditures between 1948 and 1968. Only three interpolation were necessary, although missing data at the beginnings or ends of country serie reduce the total number of observations. At least some data are analyzed for al Spanish- and Portuguese-speaking countries except Cuba and the Dominica Republic. All data are converted to constant dollars using International Mone tary Fund price deflators and dollar exchange rates.

Since no consistent breakdowns of expenditures by functional categorie exist, ministry totals must be taken as measures of outputs in each policy area. Thus education expenditures are almost always simply the total reported by the education ministry, while defense expenditures sum data for the various military ministries, general staffs, and available pension data.[4]

Using expenditures as policy outputs creates problems. Defense expenditures are complicated by the stimulation they receive from U.S. aid, which is generally unreported in expenditure totals. Eventually attempts will be made to incorporate aid into the analysis, but currently its effects have been ignored. In addition, though its redistributive impact is ambiguous, educational spending has been treated as a social development policy output. Some educational spending goes to universities, hardly an allocation benefiting the poor, but compared to other areas of the federal budget, education is relatively beneficial to the lower classes.

PRELIMINARY EMPIRICAL FINDINGS

The substantive questions posed are treated through correlation and regression techniques, primarily multivariate linear regression. Although our data are more a population than a sample, t-tests and F-tests are used for hypothesis testing.[5] Data are presented by "regimes" and by individual country-years. Regime figures are the total for each variable during the tenure of a particular executive divided by the number of years that executive held power.[6] When individual country-years are presented, the country disappears as the unit of analysis; instead, we have observations whose number sums the products of each year times the number of countries with reported data.[7] Separate country analyses were made only for the effects of prior expenditures because the limited number of observations per country prevented the inclusion of more variables.

In an earlier paper (Ames and Goff, 1973) we argued that there are compelling statistical and conceptual reasons to minimize the use of ratio variables such as a given expenditure's share of GDP or its share of total expenditures.[8] Lacking a clear resolution of the conflict over preferred operationalizations, we present data in terms of simple percentage changes, percentage changes in the expenditure's share of the total budget, and percentage changes in the expenditure's share of the GDP. Predictably, the poorest predictions are achieved when the share of total expenditures is the dependent variable, because in this case the denominator (total expenditures) is itself highly volatile.

THE RELATIONSHIP BETWEEN EDUCATION AND DEFENSE SPENDING

Education and defense spending are often regarded as inversely related. Ultimately increased spending on anything means less for something else, but the empirical relationship between any two policy areas is quite another matter. Tables 1 and 2 present correlational data for various operationalizations of

TABLE 1

Product-Moment Correlations Between Education and
Defense Variables for Individual Country-Years

Variables	Correlation Coefficient
Education ――― Defense	.85
% Change % Change Education ――― Defense	.55
Education Defense Total Expenditures Total Exp.	-.08
% Change % Change Education ―― Defense Total Exp. Total Exp.	.44
Education ――― Defense GDP GDP	.91
% Change % Change Education ――― Defense GDP GDP	.56

n=253

TABLE 2

Product-Moment Correlations Between Education and
Defense Variables for Regimes

Variable	Correlation Coefficient
Education ――― Defense	.86
% Change % Change Education Defense	.45
Education ――― Defense Total Exp. Total Exp.	-.03
% Change % Change Education ――― Defense Total Exp. Total Exp.	.29
Education ――― Defense GDP GDP	.96
% Change % Change Education ――― Defense GDP GDP	.49

n=58

defense and education expenditures both for regimes and for individual country-years.[9] In terms of the relationship between *changes* in defense and education spending the meaningful correlations are circled.[10] All are positive and significant at the .05 level.

Education and defense spending both rise and fall at the same time. Since increases in their shares of the total budget are also associated (although the relationship here is weaker), some other expenditure must be negatively related to their changes. The areas which lose when education and defense gain cannot now be specified, but clearly neither gains at the expense of the other.

THE EFFECTS OF PRIOR EXPENDITURES ON CURRENT EXPENDITURES

Tables 3-5 present the results of bivariate regressions between each variable and the same variable one or more years or regimes earlier.[11] Note that the occasional presence of an extremely low correlation coefficient should be interpreted as the absence of a trend rather than extreme volatility. For example, the variance in education spending in Ecuador is 97% explained by the previous year's spending, but although the variance in education as a percentage of GDP is 88% explained by the previous year's ratio, only 5% of the variance in education's share of total expenditures is explained by the previous year's share.

TABLE 3

The Impact of the Expenditures of the Previous Regime
on the Expenditures of the Current Regime

(Percentage of variance explained by the same
variable one regime earlier)

Education	
Education Spending	97%
Education / Total Exp.	58%
Education / GDP	95%
Defense	
Defense Spending	94%
Defense / Total Exp.	42%
Defense / GDP	67%

(All significant .05 level or better)

TABLE 4

The Impact on the Expenditures of the Current Year of
Expenditures One and Two Years Earlier

(Percentage of variance explained by the same
variable one and two years earlier)

	One Year Earlier	Two Years Earlier
Education		
Education Spending	97%	93%
Education Total Exp.	58%	50%
Education GDP	71%	35%
Defense		
Defense Spending	97%	96%
Defense Total Exp.	58%	94%
Defense GDP	71%	83%

(All sigrlificant at .05 level or better)

In fact, Ecuador's total education spending has risen in small but consistent
increments; education's share of the total budget has changed hardly at all; and
finally, education's share of the GDP has risen in steady increments.

These correlations can be compared with roughly similar data from the
American states (Sharkansky, 1968: 39-47), though our data are reported as
percentages of variance explained (R^2) rather than the more impressive simple
correlation coefficients (r) reported by Sharkansky. With some exceptions the
importance of prior expenditures seems generally less in Latin America than in
the fifty states, but such comparisons with the U.S. may be misleading. No one
has defined the limits of "incrementalism"; consequently, there is no way of
determining whether these findings meet any such standard.

Education, with the single exception of the two-year lag on education as a
percentage of GDP, seems consistently stable, confirming Schmitter's (1972)
finding that education is a relatively more incremental policy area. The simple
correlation coefficients between the two most useful dependent variables (education and education/GDP) and their predecessors one year or one regime back are
all at least .84. And 12 of 16 countries[12] have over 90% of the variance in their
education spending explained by the previous year's value.

TABLE 5

**The Impact of the Past Year's Expenditures on the Expenditures
of the Current Year by Individual Countries**

(Percentage of variance explained in each category when
correlated with the same category for the previous year)

	Expenditure	Expenditure Total Exp.	Expenditure GDP	N
Bolivia				
Education	83%	28%	86%	18
Defense	63%	65%	67%	18
Brazil				
Education	62%	49%	31%	20
Defense	63%	65%	36%	20
Chile				
Education	90%	22%	76%	19
Defense	67%	71%	55%	19
Colombia				
Education	83%	51%	68%	18
Defense	68%	56%	53%	18
Ecuador				
Education	97%	5%	88%	17
Defense	79%	27%	56%	17
Paraguay				
Education	96%	48%	75%	18
Defense	83%	69%	5%	18
Peru				
Education	98%	69%	93%	16
Defense	83%	85%	13%	16
Uruguay				
Education	47%	3%	46%	10
Defense	17%	1%	17%	10
Venezuela				
Education	97%	89%	90%	18
Defense	92%	9%	57%	18
Costa Rica				
Education	90%	96%	88%	15
Defense	75%	42%	15%	15
Guatemala				
Education	98%	42%	75%	17
Defense	90%	30%	42%	17
Honduras				
Education	97%	93%	94%	17
Defense	55%	34%	24%	17

TABLE 5 cont'd

	Expenditure Total Exp.	Expenditure GDP	N
Mexico			
Education	98%	58%	95%	16
Defense	92%	58%	60%	16
Nicaragua			
Education	92%	81%	84%	16
Defense	21%	66%	75%	10
Panama			
Education	97%	49%	78%	19
Defense	no data	no data	no data	--
Salvador			
Education	97%	87%	45%	19
Defense	89%	15%	60%	19

Defense spending is clearly much less stable than education, although a considerable part of current spending is linked to prior spending. The relative instability of defense spending may result from the devotion of a smaller component of its budget to salaries, stimulation from U.S. military aid, or sufficient military influence in the political process to command larger increases. Examination of individual cases and a more sophisticated economic model (containing measures of foreign constraints) could illuminate the causes of the volatility of defense spending.

A MULTIVARIATE "RESOURCE" MODEL

Since economic variables have claimed a position of primary importance in all prior expenditure studies, we begin by testing the effects of changes in resources. The independent variables include changes in the Gross Domestic Product, as a broad constraint on spending, and changes in total expenditures themselves, as a constraint on each policy area.[13] The equations take the following form:

$$\Delta\ DV = \partial + \Delta\ GDP + \Delta\ TE$$

where dependent variables (DV) are

education, $\dfrac{\text{education}}{\text{total expenditures}}$, $\dfrac{\text{education}}{\text{GDP}}$

defense, $\dfrac{\text{defense}}{\text{total expenditures}}$, $\dfrac{\text{defense}}{\text{GDP}}$

and where ∂ is a constant, Δ GDP is the percentage change in the Gross Domestic Product, and Δ TE is the percentage change in the total spending of the central government. These equations were also estimated with lagged values of the independent variables, on the assumption that policy-makers might use this year's increases in resources to plan next year's spending, but the explained variances obtained were always quite low and are not shown.

Tables 6 and 7 present unstandardized regression equations for the two sets of data. The entries in parentheses are the t-scores of each coefficient.

As expected, the equations fit the regime data better than the individual year data. This stems in part from the smaller number of regimes but mainly from the "smoothing" of expenditures over the course of a regime. Our discussion will confine itself to the "better" model, although the findings are quite similar in both. Once again, little will be said about the share-of-expenditures variable because of its conceptual problems.

Considering that the models only predict *changes* in spending, they seem to have done quite well, at least at first efforts. To begin, note in Table 7 the basis

TABLE 6A

A Model Using Only Economic Variables for Education Spending
by Individual Country-Years

Δ Education = 6.52 + .0896 Δ GDP + .5048 Δ TE
          (.742)   (8.20)

R^2 = 21%

Δ Education = 6.803 + .00136 Δ GDP - .3714 Δ TE
Total Exp.   (.00126)   (6.75)

R^2 = 15%

Δ Education = 7.11 - .9259 Δ GDP + .4869 Δ TE
    GDP   (7.71)   (7.97)

R^2 = 30%

N = 268

TABLE 6B

A Model Using Only Economic Variables for Defense Spending
by Individual Country-Years

Δ Defense = 1.301 + .0367 Δ GDP + .5999 Δ TE
         (.347)   (11.48)

R^2 = 35%

Δ Defense = 1.554 + .0042 Δ GDP - .2885 Δ TE
Total Exp.   (.0446)   (6.232)

R^2 = 14%

Δ Defense = 2.138 - 1.036 Δ GDP + .6236 Δ TE
    GDP   (9.795)   (11.91)

R^2 = 47%

N = 253

TABLE 7A

A Model Using Only Economic Variables for Education Spending by Regimes

Δ Education = 10.45 + .4891 Δ GDP + .6709 Δ TE
                                    (2.57)   (6.08)

R^2 = 46%

Δ Education = 12.51 + .2887 Δ GDP - .2952 Δ TE
Total Exp.   (1.799)   (3.174)

R^2 = 15%

Δ Education = 14.53 - .6647 Δ GDP + .5397 Δ TE
GDP   (4.146)   (5.806)

R^2 = 39%

N = 68

TABLE 7B

A Model Using Only Economic Variables for Defense Spending by Regimes

Δ Defense = 5.53 + .0329 Δ GDP + .5286 Δ TE
                                 (.197)   (5.44)

R^2 = 37%

Δ Defense = 2.89 - .02295 Δ GDP - .2229 Δ TE
Total Exp.   (.173)   (2.898)

R^2 = 15%

Δ Defense = 8.24 - .9434 Δ GDP + .4823 Δ TE
GDP   (7.072)   (6.23)

R^2 = 57%

N = 58

of the relationship previously found between education and defense. Changes in education and defense spending are linked strongly and fairly equally to changes in total expenditures. As total spending rises and falls, defense and education rise and fall. The shares of education and defense in the GDP tend to increase sharply when expenditures increase but seem negatively related to changes in GDP itself. This finding may appear contradictory, but it is not: a simple increase in resources does not mean more defense or education spending unless the government manages to increase its revenues. Only when the government raises expenditures will defense and education spending benefit.

Consider the strong negative coefficients associated with changes in total expenditures and changes in the education or defense share of expenditures. When total expenditures rise, education and defense rise (and increase their share in the GDP), but they *lose* relative to other categories of the budget. The areas which lose are presently unidentifiable, but some programs profit at the expense of traditional expenditures like education and defense.

Finally, two limitations on these findings: because education and defense spending are included in total expenditures, a part of their high association is spurious. Besides, the finding that total expenditure changes are generally more important than resource (GDP) changes raises more problems than it solves. How do regimes extract more resources from their economies? When can resource changes be translated into revenue increases? In effect, these findings about the allocation process underline the need for revenue analysis.

WHICH REGIMES ARE LEAST RESOURCE-DEPENDENT?

Insertion of the actual values of the changes in GDP and total expenditures for each regime into the above equations yields a prediction of education and defense spending. The difference between this predicted value and the actual value, called the residual, is a measure of the deviance of the particular case. Those regimes with the largest negative residuals are "underspenders," that is, they spent less than their increases in revenues and total spending predicted. "Overspenders" [14] (those with positive residuals) spent more than expected.

These residual scores provide the basis for testing hypotheses relating variables which are not sufficiently ordinal to be included in a regression equation. For example, if military regimes increase defense spending more than civilian regimes even after considering resource changes, there should be significant differences between the means of the residuals of civilian and military regimes.

Lacking a firm ordinal conception of regime preferences, we search informally among the most deviant (that is, least explained) cases for evidence of relationships between preferences and spending. Such a search, concentrating on the 10 regimes most "overspending" and the 10 most "underspending," reveals the non-conformity of Latin American governments to unidimensional conceptions of liberalism and conservatism plus a wide variety of allocation styles. [15]

Only two regimes followed a pattern of fiscal conservatism, underspending both on education and defense. In his long (1946-1955) reign in Argentina, Juan Peron emphasized other kinds of welfare expenditures, devoted considerable effort to income redistribution through wage policy, and perhaps saw education as sufficiently developed to allow smaller increments. Perón may have felt sufficiently in control of the military to restrict their budget, but he was removed by the armed forces, and no succeeding Argentine executive underspent on defense.

A different and somewhat surprising situation is presented by the first regime following the Bolivian Revolution of 1952, the Paz Estenssoro government of 1952-1956. Why would an avowedly radical regime spend less than expected on education? Perhaps the answer lies in the chaos engendered by the upheaval itself. Resource increases could not be translated into spending increases because tax collections were erratic, so the government was unable to begin its development program. Besides, it was forced into a rigidly conservative stabilization program. However, the two regimes succeeding Paz, that of Siles Suazo

(1957-1960) and Paz' return from 1961 until 1964, were overspenders on both education and defense.

The "reformist liberal" regime, at least in the more optimistic days of the Alliance for Progress, would cut its "wasteful" spending on defense and devote its efforts to social-development programs. Of the 58 regimes analyzed here, only one, that of Ruiz Cortines in Mexico between 1953 and 1958, was among the top 10 overspenders on education and the top 10 underspenders on defense. Mexico, of course, is something of a special case. From a high of over 60% of total spending in the 1920s, its defense budget has shrunk steadily to the present level of around 7% (Wilkie, 1967), so to some degree Ruiz Cortines' achievement is tempered by the trend he was following. Conversely, however, many regimes commonly thought to be reformist do not follow this developmental pattern, including the Betancourt regime in Venezuela, Figueres in Costa Rica, Belaúnde Terry in Peru, or Frei in Chile.

If "reformist liberals" are scarce, "reactionary" regimes are scarcely more common. Only two regimes underspent on education and overspent on defense. One was the conservative (though elected) regime of Gonzalez-Videla in Chile, and the other was the government of Castelo Branco in Brazil (1964-1966).

A much more common pattern might be called "defensive liberalism." Six regimes were overspenders both on education and on defense: the governments of Siles and Paz in Bolivia (1957-1964), José Figueres in Costa Rica (1954-1957), Villeda Morales in Honduras (1958-1963), Cháves in Paraguay (1951-1953), and Oscar Osorio in El Salvador (1950-1956). All had seen recent military overthrows and, on the theory that a fat army makes no coups, it made sense to bribe the soldiers. Five other regimes tried to expand educational spending while containing defense spending within the increases of resources. Two of these five were ousted by the military (Goulart in Brazil and Frondizi in Argentina). Two (Betancourt and Lleras Camargo in Colombia) followed unpopular military dictators and were the first of a series of civilian governments that have continued until the present. Oil has probably allowed the survival of the governments of Betancourt and his successors, and the Frente in Colombia kept a tenuous grip on power perhaps as a result of the exhaustion brought on by *la violencia* and the unity of threatened elites. The fifth regime, that of Guido in Argentina, was a provisional government installed by the soldiers after Frondizi's removal. That military expenditures did not rise excessively suggests perhaps that the complexity of Argentine society limits the power of the military over policy outcomes even though it can remove elected officials.

A MULTIVARIATE MODEL WITH ECONOMIC AND POLITICAL VARIABLES

Since considerable unexplained variance remains after the resource measures are considered, we now add a series of political variables. Tables 8 and 9 present equations for these new variables, containing both political variables and the earlier economic variables. Table 10 compares the "political" with the "non-

TABLE 8

A Model Using Both Political and Economic Variables
for Education Spending by Regimes

Δ Education = 9.54 + .5750 Δ GDP + .6834 Δ TE + .0763 LS
                          (2.92)   (5.99)   (.511)

     - 2.75 MI + 3.69 V - .0045 US
      (.613)   (1.64)   (.355)

     R^2 = 49%

Δ Education = 8.55 + .3692 Δ GDP - .2767 Δ TE + .0646 LS
TE   (2.25)   (2.91)   (.518)

     - 1.856 MI + 3.73 V - .0018 US
      (.495)   (1.99)   (.165)

     R^2 = 22%

Δ Education = 13.69 - .5993 Δ GDP + .5420 Δ TE + .1009 LS
GDP   (3.60)   (5.62)   (.799)

     - 2.49 MI + 2.24 V - .00094 US
      (.657)   (1.18)   (.097)

     R^2 = 42%

     N = 68

TABLE 9

A Model Using Both Political and Economic Variables
for Defense Spending by Regimes

Δ Defense = 12.62 + .0824 Δ GDP + .5356 Δ TE + .0119 LS
                          (.457)   (.511)   (.086)

     - 2.72 MI + 1.51 V - .0123 US
      (.671)   (.715)   (.977)

     R^2 = 38%

Δ Defense = 7.39 + .0152 Δ GDP - .2115 Δ TE + .0120 LS
TE   (.106)   (2.55)   (.110)

     - 1.67 MI + 1.391 V - .0108 US
      (.520)   (.831)   (1.08)

     R^2 = 17%

Δ Defense = 15.47 - .9155 Δ GDP + .4728 Δ TE + .0410 LS
GDP   (6.39)   (5.67)   (.375)

     - 2.63 MI + .0737 V - .0074 US
      (.817)   (.044)   (.733)

     R^2 = 58%

     N = 58

TABLE 10

The Political and Non-Political Models Compared by Regimes

(Percentage of variance explained)

	Economic Variables Only	Economic and Political Variables	Change in R^2
Education			
% Change Education	46%	56%	+ 10
% Change Education Total Exp.	15%	37%	+ 22
% Change Education GDP	39%	54%	+ 15
Defense			
% Change Defense	37%	38%	+ 1
% Change Defense Total Exp.	15%	17%	+ 2
% Change Defense GDP	57%	58%	+ 1

political" models. The four new variables represent left legislative strength, violence, military involvement, and the percentage of the population attending universities. Conceptually, the political variables make sense only at the regime level, so no data are presented for individual country-years.

Depending on one's perspective, the results of the politico-economic models are encouraging or depressing. The political variables are not consistently useful. Only in the analysis of spending on education does any political variable add substantially to the variance explained. That this area increases is not surprising because educational spending is more stable and less subject to foreign constraints than defense spending.

The two variables which seem consistently unrelated to spending changes are the legislative strength of the left and the involvement of the military. That the strength of the military should prove ineffective was foreshadowed by the deviant cases examined above. Overspenders on the military seemed as likely to be civilians as officers; perhaps civilian regimes have to placate the officers as the price of remaining in power. A related argument holds that military spending is highest when the military is an off-again on-again ruler rather than permanently in or out. To this possibility, which implies a curvilinear (parabolic) relationship between involvement and spending, we shall return in the next section.

That the left should not influence education or defense spending through its legislative power is also plausible. While in some countries, such as Chile, the party system has developed along European lines and legislators exhibit high degrees of party responsibility (Sinding, 1974), the Chilean case is more the exception than the rule. Even where parties have substantial blue-collar voting support and make explicit appeals to workers, once in power they may exert little effort to meet blue-collar needs. Moreover, the most salient issue to workers may well be wages, and wage maintenance can detract from other allocations.

The positive effects of violence upon spending are supported by a number of case studies (see Ames, 1973; Payne, 1965). Nevertheless, our violence measure is too broad. What kinds of violence elicit responses? Are certain kinds of violence counterproductive? Will "extremes" of violence lead to increased defense spending? To answer these questions measures of specific kinds of violence were substituted for the general violence levels. "Protests" (defined as non-violent protest gatherings) did not affect spending for either education or for defense. The number of people killed in violent activities was equally unimportant. "Armed attacks" had weakly positive effects on both defense and education spending (t-scores between 1.7 and 2.0). "Riots" (defined as violent demonstrations or disturbances involving large numbers of people and characterized by material damage or bloodshed) had very strong positive effects (with t-scores ranging from 3.6 to 4.4) on education increases.

These data suggest that peaceful protests are ineffective. Regimes respond when they perceive costs are increasing. They are unimpressed by deaths but quite impressed by property damage. Armed attacks are slightly effective but may also be counterproductive, because defense spending (and perhaps repression) also increases. However, because the allocational response to violence may not be linear, conclusions as to its effects should be withheld until curvilinear possibilities are explored.

TWO POSSIBLE CURVILINEAR RELATIONSHIPS

Military Involvement

It has been suggested (Schmitter, 1972) that high levels of defense spending might occur when the military are off-again on-again rulers rather than when they are either consistently non-political or permanently in power. This hypothesis can be tested by first applying our basic economic models (including changes in GDP and total expenditures) and then fitting a polynomial regression against the residuals of the first equation. Fitting this parabolic function to the residuals of the economic model proved unsuccessful. At no level did military involvement affect either education or defense spending significantly. Nonetheless, we would caution against premature rejection of the hypothesis. Perhaps defense spending jumps sharply when the military first comes into power after being less involved. Possibly civilian regimes replacing military governments bribe soldiers to stay away. Brazil after 1964 fits the first possibility; Venezuela after 1958 the second. In any event, the basic hypothesis should not be totally rejected pending more careful specification.

Violence

The relationship between violent activities and monetary allocations is complex, because the costs to a regime from pursuing any combination of symbolic, allocational, or repressive responses do not seem easily calculable or necessarily linear. Because the measures of riots and general violence were most closely related to spending increases, we estimated the equation with quadratic functions for these two variables. Both proved effective. The explained variance in the equation predicting changes in education as a percentage of the total budget increased from 22% to 38% in one case (violence) and from 37% to 52% in the other (riots). Explained variance increased by smaller but still significant amounts for the other variables.

In both cases the fitted parabola had a minimum as its turning point, that is, it was convex from the bottom, and the turning point was approximately at about the middle of the violence scores. Spending increases were highest in regimes with very low and very high levels of violence, but middle levels of violence were associated with smaller increases.

Momentarily throwing caution to the winds, we can suggest some interpretations of this finding. One explanation begins with the assumption that regimes are well enough insulated so they can ignore violence. If so, "liberal" regimes will spend more on education than "conservative" regimes, regardless of their level of violence. However, some liberal regimes are at relatively low levels of societal conflict and thus have little violence, while others are much more polarized and violent. Conceivably, then, liberal overspenders would be found at both ends of the violence spectrum, while underspenders keep violence at low levels and make no allocational response.

If we compare the most deviant cases from the purely economic equations to the most deviant cases after the addition of the parabolic violence function, we can determine which cases are best explained by the violence variable, that is, which cases are no longer deviant. Among the low-violence overspenders, the best explained cases are the Figueres regime in Costa Rica, the Villeda Morales regime in Honduras, and the Cháves regime in Paraguay. The chief high-violence underspending regimes were those of Castelo Branco in Brazil and the Panamanian government of 1949 (which had four executives). These regimes seem to fit the prediction. Costa Rica, Paraguay, and Honduras are all much less conflictual than Venezuela, where oil has caused a polarizing and destabilizing growth.

Another explanation would suggest that violence has expansionary effects on spending from about its middle level to high levels, but some sympathetic regimes spend without prodding. This implies that the Figueres and Betancourt regimes were really different, that is, Betancourt's government had to be forced to spend, but Figueres did not. Currently we lack the monographic data to resolve this question, but these regimes should not automatically be assumed to be equally "liberal."

A choice between these two explanations cannot be made without a careful lead-lag analysis plus a breakdown of education spending by grades. For example, these data appear to contradict Ames' finding (1973) that violence in Brazil in the Costa e Silva regime did compel a partial allocative (as well as repressive) response. The difference is that in Brazil the regime was responsive to university students because it was oriented to middle- and upper-class interests. When it created more universities, it did so at the expense of secondary and primary education. Class interests dictated an allocative response.

THE SIGNIFICANCE OF THE FINDINGS

Given the defining and clarifying nature of this paper, individual findings and countries have been discussed only briefly. Little more will be said now, but the value of the enterprise and the meaning of these findings need some discussion.

IS THE ENTERPRISE WORTH THE EFFORT?

We think so. With very crude models and little methodological or theoretical sophistication some simple equations succeeded in explaining significant percentages of the variance in both education and defense spending. Although the fit of the models does not approach those used in the American state policy studies, explanations of *changes* in expenditures rather than their totals were sought. These changes are a relatively small part of the total, which itself depends primarily on prior spending levels. Consequently, the importance of prior spending and resource changes now seem well established.

Perhaps the major substantive contribution is in dispelling the notion that expenditure patterns in Latin America are totally erratic. They are not. Due to the greater unpredictability of the economic environment, expenditures are less stable than those of the American states, but if this unpredictability can be incorporated into theoretical formulations and if it can be estimated quantitatively, then the predictive ability of our models will doubtless improve.

THE SIGNIFICANCE OF THE PARTICULAR FINDINGS

The measures of political variables tested here were not major determinants of education or defense spending. The initial discovery, that changes in education and defense spending were themselves related, could be explained in two ways. If political factors are important, then as the strength of the left forces the government to raise social-development spending, the armed forces respond by compelling an increase in military funding. Consequently, both rise together at the expense of policy areas which lack powerful backers. If, on the other hand, political factors are unimportant, then both education and defense spending are rising and falling as resources rise and fall.

The former hypothesis, emphasizing the importance of political factors, is denied by the weakness of the political variables in explaining changes in education or defense after resource measures are applied. With the exception of the effects of violence on educational spending, these political factors do not significantly improve an economic model.

Nevertheless, it would be premature to conclude that political factors are generally less important than economic factors in determining spending. First, our working model is not a very good approximation of the true allocation process. Second, even if no *cross-nationally equivalent* political variables systematically affect spending, many manifestly "political" influences may affect it in particular countries. That is, Latin America may not have a *common* allocation process; instead, different models may explain different groups of countries or time periods. Expenditure changes in Latin America may well prove little more "political" than in the United States (except in such cases as revolutionary Cuba), but such a conclusion is not yet appropriate.

THE FUTURE OF EXPENDITURE RESEARCH

IMPROVING THE DATA

While students of single countries are usually unable to test multivariate models, cross-national studies are hindered by the superficiality of data sets which generally show only ministerial totals. If the methodological advantages of multi-case analysis could be combined with data sets of the quality of Hayes' Brazilian study (this volume), the profundity of our analyses would increase. Since gathering such data for 20 countries is probably impossible, it might be more practical to concentrate on 8 to 10 carefully chosen cases, perhaps Argentina and Chile, Brazil, Peru and Ecuador, and some Central American nations. A project of this kind would require a group of scholars and considerable resources, but it might well yield the greatest long-run payoff.

METHODOLOGICAL TECHNIQUES

These data really form 17 time-series equations, one for each country. Such equations should not be estimated by simply combining all the data into a single multiple regression analysis. Various kinds of errors, including time invariant country effects, period specific but country invariant effects, and effects varying by time and country, may seriously distort parameter estimates. Techniques developed by econometricians (Nerlove, 1971) for pooling such time-series structures have not yet been utilized by political scientists. They might considerably increase our efficiency in processing cross-national longitudinal information.[16]

IMPROVING ECONOMIC MEASURES

Earlier it was reported that changes in price levels in the same year as expenditures were negatively related to them, while changes in the previous year were *positively* related to spending changes. Unexpected jumps in prices may cause real expenditures to fall, because while tax revenues come in slowly, prices paid for goods purchased rise. However, the following year policy-makers compensate for the losses of the previous year by raising expenditures.

Unfortunately the relationship between government spending and inflation is dynamic. Spending fuels inflation, but spending levels are affected by inflation. Moreover, policy-makers' expectations about both also affect both. As a result, a dynamic model is necessary for the correct estimation of the effects of price changes on spending. Such a model might help explain the greater year-to-year variance in Latin American expenditures.

A second improvement in the economic model would come from the introduction of other kinds of resource variables, including export prices, U.S. aid, and foreign investment. The growing literature on *dependencia* provides a theoretical justification for such variables.

IMPROVING THE POLITICAL VARIABLES

A major problem in expenditure studies has been an over-reliance on easily quantifiable variables, with a gap occurring between concepts and indicators. Researchers might profitably consider the use of different indicators to measure the same concepts as well as the use of expert rankings.

The task of relating concepts to indicators is hindered by the differences in Latin American political regimes. In some polities, for example, the strength of the left can be measured by analysis of electoral data, but where elections are non-existent other measures are needed. We agree with Frey that "the road to equivalence is through clear and common conceptualization and paramount emphasis on local validation" (1970: 248). Since electoral data must be measured on the same scale as expert rankings, this approach implies a loss of information from cases where quantitative data do exist. Such a loss in precision is an acceptable price for conceptual equivalence.

The use of expert rankings may be necessitated by the scarcity of quantifiable information for the measurement of such variables as "the ideological nature of the regime." Policy-makers are faced with the same scarcity of data. They, like us, must make educated guesses. Expert rankings have been in disrepute among

Latin Americanists since, some years ago, experts were asked to rank countries on their degree of democracy, but they have long been used in international relations. If (admittedly a big if) concepts can be made sufficiently precise, the use of expert rankings could enable more meaningful assessments of the impact of political variables.

Finally, attention should be paid to regimes' efforts to use expenditures as means of increasing political support. Allocations have programmatic purposes, but they also reward followers and bribe potential opponents. If we can predict critical times when regimes ought to expand expenditures as a bureaucratic payoff, then expenditure cycles might be discernable, and, within these cycles, we could observe shifts in allocations toward ministries with higher expenditure/employment elasticities. Moreover, the causes of high inflation, with its attendant effects on allocation, include expansion of the state sector. (For an example from Brazil, see Kahil, 1973: 330-334.) Research in this direction would at least avoid over-reliance on the questionable "programmatic" nature of expenditures.

NOTES

1. Of course useful work exists. In the area of public expenditure analysis, case studies include research on Mexico (Wilkie, 1967; Coleman and Wanat, 1973), Chile (Sinding, 1974), Cuba (Baloyra, 1974), Venezuela (Baloyra, 1973), and Brazil (Hayes, this volume). However, case studies are inherently unable to provide a basis for generalizing to Latin America as a whole because the limited number of years for which expenditures are available prevents testing complex multivariate models.

The only multi-national longitudinal expenditure study is Philippe Schmitter's "Military Intervention, Political Competitiveness and Public Policy in Latin America: 1950-1967" (1971c). While provocative and pioneering, its findings are highly questionable because of crippling methodological errors. These include using tests of significance in a manner that makes improper rejections of the null hypothesis highly probable, performing multiple regressions with excessive numbers of independent variables for the number of cases, and neglecting evident effects of serial correlation. As a result, this paper demonstrates the feasibility of expenditure analysis in Latin America, but its particular findings cannot be considered reliable.

2. The actual number of years for which we have data at this time varies from 10 to 19 among the seventeen countries. Data sources available on request.

3. Space limitations prevent discussion of a set of categories of variables which we consider indispensable to a truly isomorphic model of the expenditure process, especially one which avoids the difficulties of Dye-type models (see Rakoff and Schaefer, 1970). These categories include measures of the preferences of regimes' executives, the resources available to them (recognizing that the kind of economic indicator executives use may vary across countries), the bargaining power of left, center, and rightist groups, institutional constraints such as legislative dominance of the executive, and consideration of the uncertainty of the economic environment, especially with regards to unexpected increases in inflation. If measurable, these variables could be arranged in estimatable form, and predictions about outcomes could be made on the basis of the importance of political factors (either the preferences of executives of the power of organized interests) or economic factors (including resource changes and the uncertainty of the economic environment)

Presently, however, we are forced to consider preferences only in the discussion of deviant cases; resources must be summarized by the Gross Domestic Product; and the political environment consists of measures of the strength of the left and the military.

4. Heare (1972) includes social security expenditures for the armed forces where possible. We do not, because for many countries they are not reported separately from other social security spending.

5. We consider significance testing to be as appropriate in populations as in samples. The notion that significance testing is inappropriate in universes rests on a misunderstanding of statistical inference. Stinchcombe (1968: 23) makes this point well.

6. For example, the years 1953-1958 in Mexico are the Ruiz Cortines regime; 1959-1963 in Venezuela are the years of the regime of Romulo Betancourt. In cases where the two regimes overlap a calendar year, we have attributed the whole year to the earlier regime.

7. The number of observations for education and defense differ because no defense data were available for Panama, and because Nicaragua has fewer years of defense than of education.

8. On this problem, see also Tufte (1969; 1969-1970), Russett (1971), and Briggs (1962).

9. The number of observations equals the number for defense, because there are years with education spending but no defense data.

10. The others suffer from serial correlation problems anyway.

11. Theoretically, it makes no sense to lag more than one regime.

12. Argentina was dropped from Table 5 because the data seem untrustworthy.

13. Searches for time-dependent trends in the first differences were made in earlier versions of this paper with plots and time variables. None were found.

14. The existence of "overspenders" and "underspenders" is of course a purely artificial construct. Our own feeling is that all these regimes spend too much on defense and too little on social development.

15. The residual rankings generated by the three equations for each spending category are remarkably similar. We have only considered cases deviant on at least two of the three. Almost all were deviant on all three or on none at all.

16. A future paper will deal with the autocorrelation problems which plague the present analysis.

C. Collective Goods

Chapter 8

NATIONAL DEFENSE AS A COLLECTIVE GOOD

R. H A R R I S O N   W A G N E R

Department of Government
The University of Texas at Austin

The theory of collective (or public) goods, originally developed by economists as the basis for a theory of government expenditure, has increasingly attracted the attention of political scientists as a way of illuminating many problems of interest to them. In much of the literature on collective goods, national defense or national security is mentioned as an example of what is meant by the notion of a collective good.[1] It is odd, in light of its prominence as a paradigm case of a collective good, that the main literature analyzing national defense from this point of view is devoted to the supply of defense among alliance partners (Olson and Zeckhauser, 1966, Olson, 1967; van Ypersele de Strihou, 1968; Beer, 1972). Although the theory is clearly relevant to such questions, its original development in the context of governmental expenditures

AUTHOR'S NOTE: This paper was originally prepared for delivery at the 1973 annual meeting of the American Political Science Association, New Orleans, September 4-8, 1973. The research on which it is based was made possible by the Ford Foundation, which awarded me a Faculty Research Fellowship for the academic year 1971-1972, and the Center for International Affairs of Harvard University, at which I was a Research Associate during the same year. The underlying idea of the paper has been taken directly from the Ph.D. dissertation of my colleagues, Norman Frohlich and Joe Oppenheimer (1971), to whom I am grateful for that and much more.

would have led one to expect that it would be first applied to the question of the optimum supply of defense for a population by an established government. That is the problem that I want to explore in this essay.

This is a problem of somewhat broader significance than might at first appear. Because the objective of military security is one of the most important determinants of the behavior of governments in international politics, any argument concerning how governments decide (or ought to decide) what sort of defense policies to supply their citizens would be relevant to one of the central problems in the study of international politics: the goals that are to be ascribed to states.

Furthermore, because the theory of collective goods explicitly addresses the problem of how the preferences of individual persons are to be aggregated in an optimum way, it can also be expected to have something relevant to say about whose interests foreign policies serve, or ought to serve. This is a question that touches in turn a number of problems central to the study of international politics. One of these is the problem of collective choice as it pertains to matters of national security—the problem of democratic control of foreign policy, in both its descriptive form (how is the behavior of democracies different from that of other states?), and its normative form (to what extent should the process by which foreign policy is determined resemble the process by which other public policies are determined in a democracy?). Another is the problem raised by Marxist analysis of international politics: the relation between security interests and the special economic interests of various classes, groups, or individuals in the foreign policies of governments. And these issues are, in turn, obviously an important part of the broader class of problems concerning what James Rosenau has labeled the "linkages" between domestic and international politics, which David Vital (1969) has called the "central mystery" of the subject, and which everyone would agree to be of great importance.

I

Before discussing the concept of national security specifically, it will be helpful to bear in mind a few general properties of collective goods, as they are defined in the literature.[2] In his classic statement of the problem in 1954, Samuelson distinguished what he called "collective consumption goods" from "private consumption goods" by the fact that the former are all "enjoy[ed] in common in the sense that each individual's consumption of such a good leads to no subtraction from any other individual's consumption of that good," whereas private goods could be "parcelled out among different individuals" (Samuelson, 1954: 179). This distinction was expressed mathematically by the proposition that the total quantity of private goods consumed equaled the sum of the quantities consumed by all individuals combined, whereas the total quantity of collective goods was the same as the quantity consumed by each individual. From this difference it follows that the conditions for an optimal supply of the two types of goods must also differ. In the case of private goods, a given quantity is optimally allocated among individuals when the marginal rates of substitution of one good for another are equal to each other; and the total quantity supplied is optimal when these marginal rates of substitution are equal to marginal cost. In the case of collective goods, however, the quantity supplied is optimal only when the *sum* of all individuals' marginal rates of substitution equals marginal cost. That is, it must not be the case that any person or group of persons would *together* be willing to contribute the resources required to supply an additional unit of the collective good. Since each person consumes (by definition) the same quantity of the good, there is no problem of allocating this quantity among consumers. There is, however, a problem of allocating the cost of the good among them, and a further peculiarity of this type of good is that there is no determinate answer to the question of how this should be done.

It is important to understand what this last point means. It means, first, that there are in principle an infinite number of ways of allocating costs, all of which are Pareto optimal; second, that the economist has no compelling reason to suggest that one of these optimal distributions be chosen; and third, that the economist has no way of predicting what sort of distribution will be decided on by persons conforming to the standard behavioral assumptions of micro-economic theory.

It is instructive to remember, as the familiar Edgeworth box reminds us, that the first proposition is also true of private goods; and that the second and third are true of private goods in the case of bilateral monopoly (Shibata, 1971). That is, there is not a single Pareto optimal point at which two traders can exchange private goods: rather there is a contract curve. Every point off this curve is inferior to some point on it, in the sense that moving onto the contract curve can improve the welfare of one at no expense to the other. However, movement along the contract curve can only improve the welfare of one at the expense of the other. A single point on the contract curve can be determined by specifying a price, that is, by specifying that the two goods can only be exchanged for each other at a certain rate. If that stipulation is made exogenously, each party to the exchange can then decide what quantities of the two goods he wishes to possess, and a single Pareto optimal point will be determined. However, the price chosen will have had the effect of determining how the "gains from trade" will be distributed between the two traders.

In a competitive market, a price will be determined independently of the decisions of any pair of traders. Moreover, it will be equal to the marginal cost of the good. Thus one of many Pareto optimal points will be chosen, which has this to recommend it: that it is arrived at in such a way as to arrange simultaneously for the optimal quantity of the good to be supplied. One may still object to the resulting distribution. However, this is a problem that can be dealt with inde-pendently by a social-welfare function, or the political process.

In the case of collective goods, markets cannot develop because consumption is not exclusive. Therefore prices must be fixed, or determined by some process of collective choice. Thus the bargaining problem is not so easily circumvented. Moreover, in order for the good to be optimally supplied, it is only necessary that the cost of supplying the last unit be shared by those who consume it in such a way that each pays no more and no less than what he is willing to pay for that unit. This means that normally the prices paid should be expected to differ from person to person. But the sharing of marginal costs is consistent with an infinite variety of ways of sharing total costs. For example, in the case of two persons it would be possible for one to pay no more than part of the cost of supplying the last unit of the collective good, while the other bore the entire remaining cost of the good. This would be a Pareto optimal arrangement, in which one person succeeded in capturing all the "gains from trade" for himself.

One important suggestion for allocating the costs of collective goods has been that total costs be shared in the same proportions as benefits received. If one objected to the resulting distribution, it could be corrected by lump sum income transfers as in the case of private goods, and the separation of distributional conflicts from problems of Pareto optimality of supply and distribution could be maintained. But individuals would have powerful incentives to prevent any such allocation of costs (since they would benefit whatever they contributed). And since one would have to depend on the individuals concerned for information about the value they placed on the good, it would be difficult, if not impossible, to devise a workable method for carrying out this suggestion.

Discussion of how individuals might, in the absence of government or any enforceable collective decision rules, allocate among themselves the costs of supplying a collective good has been dominated by controversy concerning whether any of the good will be suppled at all. This is what has come to be known as the "free rider problem." The nature of this problem is clearly indicated by the example just given. The individual who avoids paying for any part of the cost of the good except for a portion of the last unit supplied enjoys a "free ride" with respect to his consumption of the rest. But this is an outcome that is, in principle, available to either person, and each may thus seek to withhold his contribution in an attempt to achieve this outcome for himself.

However, if both did so they would find themselves off the contract curve. Why, then, would this be an equilibrium outcome? It is possible that the situation in which these two persons find themselves is a prisoners' dilemma. For the collective good to be optimally supplied, the sum of their marginal evaluations of it must equal the cost of supplying the last unit of the good. However, any contribution by either person toward this cost (assuming that the good can be supplied in continuously variable quantities) could be used to increase the supply of the good only by a certain amount (determined by the production possibilities curve for the good); and it is possible that each individual's evaluation of the amount of the good supplied by his contribution would be less than any contribution he may make. But the sum of the evaluations of the two may nonetheless be greater than marginal cost. If such a condition existed, the situation would be formally identical to the prisoners' dilemma: for each person the strategy of not contributing dominates the strategy of contributing, but the outcome if both adopt this strategy is not Pareto optimal.

A number of writers have equated collective goods with the prisoners' dilemma (Buchanan, 1968: 88-91; Hardin, 1971). This has reinforced the argument of Mancur Olson (which was not based on any game theoretical interpretation of the collective goods problem) that only small groups of people will be able to supply themselves voluntarily with collective goods.[3] However, while the definition of a collective good is consistent with a pay-off distribution that conforms to the definition of the prisoners' dilemma, it is also consistent with pay-off distributions in which the strategy of contributing to the supply of the good is an equilibrium strategy. There does not seem to be anything about the definition of a collective good that *requires* that each person always value the quantity of the good bought with his contribution less than the contribution. And if he values it more, then he will have an incentive to contribute. However, the amount that he will contribute will depend on the expectation he forms about the contributions of the other(s). In other words, there will be an infinite number of equilibrium strategies, with the distribution of the pay-offs depending on which combination is chosen. The game will therefore include a bargaining problem.

Moreover, there does not seem to be any reason why dominance of the strategy of not contributing should necessarily be associated with the existence of large numbers of potential consumers. Indeed, the reverse may be true: marginal costs may decline, or marginal evaluations increase (or both) as the number of persons consuming the good and contributing to its supply increases.

If this should be the case, then the frequently asserted tendency of persons in large groups to regard the behavior of others as parameters, rather than as variables to be influenced, takes on a quite different significance than it does in the work of Olson. For it may well be that each individual will assume, not that no one else will contribute, but that the aggregate contributions of others will amount to a certain level. Each person can then decide whether it is worth his while to contribute on the basis of such an assumption.[4] However, the underlying bargaining problem would not be eliminated, and, consequently, there would be an incentive to manipulate expectations of the likely contributions of others to one's own advantage. Moreover, changes in the distribution of costs would themselves be collective goods to those who benefited from them, and persons may be willing to contribute to the support of bargaining activity to that end.

The notion that the bargaining problem associated with the supply of collective goods is the basis of much political activity is a central part of the literature on this subject (Buchanan, 1968; Breton, 1966). However, most writers assume the existence of a set of collective decision rules and a government with the power to tax; and the analysis of political activity within such a framework tends to be dominated by normative problems of aggregating individual preferences.[5] The possibility that persons would be willing to contribute toward the supply of collective goods (given appropriate mutual expectations) has, however, recently been made the basis of a theory of political leadership by Frohlich, Oppenheimer, and Young (1971). Their analysis leads to an abstract exploration of the conditions under which political organizations may arise, political competition develop, and collective decision rules emerge.

So far I have focused on two main problems: securing an optimal level of supply of a collective good, and selecting among (or bargaining over) the infinite number of Pareto optimal ways of allocating the costs of the good among its consumers. Once taxation is introduced into the picture, however, a further difficulty appears. For it then becomes possible that some (perhaps many) persons find themselves paying a greater marginal price for the good than they are willing to pay: at that price, they would rather have less of the good (how much less depends on how such a person's evaluations of marginal costs and benefits would change as the supply of the good was reduced). Since it is unlikely that any system of voting and taxation could be devised that would match each person's marginal costs and marginal benefits exactly, this is likely to be a widespread phenomenon, and, at least in principle, a further stimulus to political activity.

This summary has so far been based on Samuelson's important restatement of the collective-goods problem, which focused on one defining characteristic: that one person's consumption of the good does not diminish another's. This can usefully be called the property of *nonrivalness of consumption*. However, implicit in Samuelson's analysis (and in the discussion above) was also a second characteristic: that if a collective good is supplied to one person, it must simultaneously be supplied to all. It is clearly this second property, which can be called *nonexclusion*, that leads to the free-rider problem, and the general nature of the bargaining problem associated with these goods. Since Samuelson's formulation, it has become clear that these two properties are not the same, and that they can vary independently of each other. It has also become clear that each is really a polar case, and that it can vary continuously between the two extremes.[6] Thus private and public goods are merely two opposite corners of a two-dimensional space, defined by variations of each of these two properties. Most nonprivate goods (including defense, as well as many goods commonly thought of as private) probably lie somewhere within this two-dimensional space.

Further analysis can usefully be postponed until after a discussion of national defense. However, at this point one can already see an important difference between economists' discussions of these problems and those of political scientists. For the economist, common interests inhibit the achievement of collective goals (as compared to the exchange of private goods) and lead to conflict. All too often, however, political scientists tend to assume that common interests lead directly to group activity and the diminution of conflict. The difference lies in the economist's closer attention to the problem of individual values and individual choice. For, although two persons may agree that one thing is preferable to another (and in that sense have a common interest), they may disagree about how preferable it is, or about how the cost of achieving the jointly preferred outcome is to be shared. Moreover, some distributions of the cost can transform agreement into disagreement—at some price, some persons will find that the outcome in question is no longer preferred to its alternatives. Since national defense, or national security, is often taken to be one of the basic shared interests among members of a society, this difference is likely to lead to significant differences in analysis of what is at least the common core of all governments' foreign policies.

II

National defense may be a collective good. But what, precisely, is national defense? It cannot be equated with expenditures on defense, for the problem is what those expenditures buy. Nor can it be equated with the tanks, guns, and airplanes purchased with these funds, because they are valued not for themselves but for what they can accomplish. It is obvious that a number of different things can be done with military forces, and therefore they can be used to supply a number of different goods. I will return to this point later, because it is important for an understanding of the value that persons in a society place on the military forces themselves. However, for the moment I want to concentrate on one particular good that such forces provide—the one commonly called national defense.

What is this good? Clearly it is that of preserving the autonomy of one's own society against the threat that some other government will seek to displace one's own by military force. (There are other possible uses to which a foreign government's forces may be put from which one might want some protection, but let us ignore them for the moment.) Any society whose members were absolutely certain that this could not happen would be completely secure. More commonly, a society is not absolutely secure in that sense; rather its citizens are faced at any given moment with a certain probability that they may be defeated by some foreign government and subjected to its rule. I want to explore the implications of assuming that increases or decreases in the supply of national defense (or national security) are increases or decreases in that probability.

First, let us notice that increases in the supply of defense are not necessarily to be associated with increases in defense expenditures. It is possible that by arming itself one society may simply provoke a foreign government to attack and defeat it, in order to make itself secure. Security may on occasion be best achieved by being as militarily inconspicuous as possible.

Second, let us notice that the probability of national survival must be a subjective probability.[7] Unlike police protection, for example, where the probability of being murdered or robbed can be defined in terms of a per-capita crime rate, there is no "invasion rate" or "defeat rate" to give any objective meaning to the state of a society's military security. This is even true in time of actual war, when the war aims of the enemy can hardly ever be objectively established, and the probability of victory likewise eludes intersubjective definition.[8]

Let us ignore these implications for the moment, and assume that each person, having formulated some subjective estimate of the probability that he will be forcibly subjected to a foreign government, acts then on the basis of the expected value assumptions of modern decision theory. If we also ignore the other elements of his utility function, his welfare will be a function of three variables: the level of national security, the value he places on being a subject of his own government, and the value he places on being a subject of the government of the enemy country.[9] Expressed symbolically:

$$U = p[U(G)] + (1-p)[U(F)] \tag{1}$$

where p stands for probability that his own government will remain autonomous (and hence stands for the quantity of national defense); U(G) stands for the value the individual places on the maintenance of his own government; and U(F) stands for the value the individual places on being subjected to the foreign government in question.

This relationship can also be expressed as follows:

$$U = p[U(G) - U(F)] + U(F) \tag{2}$$

From this expression, it can be seen that as long as U(G) is greater than U(F), the individual will want p to be as large as possible. It can also be seen that the value he places on national defense (the contribution that the size of p makes to his welfare) depends on the *difference* between the value he places on his own government, and the value he places on being subjected to the foreign government. Moreover, the marginal utility of defense is constant; that is:

$$\frac{dU}{dp} = U(G) - U(F) \tag{3}$$

It is not unreasonable to ask what any of these rather simple equations can possibly mean. I have already talked about p (though I have not disposed of the difficulties associated with it). U(G) and U(F), of course, must be Von Neumann-Morgenstern utilities. One could perhaps imagine a person determining these values for himself as follows. He would try to imagine as concretely as possible what his life would be like as a subject of the foreign government, under the conditions that would be likely to emerge as the result of military defeat. He may then imagine that he was about to be forcibly transported to that country, where he would occupy a station identical to the one he anticipates as the consequence of military defeat. He could, however, by paying a certain monetary price, arrange to stay at home and live his life as he had expected to live it. He could then try to determine how much he would be willing to pay for such a "ticket to stay home." If he had determined for himself a utility function for money, then he would by implication have determined the value of U(G) - U(F).[10]

Alternatively, the individual could determine the value he placed on increments of defense in monetary terms directly, by imagining that he was being confronted, not with being shipped abroad, but with tickets to a lottery, in which he would be given a ticket to say home if he won, and would be shipped abroad if he lost. He could then ask himself how much he would be willing to pay to avoid such lotteries, allowing the probability of winning to vary from zero to one.

Mention of the monetary value of defense is important for reminding us of another determinant of a person's evaluation of it. Because national defense, by this definition, is a probability, persons may differ in their evaluation of it not only because of differences in their evaluation of membership in the two societies, but also because of differences in their attitudes toward risk. (Evaluations of risk are included in the process by which Von Neumann-Morgenstern utilities are determined, and therefore are included in U(G) and U(F) in the equations presented earlier.) If we assume (as is plausible) that any given person is averse to risk, then, while the marginal *utility* of defense will be constant, the marginal rate of substitution between money and defense will be increasing. That is, the more defense supplied, the more such a person would be willing to pay in monetary terms, for the next increment of it, and vice versa (Raiffa, 1968: 66-70).

In speaking of the evaluation of risk, I have already mentioned the likelihood that persons will differ in this respect. Let us look more closely at the other main source of differences in the evaluation of national defense, the size of U(G) - U(F). What factors are likely to influence the size of this number for any individual? Clearly the size of this term is a function of the value that such a person places on the whole stream of goods that he associates with his own government, as well as those that he predicts would be his lot in the event of national defeat. And each of these is itself a function of two other factors: the goods that the person in question has access to, and predicts he would have access to in the event of defeat; and his evaluation of those goods. There may be important differences among people in both these respects.

First, persons who have access to exactly the same stream of goods in their own society, and make exactly the same predictions about their likely fortunes in another, may nonetheless differ in their evaluations of one or more of these goods. (For example, they may differ in the relative values they assign to freedom of opportunity as opposed to the guarantee of some minimum level of economic well-being). Second, persons may differ in their access to the goods provided by their own government, or in their predictions of their fate under another, or in both. This may lead to differences in the size of U(G) - U(F) among them. For example, a peasant may predict that his life would hardly be altered by being a subject of another government, while a member of the governing elite of his society would anticipate a marked worsening of his own position. Finally, for each person the size of U(G) - U(F) will be influenced by the information he has, not only about the degree to which his own government can be said to be responsible for various valued aspects of his situation, but also about the quality of life he can anticipate in the event of national defeat. And the latter is, in turn, likely to be affected not only by the information the person has about the war aims of the enemy, but also by the information he has about the character of life in the enemy country itself.

So much can be said about the utility of defense. However, if one is interested in the monetary demand for defense, one must also bear in mind that this will probably increase with income, simply because individuals with more income have more money to spend. This effect is independent of the fact that the size of U(G) - U(F) may also be positively related to income. There may also be other income effects, however, some of them in the opposite direction, as a result of the fact that higher income may lead to better information, which may in turn influence both the size of p and the size of U(G) - U(F). Thus differences in income are likely to be associated with differences in the monetary demand for defense.

The conclusion that emerges from this analysis so far is that, even if national defense is assumed to be a pure collective good, there are likely to be significant differences in the evaluation of it among the members of all societies. In some societies, there may be some (perhaps many) persons for whom U(G) is smaller than U(F). Even in societies where this is not the case, the size of U(G) - U(F) is likely to vary among persons. Moreover, this could be the case even if everyone agreed entirely about the nature of the international political situation, and the consequences of various proposed defense programs. Of course, when one adds that people can in no case be expected to agree about these matters, then the probability of differences in their evaluations of any particular defense program is greatly increased, since they will then not agree about the existing size of p, or about the size of p that would result from adopting the defense measures in question. However, it is important to emphasize that there are grounds for disagreement even apart from this possibility, and that the significance of the latter source of disagreement will be determined by the former.

I want to continue to explore these problems associated with defense as a pure collective good; however, it may be useful to pause at this point and notice the ways in which it may be impure, and what significance this may have for the present argument. First, the subjectivity of p (which leads to differences in consumption units among individuals) is itself a departure from standard assumptions. Clearly the supply of a certain level of p to one person may also interfere with the supply of the same level to another. For example, suppose that one person believed that p could best be increased by building a larger army, while another believed that a larger army would simply provoke the enemy into attacking. In such a situation, it would be impossible to increase both persons' supply of national defense simultaneously.

Second, as the above example indicates, the probability of continued national autonomy is itself really a function of two other probabilities: the probability that the enemy will not attack, and the probability that if it does attack it can be defeated. The former is much more likely to be a pure collective good than the latter, since it may not be possible to keep the entire national territory out of the enemy's hands if it attacks. Thus, it may not be possible, again, to increase everyone's supply of national defense simultaneously. (This is even more obviously the case if one expands the concept of national defense to include not only preservation of autonomy but also security from loss of life and property through enemy attack.)[11]

Of course, for p to have any significance at all, it must be the case that the collective goods underlying U(G) and U(F) must not be pure collective goods. That is, at a minimum the members of one society must be excluded from enjoyment of the collective goods provided to members of another. However, this need not be the case for all collective goods. Indeed, one interesting (but little explored) aspect of international politics concerns those goods that are supplied on a nonexclusionary basis across national boundaries. Among these, in some situations, would be national defense itself. Certainly the American government currently supplies defense with its own military forces to the citizen of many countries.[12]

Even if the goods in question were pure along the other dimension (that is, there was no rivalness of consumption) there may be good reason to supply them exclusively to members of one society. For example, a group of people may find it easier to solve the allocation problem associated with determining an optimal supply and an acceptable distribution of costs for the collective goods made available so long as others were excluded from participating in this process. However, another good reason for exclusion would be the impossibility of increasing all person's supplies of some collective goods simultaneously. One group may therefore seek to preserve a certain homogeneity of values by excluding others either from consuming the goods supplied or from participating in decisions about them.[13]

These are all factors that influence the size of U(G) - U(F). But let us return to consideration of p. Clearly if it is impossible to increase p simultaneously for everyone, then the potential for conflict over defense questions is greatly increased. However, I have not said everything there is to be said about defense as a pure collective good. Let us therefore return to that subject.

If everyone in a society agrees that U(G) is greater than U(F), they will agree in wanting p to be as large as possible. But my earlier argument implies that they will not agree about the marginal value of increases in p. That is, when asked how much of some other good they are prepared to surrender in order to achieve some particular increase in p, they are likely to give different answers. To understand conflicts over defense policies, therefore, it is necessary to consider the costs of defense.

If p can be maximized by being militarily inconspicuous, then national defense is not likely to be very costly. Let us concentrate for the moment, however, on the case where increases in p require relatively costly increases in the size of the military forces available. Any marginal increase can only be purchased at a certain monetary cost, which is to be shared among persons in the society in a certain way. For each person, there will be three relevant aspects of the situation: (1) the value he places on the increment of national defense purchased with all contributions toward its cost combined; (2) the value he places on the increment in national defense purchased with his own contribution; and (3) the value he places on the share of the cost allocated to him.

For convenience, let us label the cost of defense C, and each individual's share C_i. Then $p = f(C)$. The marginal utility derived from increasing a person's own expenditure on defense will be $\frac{dU_i}{dC}$. The marginal utility to the same person from the collective expenditure on defense will be $\frac{dU_i}{dC}$. For the sake of simplicity, let us re-label $U(G) - U(F)$, for any individual, as D_i. Equation (2) can now be expanded to include i's share of defense costs:

$$U_i = pD_i + U_i(F) - U_i(C_i) \qquad (4)$$

Holding $U_i(G)$ and $U_i(F)$ constant, and differentiating, we have

$$dU_i = D_i dp - dU_i(C_i) \qquad (5)$$

Therefore,

$$\frac{dU_i}{dC_i} = D_i \frac{dp}{dC_i} - \frac{dU_i(C_i)}{dC_i} \qquad (6)$$

And,

$$\frac{dU_i}{dC} = D_i \frac{dp}{dC} - \frac{dU_i(C_i)}{dC} \qquad (7)$$

But $\frac{dU_i(C_i)}{dC} = \frac{dU_i(C_i)}{dC_i} \cdot \frac{dC_i}{dC}$. Equation (7) can therefore be expressed as:

$$\frac{dU_i}{dC} = D_i \frac{dp}{dC} - \frac{dU_i(C_i)}{dC_i} \frac{dC_i}{dC} \qquad (8)$$

$\frac{dC_i}{dC}$ can be interpreted as i's marginal cost share. Since it will be less than one, $\frac{dU_i}{dC}$ will be greater than $\frac{dU_i}{dC_i}$, unless marginal costs are increasing.

If there is some $\frac{dC_i}{dC}$ such that $\frac{dU_i}{dC}$ is positive for all individuals, then defense is suboptimally supplied and all could be made better off by increasing it. However, it may be that $\frac{dU_i}{dC_i}$ is negative for some or all persons. In that event the situation is a prisoners' dilemma, and i will prefer not to pay any share of the cost. Moreover, if $\frac{dC_i}{dC}$ is sufficiently large, $\frac{dU_i}{dC}$ may be negative (even though for some smaller share of the cost it would be positive). In that event, i would be made worse off by increasing the supply of defense; if $\frac{dC_i}{dC}$ cannot be reduced, he will therefore oppose any increase in defense spending. In any case, i will want $\frac{dC_i}{dC}$ to be as small as possible. This will be zero if the situation is a prisoners' dilemma; if not, what is possible depends on the bargaining that takes place, since his cost share will be a function of the decisions made by others.

It is interesting to distinguish between situations in which cost shares are fixed, and situations in which they are allowed to vary (and may therefore be influenced). If they are allowed to vary, there is an incentive to engage in bargaining (or to try to evade one's taxes, if contributions are compulsory). However, this does not distinguish defense expenditures from any other collective good simultaneously supplied, and, so long as D_i is positive for all persons, would not lead to any disagreements about the level of defense effort. If cost shares are regarded by each individual as fixed, however, then there may be some level of defense at which some persons will want more defense spending, and some will want less.

In most societies, conditions are somewhere between these two extremes. That is, both the level of defense spending and the allocation of cost shares can be varied, but decisions about each are normally made somewhat independently of the other. Thus conflicts over programs and conflicts over taxation both exist, although somewhat insulated from each other. Moreover, in societies where D_i is, for each individual, very large and there is a large population with a large per capita income, many different distributions of cost shares would leave $\frac{dU_i}{dC}$ positive for all individuals so long as defense costs are monetary costs. However, where costs shares include military service this is less likely to be the case. Of course, so long as one is talking about monetary contributions toward the purchase of tanks, ships, and airplanes, it is likely that for most people $\frac{dU_i}{dC_i}$ is negative; that is, what one person's money can buy in the way of military equipment is not likely to be, for him, worth the cost. But there is no reason to assume this to be the case for individual contributions toward national defense of all kinds.

More could probably be said about conflicts over defense expenditures within the limitations of the above analysis. However, its relevance would be limited by the fact that some important constituents of the situation have been left out. One is these is the relation between the supply of defense and the supply of other collective goods.

III

It is common to think of defense and other collective goods competing with each other for scarce resources. However, it is possible that the quantity of resources required to produce a given increment in defense may not be an adequate measure of its costs. It may either overstate or understate the real costs of defense to any given person, since defense may be either directly complementary to or competitive with the supply of other collective goods. Thus the real costs, and real benefits, of defense expenditures for each individual can only be evaluated by taking these relationships with other collective goods (and perhaps some private goods as well) into account. Since evaluations of these other goods are also likely to differ, and since some of them may involve some rivalness of consumption, the potential for conflict over defense will be increased. Moreover, such relationships obviously will complicate the problem of allocating defense costs. And since the nature of these relationships may vary, depending on what sort of defense policy is adopted, there will be an even greater incentive for conflict over defense policies that is separated from conflict over allocation of costs.

Before introducing other goods into the analysis, let us notice one relationship of this sort among the variables that have been examined whose possible existence has so far been ignored. This is some interdependency between p and D_i (or $U_i(G) - U_i(F)$). In particular, it is possible that in some situations increases in p may only be obtained by taking measures that would have the effect of diminishing D_i. For example, it may be necessary to introduce such a degree of regimentation into everyone's daily life as to seriously diminish the difference for an individual between life in his own society and life in another. Beyond some point, every increase in p might be fully offset by decreases in D_i, leaving an individual at best indifferent to any increase in the supply of defense, and at worse worse off as a result of it. (Of course, the expected duration of such defense measures would be of great importance.) The addition of such effects as these would make it more difficult to find some method of allocating costs such that $\frac{dU_i}{dC}$ was positive for all persons.

The same sort of relationship may exist with other goods. Here I will do no more than give one or two examples to illustrate the sort of effect that is possible—indeed, likely. First, let us consider the complementarity between defense and other goods. Suppose that the members of one society place some value not only on their own defense, but also on the defense of other societies, such as the value that persons of East European background place on the independence of Eastern European countries from Soviet control. Such persons would have two independent reasons for valuing American efforts to protect (or secure) the autonomy of these countries: one based on the contribution of their defense to the security of the United States, and another based on their independent valuation of the defense of Eastern Europe. One would expect such persons to place a higher marginal value on defense expenditures than other American citizens, other things being equal.

Or consider (to borrow a theme of the left) a businessman with extensive investments abroad. There may well be considerable complementarity between efforts to increase national security (or p), and efforts to increase the security of his investments. For such a person the real benefits of defense expenditures are much greater than would be indicated merely by their effect on p.

It is easy to see how complementarities such as these can be converted into competition. For increases in p may require some sacrifice of the defense interests of other countries, or some cutback on efforts in areas of greatest vulnerability of private foreign investment. In such cases the real costs of defense for some persons are much greater than the size of the defense budget would indicate. Indeed, decreases in defense spending, accompanied by increases in p may even leave some persons worse off.

These examples are enough to illustrate the point. Clearly, the effects of a particular size and pattern of defense expenditures on many other possible collective goods are no less subjective than is p; and, consequently, conflict is likely to be further exacerbated by intellectual disagreement. However, let us, as before, ignore that point and proceed. Let $U_i(X)$ stand for the value of any and all other goods whose supply is affected by expenditures on defense, and assume that variations in p affect $U_i(G)$ (and consequently D_i), but not $U_i(F)$. Then equation (7) must be altered as follows[14]:

$$\frac{dU_i}{dC} = D_i \frac{dp}{dC} + p\frac{dD_i}{dC} - \frac{dU_i(C_i)}{dC} + U_i(X) \frac{dp}{dC} + \frac{pdU_i(X)}{dC} \qquad (9)$$

Clearly the potential for divergent evaluations of defense expenditures has been greatly increased. Moreoever, it is even more likely that $\frac{dU_i}{dC}$ will be positive for some and not for others, given some method for determining $\frac{dC_i}{dC}$.

Furthermore, the possibility for some conflict of interest with respect to $\frac{dp}{dC}$ (the marginal productivity of defense spending) emerges. Previously one could assume a common interest that this be as large as possible. However, there may be some relation among $\frac{dp}{dC}$, $\frac{dD_i}{dC}$, and $\frac{dU_i(X)}{dC}$ such that they cannot all be increased simultaneously—that is, some defense programs may have strong complementary effects on other goods and others may not. Disagreement about the marginal value of these other goods will lead to disagreement about the most efficient way to spend money on defense. Some persons may support relatively inefficient defense programs because the effects of defense expenditures of that sort on other goods of interest to them compensate for the relatively high marginal cost of defense. Other persons, valuing these other goods much less (or not at all), may find the marginal cost of such defense programs greater than the marginal benefits they produce, and in any case could increase the ratio between benefits and costs to themselves by adopting a different pattern of defense expenditures.

In this connection, it may be useful to recall that p is itself a function of two other probabilities: the probability that the enemy will not attack, and the probability that it can be defeated if it does. These were labeled earlier p_1 and p_2. The first is in turn a function of any and all efforts to affect the enemy's intentions (which may usefully be divided into efforts at appeasement and efforts at deterrence), and the second is a function of any and all efforts to influence the capabilities of one's own government relative to the enemy's. Debate about the relative merits of efforts to increase p_1 or p_2 is one of the most persistent lines of division over defense policy and can be associated with differences in criteria for decision-making under uncertainty; such disagreement can be affected by whether one believes oneself completely ignorant of the enemy's intentions or not. However, the above analysis indicates another possible basis for such a disagreement: the existence of conflicts of interest concerning defense programs designed to influence one or the other of these probabilities. Programs to have one or the other type of effect may be directly complementary to or competitive with the production of other valued goods, and differences over the merits of these other goods may thus lead to conflict over allocation of effort between these two types of defense programs. (Of course, the same could be said, with respect to p_1, of the allocation of effort between appeasement and deterrence.)

The purpose of this analysis so far has been not to provide a description of political conflict over defense issues in any particular society, but to show how political conflict is possible with respect to what is commonly thought of as a basic common interest: the preservation of the political autonomy of a society that is preferred to any other by all its members. It may be useful to summarize briefly the bases for such conflict. First, since national security is a probability, persons may differ in their evaluations of it because of differences in their attitudes toward risk. Second, the contribution that the level of national defense makes to a person's welfare is a function of the difference between the value to him of his own government and the value to him of being subjected to a potential enemy government. This is, in turn, a function of his access to various collective goods provided by his own and any alternative government, and of his evaluation of those goods. Individuals may differ in both these respects. Third, differences in income levels will lead to differences in the willingness of persons to contribute monetary resources toward the supply of defense. Finally, the supply of defense may be either complementary to or directly competitive with the supply of other goods; persons may differ in their degree of access to and evaluation of these other goods, and these differences will influence both their evaluation of any particular pattern of defense expenditures and their judgment of the relative efficiency of alternative patterns of defense expenditures.

Because of these differences, it may well be the case that some particular allocation of the marginal costs of defense will lead some persons to favor an increase in defense expenditures, and others to be opposed to it.[15] Moreover, some persons may favor one pattern of defense expenditures, and others favor another. Finally, because defense is a collective good, all persons will have an incentive to try to shift the burden of paying for it onto others; opposition to any particular level of defense spending may be a good tactic for achieving this. All these propositions are based on the assumption that people agree about the state of the world and the effects of various courses of action, and that defense is a pure collective good. If they disagree (as they will), and if there is some rivalness of consumption with respect to defense, then the bases for conflict will be multiplied.

IV

Perhaps the significance of some of the factors mentioned above, and their potential relevance for some of the concerns of political scientists, can be better understood by asking a hypothetical question. Suppose one group of people who place a high marginal evaluation on some particular pattern of defense expenditures wishes to increase the willingness of others to contribute resources in support of it. How may they affect the incentive that other persons have to contribute to defense? (Let us assume that they are able to influence both information and outcomes.)

One obvious point of influence would be the size of D_i. This could be influenced, first by shaping the information available about the enemy's war plans (which would influence an individual's estimate of the consequences for him of defeat), or the information available about his prospects under an enemy government. By painting as black a picture as possible of either or both of these bases for an individual's estimates of $U_i(F)$, the size of D_i could be increased, and hence the marginal utility of defense expenditures for an individual would be increased.

Second, it would be possible to increase D_i by actually increasing the supply to an individual of various collective goods of value to him from his own government. This would lead to an increase in $U_i(G)$. Thus, a political elite finding itself under pressure as the scale of international military conflict increases may develop an interest in increasing the supply of other collective goods to its citizens in order to increase their interest in the supply of defense. Any increase in their welfare for which the government was responsible would have this effect. Special recognition for linguistic, religious, or cultural interests can (if the society is sufficiently homogeneous along these lines) sometimes be an especially inexpensive way of achieving this objective.

Third, one can attempt to exploit any complementarities that may exist between some defense programs and other collective goods of value to those whose support is being sought. These would include both the impact of defense expenditures on the domestic environment (for example, the impetus to technological development) and their impact abroad (for example, their effect on business, ethnic, or ideological interests abroad).

Finally, since p is itself subjective, one can try to influence the information on which an individual's estimate of $\frac{dp}{dC}$ is based, leading him to believe that it is very large. At the same time, one may try to convince him that the existing level of p is quite low.

It is sometimes suggested (or assumed) that the marginal value of defense for the less privileged members of a society will be less than that for members of the elite. The present analysis provides some support for such an assumption, both in its analysis of the components of D_i and in its suggestion that willingness to bear the costs of defense may be positively related to income. However, as the remarks above suggest, it also highlights some elements of the situation that may work in the other direction.

Clearly, the information available to elite and nonelite persons will be important. For example, better information about the quality of life in the enemy country, or about the consequences of defeat, may lead to a smaller value for D_i for members of the elite than would otherwise be the case. Moreover, better information about the world may lead elite persons to assume a higher existing value for p, or a lower value for $\frac{dp}{dc}$, than nonelite persons.[16]

But there are other factors besides differences in information that may narrow the divergence between elite and nonelite persons in their marginal evaluations of defense. First, nonelite persons may place a higher value on linguistic, religious, and cultural interests than members of the elite; if these interests are important components of $U_i(G)$, they may at least partially counterbalance the special privileges of the elite with respect to other goods.

Second, members of the elite may have greater confidence in their ability to adapt to changing circumstances than nonelite persons. This may lead them to expect that, in the event of defeat, they may manage to land on their feet and adapt to alien rule. Such calculations would tend to diminish somewhat an otherwise large D_i. Similarly, differences in attitudes toward risk may narrow the differences between elite and nonelite persons with respect to the monetary value they assign to defense.

Third, there may be complementarities between defense programs and some domestic goods of value to nonelite persons. For example, military service is often a route to personal advancement for underprivileged people; even when it does not lead to greater economic opportunities, it may nonetheless give one a social status greater than one would otherwise have.

Finally, there may also be complementarities between defense programs and nondomestic goods of value to nonelite persons. For example, while writers on the left emphasize the special interest that U.S. businessmen with foreign investments may have in the defense policies of the American government, one must also remember the Polish members of the U.S. working class, and their enthusiastic support for a hard line with respect to the Soviet Union.

These remarks have been intended to show the connection between the earlier, somewhat formal analysis and some of the traditional concerns of political scientists interested in defense policy and international politics. They are relevant to the role that propaganda and the control over information may play in the politics of defense policy, and to the question of what lines of cleavage may emerge with respect to defense policy. However, they do not constitute the basis for an anlysis of political bargaining about defense policies, or for any predictions concerning the results of such bargaining.

V

It would not be useful to develop a formal model of the politics of defense apart from a more general model of political conflict as well as a careful analysis of the institutional setting in which it takes place.[17] Rather than pursue any such general problem here, I will concentrate on two questions about the relation between conflicts concerning defense and those over other collective goods. The first is: Are there any peculiarities of defense that may sharply distinguish conflict over defense policy from other political conflicts? The second is: Are there any important effects on the outcome of conflicts over defense that can be attributed to the nature of the political decision rules within which such conflict takes place?

The answer to the first question seems to be, in general, No, so long as one is considering such goods without reference to the process by which decisions about them are reached. For example, one is sometimes tempted to assume that the marginal value of defense can be expected to be greater than the marginal value of other collective goods. But this need not, in general, be true. If, for example, D_i is very small, it may well be that a dollar spent to increase the components of $U_i(G)$ will increase an individual's welfare more than a dollar spent to increase p, even though p might be significantly less than one. Thus, an individual might object vigorously to efforts to increase the supply of defense at the expense of other collective goods, even in times of some national danger.

It appears that if there is anything that distinguishes conflicts over defense policy from any other political conflict, it is something that has not been discussed yet: the costs of bargaining. So far, the benefits and costs of bargaining over defense policy have been assumed to be the gains or losses to any individual resulting from changes in cost shares, in decisions about whether to increase or decrease the supply of defense, and in patterns of defense spending that affect the marginal productivity of defense spending. However, the resolution of conflict over such matters takes time; and p may be declining rapidly as time passes. Moreover, political conflict is difficult to conduct in secret, and the publicity associated with it may also reduce p.

It would require a separate essay to discuss adequately the question that has just been raised. I will restrict myself to a few brief comments. First, such decision costs are not unique to defense policy; for example, bargaining over methods to control inflation can also be costly in the same way. Second, not every aspect of defense policy is very costly in this respect, nor is any particular aspect always equally costly. Third, the costs of bargaining over defense, as defined here, are for any person a function of the marginal value of defense to him. The higher the marginal value one places on defense, the greater the marginal cost of haggling about it. Thus, persons placing a low value on defense may not be greatly deterred by the costs of efforts to oppose a greater allocation of collective resources to defense expenditures. The fact that bargaining is itself costly may actually give such persons a bargaining advantage over those who place a high marginal value on defense, and increase the incentive of the latter to give the former a greater stake in defense by increasing the supply of other goods to them. Finally, since the costs of bargaining over defense are not distributed equally, increasing or decreasing them can be expected to affect the outcome of such bargaining. High decision costs will work to the advantage of some and not to others, and vice versa. Hence, one would expect efforts to manipulate information about such costs to be a normal part of the political process, along with efforts to manipulate information about p, $\frac{dp}{dc}$, and the components of $U_i(F)$.

What of the effects of the nature of a society's political constitution on its defense policies? Define a constitution as a set of rules specifying a set of decision roles, prescribing how the occupants of such roles are to be chosen, and specifying that the consent of the occupants of certain decision roles is a necessary and sufficient condition for a decision binding on everyone. Assume that all such sets of rules can be roughly placed among a scale according to the proportion of the total number of persons affected whose consent is required for a decision to be made. At one extreme the unanimous consent of every person would be required; at the other extreme all decisions would require the consent only of one specific person. (In practice, a lack of time and information would prevent the realization of either extreme when the number of people was very large, or the number of decisions to be made was very large or they were very complex.)

Assume further that the willingness of an individual to support a set of decision rules at any particular point on this scale is a function of his estimate of the value to him of all the decisions likely to emerge from such a set of rules, minus the cost to him of the process by which decisions are made. Assume also that the expected value of the decisions made by a certain set of rules to any given individual increases as the values of the persons in the community for whom decisions are to be made become more homogeneous. Thus, if a person's values are identical to everyone else's, or if he is indifferent among outcomes, then the collective decisions could be expected always to conform to his own preferences. If not, then he could not expect always to get his own wishes. And so long as he could not predict exactly how political conflict would develop, the probability that decisions would depart from his own desires could be expected to increase as the number of persons whose consent was required diminished.[18]

It follows that the willingness of any individual to support the maintenance of a relatively dictatorial set of decision rules depends upon his indifference among outcomes, his belief that the values of other persons are very similar to his, or his belief that the marginal decision costs resulting from increasing the number of persons whose consent is required are high and increasing. Thus persons with a strong interest in maintaining a dictatorial set of decision rules have an incentive to try to make values in their society more homogeneous, and to convince others that the costs of a greater degree of participation would be quite high.

Decisions about defense policy may have special relevance for the latter objective. By maintaining a state of affairs in which political bargaining threatened significant reductions in p, everyone's incentive to support such a set of decision rules would be increased; however, the effect would be greater on those with a high D_i than on those with a low one. In many situations this would imply that such a crisis atmosphere would have a greater effect on the incentives of potentially dissident members of the elite to stay in line than on nonelite persons. However, such a crisis atmosphere, by cutting off information about life in potential enemy societies, would also be useful in facilitating the manipulation of $U_i(F)$, and hence D_i, for all members of the society.

Anyone attempting to use defense policies for such ends would probably be a member of the political elite and would, for that reason, likely have a high value for D_i. Thus his own personal marginal evaluation of defense would be extremely high. However, high values of p would also tend to undermine support for the rules that define his political role. Such a person is therefore likely to be an example of the possibility, mentioned earlier, that D_i may itself be negatively related to p. For such a person the optimum value of p probably will be significantly lower than one, though obviously greater than zero.

In any society it would be true that national defense as a collective good may be one of the bases on which political leaders seek to elicit support; and in many societies some political leaders would find this a more advantageous basis than other collective goods. Such political leaders would also have an incentive to use defense policy decisions to manipulate others' information about the international environment. Moreover, in any society some political leaders may derive some bargaining advantage from fostering the impression that the costs of haggling over defense decisions are high. However, in societies with relatively participatory decision rules, the latter effort may prove to be a threat to the continued importance of some decision roles, and thus the occupants of those roles may have some incentive to counter that impression and alter the policies that foster it. In societies with relatively dictatorial decision rules, on the other hand, all members of the political elite may have a sufficient personal interest in maintaining the roles prescribed that they all have some stake in the continuance of such defense policies (even though their effect is to inhibit political conflict among themselves).

VI

I am under no illusion that this essay constitutes a valid descriptive or normative theory of anything. I have merely tried to offer what seems to me one plausible way of representing some of the concerns of students of foreign policy-making and international politics in the framework of analysis that has grown up around the nation of a collective good. Some of what I have said has been merely illustrative and is not intended as a full development of the theme discussed. Some of what I have said may seem implausible; one may then want to revise the assumptions on which it is based or reconsider the bases for one's preconceptions. Some of what I have said may seem merely to restate common sense, in which case it may nonetheless be interesting to see one set of fairly simple assumptions from which common sense can be derived. In any case, this analysis may be a stimulant to make more explicit the inferences that underly such literature as we have on this subject.

NOTES

1. Indeed, in an article criticizing Samuelson's formulation (1954), Julius Margolis (1955) wrote: "Possibly the only goods which would seem to conform to Samuelson's definition are national defense and the aged lighthouse illustration."

2. The best general survey of this subject for political scientists is probably Buchanan (1968).

3. In the case of Buchanan, this is based on the idea that only small groups can arrive at a negotiated solution to the prisoners' dilemma game. See also Olson (1965).

4. A formal representation of an individual's decision problem in these circumstances may be found in Frohlich and Oppenheimer (1970). Unfortunately, in this article Frohlich and Oppenheimer treat the decision of whether to contribute or not as a problem of decision-making under uncertainty (which they analyze in a Bayesian fashion), rather than a game theoretical one, and therefore the relation between their analysis and Olson's or Buchanan's is not made entirely clear.

5. The most important exception to the first part of this statement is Buchanan and Tullock (1962), and to the second part is Downs (1957).

6. These distinctions were first made by Head (1962). See also Buchanan (1968: chapters 4 and 9) and Frohlich and Oppenheimer (1971: chapter 2).

7. At various points in this paper I will assume that it is meaningful to speak of "subjective probabilities" as a way of describing how people behave under conditions of uncertainty. For a very helpful discussion of this notion, although in a normative context, see Raiffa (1968).

8. Thus the quantity of defense supplied will not be the same for all citizens. This fact does not in itself violate the assumption of a pure collective good.

9. I am ignoring the possibility that the threat of foreign attack may come from more than one country.

10. For a discussion of what this would in turn involve, see Raiffa (1968: chapter 4).

11. For a discussion of this aspect of the problem, see van Ypersele de Strihou (1968: 265-276).

12. This fact, of course, gives the citizens of one country an interest in the political decisions of another. It may be worth pointing out that equation (1) implies another reason for such an interest as well: so long as p is less than one, any person's utility can be increased by increasing U(F) as well as U(G). This can be done by improving one's own personal prospects in the enemy country, or improving the general quality of life in that country. Thus enhancement of the quality of life in the Soviet Union would, on these assumptions, increase the welfare of American citizens for reasons entirely independent of the fact that such changes might lead to an increase in p.

13. This discussion is based almost entirely on Frohlich and Oppenheimer (1971: chapters 5-10). See also Breton (1965) and Mueller (1971).

14. The supply of X is presumably contingent on maintenance of i's government, and hence is available only with probability p. Strictly speaking, therefore, $U_i(X)$ could be included in $U_i(G)$, and hence D_i. However, it is useful to separate out those goods that require some manipulation of the external environment as defense-related foreign policy goods. Thus $U_i = pD_i + U_i(F) - U_i(C_i) + pU_i(X)$.

15. Improper allocation of marginal costs would lead to disagreement even if everyone's marginal evaluations were the same. However, such differences make it more difficult to match marginal costs with marginal benefits.

16. If one assumes that willingness to rely on subjective probability estimates of the enemy's intentions depends on how much information one has about the enemy, and that access to such information is more likely to be open to elite than to nonelite persons, then preferences for p_1 as distinguished from p_2 may also be class-related. On these grounds one would expect an affinity between lower-class persons and the military (specialists in dealing with enemy capabilities) and between upper-class persons and diplomats (specialists in dealing with enemy intentions).

17. For models built explicitly around the notion of a collective good, see Downs (1957), Buchanan (1968), Frohlich, Oppenheimer, and Young (1971), and Frohlich and Oppenheimer (1971).

18. For a discussion of collective decision rules in these terms, see Buchanan and Tullock (1962).

Chapter 9

THE ECONOMIC THEORY OF ALLIANCES: REALIGNED

TODD SANDLER

Assistant Professor of Economics
Arizona State University and SUNY at Binghamton

The post-World-War-II period has witnessed the rise, and sometimes fall, of defense alliances in which defense is produced and shared by the member nations. Most notable of these postwar alliances have been NATO for the non-Communist countries and the Warsaw Pact for the Communist bloc countries. Other post-World-War-II alliances include SEATO, CENTO, Rio Pact, and the Arab League Nations (Russett, 1970). The formation and stability of a defense alliance lends itself to an economic analysis in which two or more nations form an organization for the purpose of sharing a pure or impure public good. Once an alliance is formed the production of the defense good within one of the allied nations provides spillover benefits to the other ally. Thus, each nation must make production and consumption decisions with respect to both the private good and the defense good by accounting for the production decisions within the other nation.

An earlier analysis (Olson and Zeckhauser, 1966) examined the economic theory of alliances and explicitly accounted for community taste for the defense good. Unfortunately, the production constraint that is indicative of the tradeoff between private and public good production was not an integral part of the analysis. This omission limited their analysis since no Pareto efficient movements could be analyzed within their graphical model.[1] In a more recent article by William Loehr (1973), the production constraint has been added and Pareto efficiency has been examined within a trading situation.

Unlike the previous analyses, this paper indicates that the relative sizes, as reflected in the factor endowments of the allies, are instrumental in determining alliance stability. A previous investigation (Olson and Zeckhauser, 1966: 269) has suggested that alliance instability is due to the inferiority of the collective good. This paper examines more explicitly alliance stability from both the demand and supply sides. Most importantly, the model presented here analyzes the use of taxing schemes for the purpose of inducing Pareto optimal resource movements within the alliances. These tax-induced moves, which account for the publicness of the commonly shared collective good, are analyzed by examining relative productive efficiency and the income elasticity of demand for the collective good. Taxation is seen to promote stability by allowing all allies to gain by the alliance whereas prior to taxation only the smaller nation gains in many instances. The introduction of interregional taxation allows for interregional movement of resources that has been absent from the other investigations.

An extension of this paper permits the theory of clubs to be applied to the issue of alliances in order to determine optimal alliance size. The situation of optimal alliance size is analyzed under the alternative assumptions of defense being a pure public good and an impure public good. Another important extension breaks with tradition and analyzes the economic gains from an alliance within a dynamic framework. The dynamic consideration focuses on the growth capabilities of the allies and the generation and provision of defense spillovers over time. Some of the static policy recommendations for taxing mechanisms may have to be altered in light of the dynamic argument.

The paper is divided into five sections. Sections 1 and 2 deal with the basic model under two alternative situations. Section 1 analyzes alliances when no great size disparity exists between allies, while section 2 examines alliances when significant size differences are assumed. Both sections consider the efficacy of a taxing scheme and Pareto efficient movements. The third and fourth sections consider extensions of the model, and the remaining section draws conclusions.

BASIC MODEL–CASE 1: NO GREAT SIZE DISPARITY

This model examines the formation of a military alliance from an efficient resource allocation approach. Expenditure on defense is treated as a pure public good[2] (Samuelson, 1954) from the viewpoint of the allied nations—thus, one unit of defense produced in any allied country provides one unit of defense services to all countries in the alliance. This model examines an alliance that consists of two nations such that there is no great disparity between nations with respect to factor endowments. Each nation produces the same two goods in which one good is a private nondefense good and the other good is defense. Although the private good and the defense good are produced with different factor proportions by utilizing different linearly homogeneous production functions, it is assumed initially that the production processes employed in producing the two goods do not vary between countries.[3] Initially, intraregional resource mobility is assumed although interregional resource mobility is allowed at a later stage of the analysis. In addition, this model assumes the existence of a social welfare function within each of the countries so that each nation's populace reveals its preferences for the two goods with a community indifference map.[4] Within the respective countries, defense expenditure is provided by the government from funds collected from taxation of the country's citizens.

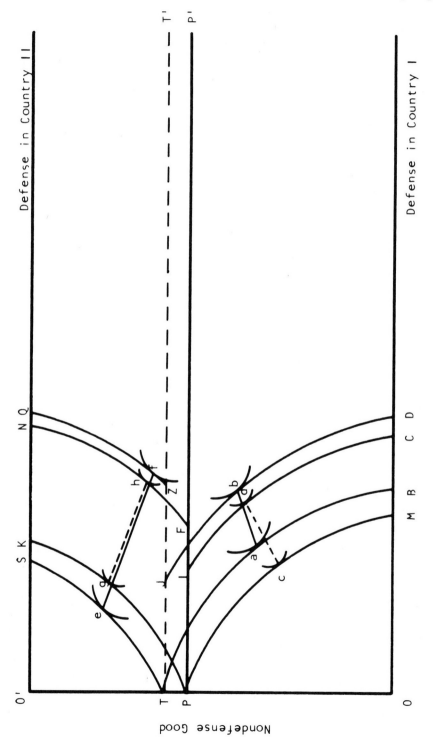

Figure 1

Figure 1 represents a "modified Edgeworth box" diagram.[5] The figure depicts the production possibility constraints and the community indifference curves for both allied countries. On the two horizontal axes the amounts of the defense good in the respective countries are measured; the vertical axis measures the amount of the nondefense good, which is private between nations. The total feasible amount of the nondefense good within the two countries combined is OO ' in which OP is the maximum production possibility quantity in country I and O ' P is the largest feasible amount for country II. The bottom half of Figure 1 (below line PP ') depicts the production possibility frontier, associated consumption possibility frontiers, and community indifference curves for country I, whereas the top portion of the diagram depicts these curves for country II. The graph for country II has been turned on its head so that O ' is the origin and increases in region II's nondefense good are measured in a downward direction.

Prior to the formation of the alliance, the relevant production constraint for nation I is production possibility frontier PM and for nation II it is production possibility frontier PK. Given the community indifference map within each of the countries, equilibrium will occur at the tangency point of the community indifference curve and the production possibility frontier. Therefore, equilibrium is at point c for nation I and at point g for nation II. At these tangency points equality of the marginal rate of transformation and the sum of the marginal rate of substitution of the respective country's residents[6] is assured.

Since alliance formation creates a spillover situation, the amount of defense that is available to each country is equal to the quantity of defense produced both at home and within the ally. Within Figure 1, if the production of the defense good in country II is equal to MC units, then country I experiences spillovers equal to MC units. Geometrically these spillovers can be taken into account within the diagram by a horizontal outward shift of country I's production possibility frontier PM to position IC such that MC units of the defense good has been added to each coordinate pair on the original frontier.[7] In a similar manner, production of the defense good within country I shifts the production possibility frontier PK in country II to position FN whenever country I produces KN units of defense. These post-spillover frontiers represent the consumption possibility frontiers for the respective countries. The post-alliance equilibrium position may rest at the position of tangency of the consumption possibility frontier and the indifference curve. Inasmuch as the presence of defense spillovers will affect the output decisions for defense within each of the countries, positions d and h may not be final equilibrium positions. In order to derive the final equilibrium position, production reactions curves for the public good must be found—consumption expansion paths cd and gh can be utilized in this derivation.[8]

Figure 2 illustrates the production reaction paths P_I and P_{II} for the respective regions. On the vertical axis is measured the quantity of the defense good produced in country I; the horizontal axis measures the quantity of the defense good produced in country II. Thus, the production reaction path, which is

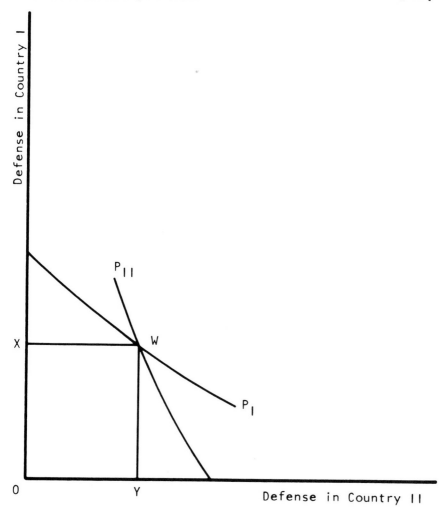

Figure 2

derived from both the production constraint and the community taste patterns, depicts the amount of the defense good that the respective country will produce for varying amounts of defense production within the allied country. Stable equilibrium occurs at point W where country I provides OX units of defense and country II provides OY units of defense. Although point W is derived by considering production interdependence in the form of spillovers, this point does not account for the preferences of both nations' individuals when production decisions are reached in each nation. Previous literature has indicated that the equilibrium point W is not Pareto optimal because there is no assurance that the sum of the marginal rates of substitution for all residents within both nations is equated to the marginal cost of production.[9] In fact, point W represents the independent adjustment equilibrium in which the sum of the marginal rates of substitution for the residents of only one nation is equated to the marginal cost. Since Pareto optimality is not reached at point W due to a failure to adjust for consumption interdependence, there is room for Pareto optimal taxing arrangements.

The question of equilibrium instability has been raised by Olson and Zeckhauser in their discussion of defense as an inferior good.[10] The possibility that defense can represent an inferior good seems to be objectionable. If defense is an inferior good, an increase in a nation's income would induce an absolute decline, or at best no change, in the consumption of the defense good. Inasmuch as defense is desired for the purpose of protection of national income and lives, it seems reasonable that increases in national income would always enhance the consumption of the defense good because much more would be at stake. Although defense as an inferior good is theoretically feasible, it is likely to be of no practical significance.[11]

Returning to Figure 1, the efficacy of a taxing scheme that could move both countries to a higher level of welfare is examined. The situation in which country I receives a net tax payment from country II is illustrated in the diagram. The tax represents a flow of resources from country II to county I which shifts out the production possibility frontier of country I to position TB, and the tax shifts country II's frontier to position TS. Spillovers are now shown by shifts of the production possibility curves along line TT ' —the pre-tax situation utilized line PP '.[12] The shifts in the respective production possibility frontiers is indicative of greater output potential for country I at country II's expense. In addition, the movement of line PP ' to position TT ' highlights that the nondefense good is purely private between the two countries.

In order to find the new points of equilibrium the post-tax consumption expansion path ab for country I and ef for country II must be consulted, revealing some important results. The final equilibrium consumption possibility frontier for country I must lie to the right of the pre-tax equilibrium consumption possibility curve or else country I's welfare would decrease because of the tax. In addition, country II's post-tax equilibrium consumption possibility curve must lie to the right of country II's original production possibility curve (PK) if the alliance is to improve the welfare of country II.

If point f represents the post-tax equilibrium in country II and point b represents the post-tax equilibrium in county I, then both countries have reached higher levels of welfare through the tax as compared with pre-tax equilibria h and d. Even though country II has lost productive capacity, the country can be compensated by an increase in defense spillovers made possible by county I's increased production of defense. This increase in defense spillover releases resources from defense good production in country II and these resources can be re-employed in private good production. For country I the situation is reversed since it gains productive capacity but loses some spillovers

Figure 1 represents only one of a number of possibilities, since the taxed country may not get to a higher level of welfare when spillover compensation is inadequate. Although country II is taxed by the other member of the alliance, it is to its advantage to remain in the alliance as long as the post-tax equilibrium is on a higher level of welfare than the level associated with the community indifference curve through point g. Unlike many public goods such as mosquito spraying, defense benefits can lend themselves to exclusion. Hence, in the absence of the alliance no defense spillins will be experienced. Therefore, even if the taxing scheme does not move both nations to a higher level of welfare, it is still to the advantage of an allied country to be taxed when taxation is necessary to keep the alliance intact.

It is of interest to examine what conditions should prevail if the taxing scheme is to increase the economic well-being of both participants as compared to the no-tax situation. In examining these conditions, the assumption of identical production processes within the allied nations is dropped so that one nation is a more efficient producer of the defense good. As discussed above, in order to compensate the "taxed" country, large spillins of defense must be present. It is these large spillins that allow some productive factors to be reallocated to the nondefense-good production within the taxed country. Thus, anything that promotes large spillins is beneficial to the taxed country. A tax-induced flow of resources from the less efficient producer to the more efficient producer of the defense good will mean a greater outward shift of the production possibility frontier with respect to the defense good within the recipient country.[13]

In addition to the supply side elements, the demand side must be examined as well. If the defense good has a high income elasticity of demand, then increases in income arising from spillins and taxes are spent primarily on defense within the recipient nation. In the special case where all indifference curves have the same slope along a line perpendicular to the ordinate, then defense is a superior good and any increase in spillins will mean no reduction in defense expenditure.[14] Therefore, the taxed country has a greater chance of benefiting from the tax when the productive efficiency is greater in the tax recipient nation and the income elasticity of demand for the defense good is high. A high income elasticity for the defense good within the taxed country will be beneficial to the tax recipient nation because the production of defense within the taxed nation will not be cut back as significantly when the increased spillins are experienced in the taxed nation. Thus, a high income elasticity of demand for the defense good within both countries helps to insure a greater possibility of Pareto optimal tax movements.

CASE 2: DISPARATE SIZE

This case analyzes the situation in which two prospective allies have significantly different factor endowments so that the production possibility frontier of the large nation dwarfs the frontier of the small nation. The assumptions, previously stated for the first case, are assumed to hold for this case. Also, the absence of taxation is assumed to hold initially. Most importantly, defense is viewed as a "good" over commodity space so that bliss and saturation points are ruled out.[15] The analysis of this case indicates that in the absence of a taxing arrangement, the alliance will probably be unstable when only static considerations are analyzed.

Figure 3 shows the modified Edgeworth box for case 2. Country I's curves are depicted in the lower portion of the box; country II's curves are depicted in the upper portion. In the absence of an alliance, equilibrium will occur at position c for country II, and at position a for country I. At these equilibrium positions, the sum of the marginal rates of substitution for the country's residents is equal to the marginal rate of transformation. As before, in order to determine a position of final equilibrium that would account for defense spillins, the production reaction paths must be derived.

Unlike the previous case, the consumption expansion path for country I is no longer a strictly monotonically increasing path. In Figure 3, the consumption expansion path for country I is *abd*. Point b on the expansion path indicates the position where country I has sufficient defense, provided by spillins b, relative to the nondefense good so that the country will use all of its factors to produce the nondefense good. Note that defense is still a good in the normal economic sense; however, relative to the nondefense good, country I will not willingly produce the public good. If more spillins come in past point b, country I will get to a higher level of welfare as long as it does not lose any of the private good. Therefore, with spillins equal to Pd, country I will be on indifference curve I which represents a significantly greater level of well-being than the level associated with point b. Once point b is reached, the possible equilibrium positions will be along line PP ' and all the remaining possible equilibrium points are corner solutions.[16]

The consumption expansion path for country II appears in the same form as before.[17] In Figure 3, country II's consumption possibility frontier TS, which corresponds to a situation where MS units of defense spill in, is shown. Points c and e on the consumption expansion path, and other points derived in a similar manner by varying the amounts of spillins, are used to derive country II's production reaction path shown in Figure 4.[18] Production reaction curve P_I indicates that when defense production is Ob units in country II (where Ob units is equivalent to Pb units in Figure 3), then there is no defense production in country I.

The production reaction paths of Figure 4 underscore the special circumstances of case 2. Both the great disparity of factor endowments and the indifference map of country I cause the production reaction path of nation II to lie outside of the respective path for nation I. Equilibrium will be stable with country II supplying the entire production of the defense good.

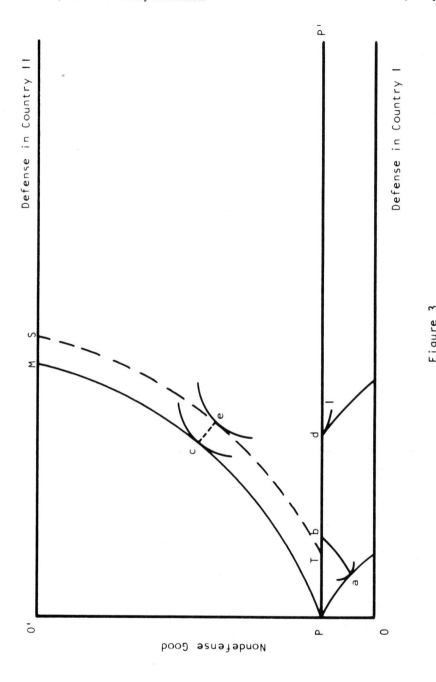

Figure 3

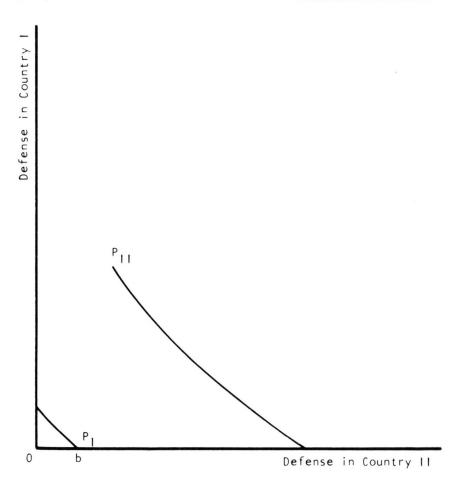

Figure 4

Returning to Figure 3, final equilibrium is at point c for country II and at point d for country I. Since the equilibrium precludes defense production within country I, country II remains at its prealliance equilibrium whereas country I is significantly better off. In effect, the large nation has supplied the defense needs of the small nation, and this, in turn, allows the small nation's resources to seek other employment. Thus, the alliance is definitely to the advantage of the small nation, and may not be to the advantage or disadvantage of the large nation. This proposition would be especially important whenever defense is not a pure public good so that provision of defense causes some negative spillins (congestion costs) to the nation providing the defense. In this situation, provision of defense by nation II for nation I would reduce the amount of defense provided within nation II.[19] Thus the alliance would move country II to a lower level of

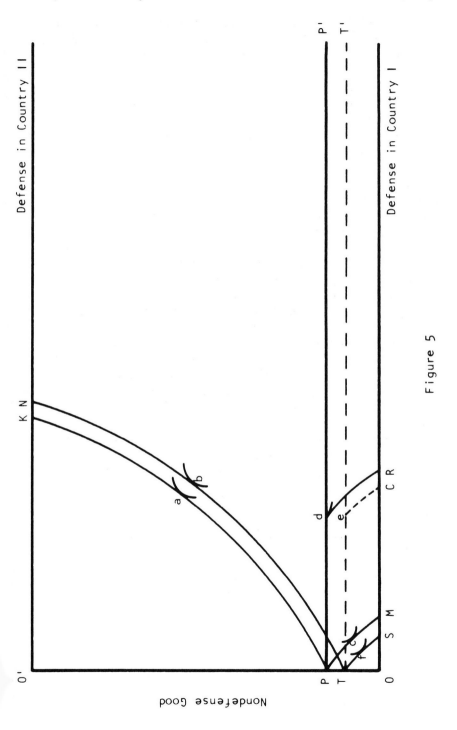

Figure 5

economic welfare as compared to the no-alliance situation. In the absence of a taxing scheme, country II at best does not benefit[20] from the alliance, and may significantly lose when defense is impure in nature. Inasmuch as the benefits of the alliance are very one-sided, the stability of the alliance may be questionable, unless some means of taxation is introduced.

The introduction of a taxing system in which taxes flow from nation I to nation II is shown in Figure 5. The tax-induced resource movement shifts nation II's production possibility curve PK to position TN. Equilibrium changes from point a to b in country II and a higher level of economic welfare is reached. For country I the situation is somewhat more complex, because the tax causes two opposing changes. First, the tax reduces the productive capacity of country I so that the production possibility curve shifts from position PM to TS. Secondly, with defense as a normal good in country II, the increase in the productive capacity in country II induces an increased production of the public good, which in turn enhances spillins for the ally. Whether country I can benefit from the tax depends upon the strength of these opposing effects. The strength of the opposing effects depends upon the income elasticity of demand for defense within both countries[21] and the shifts of the production possibility frontier. Within Figure 5 the new equilibrium in country I is at point e after the increased spillins are accounted for. Thus country I can lose some welfare from the taxing scheme as compared to the no-tax alliance. Nevertheless, it is to country I's advantage to be taxed whenever taxation means stability of the alliance because the level of satisfaction associated with point e is certainly higher than the level associated with point c (no-alliance equilibrium). In addition, the strength of the alliance is enhanced because both nations reach a greater level of welfare due to the alliance.

The existence of a corner solution for country I severely restricts the possibility that country I can benefit from the tax. Figure 6 serves to illustrate this point. In the figure, two consumption possibility frontiers that account for

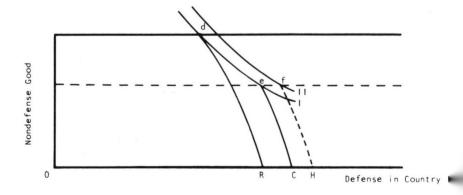

Figure 6

spillovers both before and after the tax are shown. Frontier dR is the pre-tax consumption possibility frontier with equilibrium at point d. Unlike Figure 5, the increased spillovers, which are derived from the tax, move the consumption possibility frontier for country I to position eC. Although the post-tax consumption possibility curve lies to the right of dR, the level of economic welfare has remained unchanged at point e. If the post-tax frontier had been between frontiers dR and eC, then the level of welfare would be less. Thus, the position of the frontier to the right of the pre-tax frontier does not allow welfare statements without prior knowledge of the indifference map whenever corner solutions exist. As long as the frontier lies significantly to the right, such as frontier fH, then welfare may be improved. This example should illustrate that it is unlikely that the tax will benefit country I as compared to the no-tax alliance situation.

EXTENSIONS: OPTIMUM ALLIANCE SIZE

The theory of clubs (Buchanan, 1965) can be used to determine optimum alliance size. Optimum alliance size would occur when the marginal benefit that a member secures from an additional ally is equal to the marginal cost from adding the ally. When defense is examined as a pure public good, the theory of clubs (Buchanan, 1965: 5-7) would indicate that optimum alliance size entails an unlimited number of members. This result is derived by considering the situation in which the amount of defense for the alliance is set at some predetermined level that is deemed adequate to ward off attack. For this fixed amount of defense, the addition of an ally will lower the cost whenever the ally shares in the provision of the defense. The benefit that each country derives from the alliance would remain unchanged—hence, marginal benefit is zero and marginal cost is negative. Inasmuch as marginal benefit exceeds marginal cost, additional members should be added.

Of course, whenever the prospective ally refuses to share in the cost, then the additional member would neither enhance nor detract from the net benefit of the existing membership. If additional members give direct benefit to the alliance membership because larger alliance size would indicate greater potential strength against enemies, then there would be economic incentive to expand membership even though cost per member may increase.[22] The most important qualification arises when defense is an impure public good so that the total benefit per ally may decline after a point when congestion begins to set in. When this situation exists, then the membership should be expanded until marginal benefit of an additional ally matches the marginal cost of adding an ally, and a finite number of allies would be optimal.

When spillins are explicitly accounted for in the analysis, the facility to be shared will increase in size whenever the prospective entrant is producing the defense good after receiving the spillins. In addition, it is necessary that other members do not as a group reduce defense production by an amount equivalent to the defense production added by the ally. If the facility to be shared is increased, then additional members will mean both increased benefits and reduced cost from decreased production reactions.[23] For this situation, optimum membership would include unlimited numbers of allies—hence, an effective alliance may have a tendency to expand.[24]

FURTHER EXTENSION: A DYNAMIC CONSIDERATION

Up until now, this paper has followed previous investigators by analyzing the economic theory of alliances from a static viewpoint. This section breaks with tradition because the dynamic consideration of growth is brought into the spotlight. Our previous static policy recommendation, that taxes may be a necessary measure to insure alliance stability in the face of significant economic size differences among allies, may have to be modified when dynamics are investigated.

Economic growth is achieved by investment in both machines and humans. In addition, infrastructure, which includes communication systems and transportation networks, promotes growth by providing the necessary environment for growth. Research expenditures and the resulting technological changes are also required ingredients for a growing economy. Defense expenditure inhibits growth because it takes resources away from nondefense expenditures, such as investment, public education, and infrastructure, and redirects the resources into defense items, which are more of a consumption nature. Bombs, tanks, and warplanes cannot be used as resources to permit the creation of new products. Two of the feedbacks into the growth process, which defense expenditure does provide, are research and technological spillovers that may be derived from defense good development. Although some research and technological spillovers are provided by defense expenditure, these spillovers usually are far smaller than the spillovers provided by nondefense expenditures since the route is more direct for nondefense good development (Russett, 1968: 133-137). Another useful growth promoting feedback that is provided by defense expenditures concerns training and education. Nevertheless, after accounting for technological spillovers and education provisions, defense spending is unquestionably a drain on economic growth since a majority of defense expenditure is a public consumption item with no feedback into the provision of goods and services. This is highlighted when the rapid obsolence of defense goods is recognized.

Consider a situation analogous to case 2 in which significant economic size differences exist between two allied nations. In the absence of a taxing mechanism, the previous analysis indicated that the larger nation would have to provide defense spillovers with little or no benefit of reciprocal spillovers. From a dynamic approach, it may be to the benefit of the larger nation to provide all defense expenditure in the form of spillovers to the smaller ally for a number of years without resorting to a taxing scheme whenever significant growth potential exists in the smaller nation. By providing defense for the small ally, the large ally can allow the smaller nation to concentrate on nondefense goods, which, in turn, permits more rapid economic expansion within the smaller ally. Increased economic growth means that at a future date the smaller ally will be able to provide a much greater amount of defense goods and hence render a significant time stream of defense spillovers for the larger nation. This argument may best be described as an "infant economy" rationale for the free provisions of defense spillovers by a large ally.[25] Thus, taxing restraint by the larger nation in the short run may mean a much improved position in the long run.

In order for the large ally to experience significant long-run benefits by freely providing defense services, three important considerations must be recognized. First, the larger nation must make sure that the smaller nation will try to achieve its growth capabilities by directing defense-released resources into growth-promoting activities. A problem will arise if released resources are channeled into private consumption, which has little or no growth-inducing effect. Second, once adequate growth is achieved in the small ally, the free provision of defense spillovers without reciprocity must stop.[26] Unquestionably, both of these considerations require a great degree of cooperation. Thirdly, the smaller nation must possess a large growth potential.[27]

CONCLUSIONS

This paper has examined the stability of alliances with respect to the level of economic welfare of the participants. In the absence of a taxing scheme, the model indicates that the stability of an alliance may depend on the relative sizes, as reflected by factor endowments, of the allies. Greater size disparity is more indicative of instability, since the smaller nation may not willingly produce spillins for the other nation. The introduction of a taxing scheme in which one or more nations must contribute to the alliance increases the stability of the alliance, since all allies would experience increased welfare as compared to the no-tax situation.

This paper also examined briefly the question of instability arising from inferiority of the defense good and dismissed the possibility as unlikely. An extension of the model examined optimum alliance size. In addition, a dynamic extension, which considered growth potential and defense expenditure, was presented. The dynamic extension indicated that the static policy of a taxing mechanism may not be optimal when long-run effects are examined.

NOTES

1. This is true of Olson (1971: 866-874).
2. The analysis can be easily altered to allow for an impure public good by assuming

that a unit of defense provides less than one unit of defense services to all countries in the alliance.

3. The assumption of linearly homogeneous production functions and different factor proportions between industries insures that the production possibility frontiers are convex to the origin. The assumption of identical production functions between countries is for analytical simplicity and does not change the conclusions of the model. When Pareto efficient taxing schemes are examined, the production functions between countries are allowed to vary. See Sandler and Shelton (1972: 737-739).

4. Community indifference curves were utilized in the original alliance article by Olson-Zeckhauser (1966: 268). Each community indifference curve assumes the same income distribution between individuals of the economy.

5. The tool of the "modified Edgeworth box" diagram can be reviewed in Pauly (1970: 572-85) and Sandler and Shelton (1972: 736-753).

6. It is necessary to consider the sum of the marginal rates of substitution of the nation's consumers since defense is a pure public good. See Breton (1970: 889).

7. If defense is not purely public so that a unit of defense in an ally provides less than a unit of defense within the other country, then the shift in the consumption possibility curve will be parallel and the shift will be less than the amount of defense production within the ally. Spillovers are no longer equal to production but they are proportional to production.

8. Since the derivation of the production reaction paths has appeared elsewhere, the rather detailed derivation is not repeated here. See Breton (1970: 893-895).

9. Pauly (1970) and Buchanan (1968: 20-22) state this condition as

$$\sum_{i \text{ in } I} U^i_c/U^i_r + \sum_{i \text{ in } II} U^i_c/U^i_r = f_c/f_r.$$

The U^i_c represents the marginal utility derived from the public good to individual i. Similarly, U^i_r is the marginal utility derived from the private good to individual i. The f ratio is the marginal rate of transformation or marginal cost.

10. The situation of inferior goods can be depicted by an exchange of production reaction curves for the two countries (Figure 2). With this unstable equilibrium, one country would supply the entire amount of the defense: Olson and Zeckhauser (1966: 269).

11. The situation in which defense behaves as an inferior good must not be confused with the situation where defense is not a good at all—as in the case of a neutral country. This issue is dealt with later in the paper.

12. Lines PP ' and TT ' are known as lines of truncation. We have assumed parallel shifts of our frontiers for the sake of simplicity. If a relatively large amount of a factor more suited to either the private or public good relocate, then a non-parallel shift would be appropriate. The basic results would not be altered, hence, the simpler case is analyzed in the text.

13. If the recipient country is a more efficient producer of the nondefense good as well, then the dimension of the box with respect to the private good will increase.

14. This holds because spillins do not change the slope of the consumption possibility frontier as compared with the production possibility frontier.

15. The introduction of bliss points would break the normal monotonicity assumption of the indifference classes so that more of a good would mean less satisfaction (i.e., positively sloped indifference curves) past the bliss point. This assumption is in keeping with the evaluation curves (Figure 3) of Olson and Zeckhauser (1966: 269).

16. The marginal rate of transformation is not equal to the sum of the marginal rates of substitutions.

17. Of course, there is some amount of public good spillovers which could force production of defense to zero within country II. However, within the example this possibility is not relevant since country I is incapable of producing the required amount of spillovers for this to occur.

18. Extending P_{II} until it intersects the ordinate would indicate the required amount of spillins that would induce country II to stop producing defense domestically.

19. This would be depicted in the box by a horizontal inward shift of country II's production possibility frontier PM by a proportion of the amount of the spillout.

20. This proposition would be modified if the alliance gives satisfaction to country II because country I's welfare affects country II's satisfaction—i.e., interdependence of utility between nations. In addition, this proposition needs modification, whenever nation II receives benefit by having allies where first-line defenses can be set up against attack. Also, political gains, which are not depicted by the diagrams, may modify the proposition. Thus there may be some spillins of benefits that are not depicted in the diagram.

21. This follows because the indifference map will partially determine the increase in defense good production.

22. The previous stated maximum rule would still hold.

23. This assumes that defense is not a superior good.

24. Organizations such as the United Nations may fall into this situation.

25. The argument is somewhat similar to the "infant industry" rationale for protective tariffs in which an infant industry is protected initially so that with economies of scale and technological advance it may become able to compete without protection in the future.

26. An economic optimum is achieved for the larger nation when the discounted value of the marginal cost of free defense spillovers provision, which includes foregone taxes and congestion costs whenever the defense good is impure, must be equated to the discounted value of the marginal benefit, which includes the stream of defense spillovers resulting from the restraint policy.

27. A similar argument can hold for case 1 of this paper when the two allies have significantly different growth potential.

SECTION III

METHODS

Chapter 10

COMPARATIVE POLICY ANALYSIS AND THE PROBLEM OF RECIPROCAL CAUSATION

E D M U N D P. F O W L E R
Glendon College of York University

and

R O B E R T L. L I N E B E R R Y
Northwestern University

The most general and often the most provocative questions in the social sciences rarely lend themselves to rigorous analysis. One such problem in public policy analysis concerns the mutual interaction between political systems and their socioeconomic environments. While research on the policy outputs of state and local governments has burgeoned in the last decade, it has been limited by a unidirectional causal model which cannot capture a dynamic world of system-environment transactions. In this paper, we cannot unravel the tangled skein of reciprocal causation, but we can draw attention to its existence. Our own answers to the problem we pose may be wrong-headed, trivial, or unproductive. But even if they are, the problem will not disappear. We develop explicitly three models which have implicitly guided research on public policy. Second, we suggest one method (among several) for dealing with the problem. And third, we illustrate the method by testing some hypotheses about the relationship between urban policy and urban socioeconomic environments.

THE PROBLEM

Unquestionably, comparative policy analysis has rescued state and local politics from the "lost world" to which Lawrence J. R. Herson (1957) once

AUTHORS' NOTE: We are indebted to the Canada Council for financial assistance, and to Hubert Blalock, Larry Dodd, Roger Hanson, Rick Hofferbert, Jehuda Kotowitz, and William Loehr for invaluable advice. We eagerly absolve these significant others from culpability for our errors.

rightly consigned it. This stream of research is heavily indebted to the Eastonian (Easton, 1957) input-output-feedback trilogy, which posits an open system with interchanges between the political system and its environment. Unfortunately, most research in the ever-popular Easton tradition pays little more than lip-service to the dynamic character of the model, or to the practical possibility that "outputs" actually affect "inputs" as well as vice versa. The feedback loop is included in diagrams but never in research designs. Instead, the most popular application assumes that certain social and economic characteristics of the environment, combined with various structures of government and informal political processes, produce different "levels" or "packages" of public policy.[1] Citizens and interest groups are seen as independent variables.[2]

At the same time, there coexists another equally lively body of writing—also perfectly consistent with the Easton model—which takes policy as its independent variable and environmental change as the dependent variable. As social scientists, as policy advisors, and as citizen-activists, political scientists cling fervently to the belief that policy can and should alter the human and economic problems of an urban civilization. Much of this literature falls under the rubric of policy impact or policy evaluation research. The great debate between Coleman (1966) and his critics (for example, Mosteller and Moynihan, 1972) over educational policy, Sharkansky's (1967b) work on state expenditures and state service levels, Kaiser and Weiss's (1970) work on the consequences of local land use control, and related work form an alternative paradigm about the relationship between the policies of government and the environment.[3] Economists (Tiebout, 1968) often talk in terms of the citizen-consumer's response to public policy, which influences his choice of home and therefore the socioeconomic mix of the community.

We have here, then, two streams of analysis—both, we think, among the most provocative in contemporary policy analysis—independently researching opposite sides of the Easton model and never do the twain meet.

These two bodies of research suggest clearly the thesis of the present paper: there is a reciprocal relationship between inputs and outputs in the urban system. The reciprocity problem is a significant one for two reasons, one theoretical and one methodological. Theoretically, inattention to the reciprocity problem ignores realities of a dynamic, open system. In some respects this is an ironic twist because the intellectual progenitor of comparative policy analysis, David Easton, carefully expounded a model whose essence was dynamic and transactional rather than static and unicausal. Methodologically, when the causal connections between any two variables are reciprocal, estimates of the relationship between them are artificially inflated.

THE PARADIGMS

With particular reference to the urban community, it is possible to identify three paradigms which purport to explain the relationships between outputs of a system and the composition of its socioeconomic environment.

SOCIOECONOMIC DETERMINISM PARADIGM

One genre of public policy studies has implicitly or explicitly subscribed to a causal theory which may be called the "socioeconomic determinism" paradigm. Somewhat Marxian in its emphasis upon the primacy of social and economic forces and its de-emphasis of political forms as independent forces, this theory assumes that variations in socioeconomic attributes "cause" variations in types of levels of policy outputs. One well-known example of this paradigm in classical economics is Adolph Wagner's "law" holding that urbanization is inexorably associated with increases in government spending. In contemporary political science, Dawson and Robinson's (1963: 266) research begins "with the assumption that public policy is the major dependent variable that political science seeks to explain. The task of political science, then, is to find and explain the independent and intervening variables which account for policy differences." Thomas R. Dye's (1966) work on state politics began with a causal model which assumed that public policies were dependent variables, economic systems were independent variables, and governmental structures were intervening variables. The particular propositions which allegedly provide linkages between politics, economics, and policy are not always spelled out, but Davis and Harris (1966: 262) make explicit one possible set of assumptions. Using five major independent variables to explain urban expenditures they hypothesize that "the larger the value which an 'interest-group' or 'taste-determining' variable assumes, the greater effect it has upon politicians' decisions concerning the expenditure-taxation mix."

One of the most direct statements of the Socioeconomic Determinism paradigm is Edward C. Banfield's (1965: 7-8):

> One would like to be able to show how particular causes produce particular effects. If one could trace out *several* links in a causal sequence, that would be especially satisfying. Thus, one might begin by showing how certain "starting place" characteristics of a city, such as its size, rate of growth, economic function, rate of home ownership, or the class or ethnic composition of its population exert a causal influence on the form and style of its government. . . . A second link might be established by showing the causal connections between form and style on the one hand and the content of the city government's policy on the other hand.

These and similar epistemological underpinnings of the Socioeconomic Determinism paradigm are so common that they may be taken as the conventional wisdom of policy analysis.

ECONOMIC DEVELOPMENT AND SOCIAL CHANGE PARADIGM

However commonplace, the Socioeconomic Determinism paradigm stops just short of some important questions. Banfield and Wilson (1963: 56) have argued that

Causality may run in the other direction as well: if the ecology of the city determines the style of its politics, so may the style of its politics determine its ecology. In other words, the kinds of people who live in the city, their distribution in natural or other areas, and the conceptions that they have of the public interest both affect and are affected by political circumstances.

Indeed, political scientists, economists, and political activists alike take environmental change to be a principal function of policy. Provocatively titled and controversial theories, such as Rostow's (1960) "take-off" theory, Hirschman's (1958) theory of "unbalanced growth," and Rosenstein-Rodan's (1963: 143-150) "big push" theory all emphasize the role of governments in stimulating economic development at the national level. Governments are said to manipulate (or prevent) social change through public policy, whether the intended change be the elimination of illiteracy, the amelioration of poverty, or the promotion of school integration. At the urban level, zoning is perhaps the most obvious policy through which communities manipulate their social and economic environments. According to Robert Wood's (1964: 74) New York regional study:

By far the most universal of the policies employed to guide growth in the region is the control of land use; and by far the most popular control device is zoning.... [P]lanning, zoning, and promotion ... represent ways by which [local governments] can keep "undesirables" out and encourage "desirables" to come in, if they choose. And of course, the definition of desirables and undesirables varies from place to place.

In suburban areas, zoning is often flexible enough either to maintain a simon-pure residential haven (social zoning) or to attract industries which contribute more in tax dollars than they consume in services (fiscal zoning) (Sacks and Campbell, 1964). Whatever its policy content, zoning is a familiar urban policy for environmental control. Its popularity is documented by the disgruntled property owner in Greenwich, Connecticut, who complained that "no one can get elected unless he swears on the Bible, under a tree at midnight, and with a blood oath, to uphold zoning (The New York Times, 1967).

Although zoning is the most obvious (and, regrettably, the least measurable and least researched) example of environmental control through public policy, the fiscal packages of urban governments can also be designed to produce or alter economic development. Urban administrators and planners have now developed sophisticated simulation models designed to test the effects of alternative expenditure-taxation mixes upon future states of metropolitan development (Fagin, 1967).

After being virtually wedded to the Socioeconomic Determinism paradigm in the earlier days of policy research, public policy analysts have recently recognized the potential effects of policy as an independent variable. Taking their cue from a hitherto underrecognized passage in Easton's *Systems Analysis of Politi-*

cal Life, in which he distinguished between policy outputs and outcomes. Ranney (1968: 8-9), Sharkansky (1970a: chapters 4 and 6), and others have emphasized that policy analysis need not stop with expenditures and taxes.[4] These writers stress the need for policy *impact* research, where the consequences of policy for environmental change is the central concern. While some of the socioeconomic determinism research has been able to predict with almost uncanny accuracy the levels of public expenditures, using regression analysis,[5] relatively little is known about the impact of state and local policies. If impact research constitutes a second plateau in research on state and local governments, then recognition of the reciprocal interaction of policy and environment logically constitutes the next research issue.

RATIONAL ECONOMIC MAN

A third paradigm has informed discussion of urban policy, particularly in economics and, to a lesser degree, in political science. Like the Economic Development and Social Change paradigm, it posits a causal arrow flowing from policy to environment. We call this the "rational economic man" paradigm. In this model, the crucial intervening variable is the mobility of persons and plants. It assumes that policy affects the socioeconomic composition of the environment because *persons and production move about in order to obtain a desired mix of services and taxation.* Although limited in reality by the existence of cost-space friction, the Rational Economic Man (or Firm) theory rests upon familiar assumptions about economic man, behaving rationally, counting costs and marginal utilities. A prototypical statement linking municipal public policies and the mobile economic man is by the economist Tiebout (1968: 358):

> Consider for a moment the case of the city resident about to move to the suburbs. What variables will influence his choice of a municipality? If he has children, a high level of expenditure on schools may be important. Another person may prefer a community with a municipal golf course. The availability and quality of such facilities as beaches, parks, police protection, roads, and parking facilities will enter into the decision-making process. Of course, noneconomic variables will also be considered, but this is of no concern at this point.
>
> *The consumer-voter may be viewed as picking that community which best satisfies his preference pattern for public goods.*

If the rational man (or firm) prefers a high level of public services, he will locate himself accordingly, other things, as they say, being equal.[6] The problem with the theory is that other things are almost never equal, as economic men behave only slightly more rationally, if at all, than political men. Nonetheless, the image creeps frequently into scholarly literature (for example, Wood, 1958: 209) on the suburban migration. In fact, the assumption that "the citizen-consumer votes with his feet as he transfers his loyalty from some municipal Macy's to some municipal Gimbel's" (Long, 1967: 245) has underpinned some elaborate defenses (Ostrom, Tiebout and Warren, 1961; Warren, 1964) of the fragmentation of metropolitan government, on the grounds that optimality of choice is maximized.

Necessarily, since both posit a causal arrow flowing in the same direction, there is some theoretical overlap between the Rational Economic Man and the Economic Development and Social Change paradigms. It seems to us that the most useful distinctions between them are these: (1) The Economic Development and Social Change paradigm assumes for the most part a constant population alterable through public policy, while the Rational Economic Man paradigm assumes a perpetually mobile population; (2) public policy ordinarily affects economic development and social change in a fashion which may be characterized, following Merton, as *manifest*, that is, it is intended and anticipated, but it affects mobility mainly in a *latent* fashion; (3) the Economic Development and Social Change paradigm focuses upon the *production* of public goods, while the Rational Economic Man paradigm focuses upon their *consumption*; and (4) the Rational Economic Man paradigm emphasizes a micro perspective, while the Economic Development and Social Change paradigm emphasizes a macro perspective. Granted that there are similarities between two models which posit causal arrows from policy to environment, both are sharply distinguished from the conventional model of public policy analysis, the Socioeconomic Determinism paradigm.

THE BETE NOIRE: THE PROBLEM OF RECIPROCAL CAUSATION

Logically, if we assume an open system in which system-environment relations are reciprocal, the Socioeconomic-Determinism and the Economic Development-Rational Economic Man paradigms are not incompatible.[7] Methodologically, they have been mutually exclusive because of the bête noire of reciprocal causation in statistical analysis. Statistical techniques conventionally used in political science have difficulty in coping with reciprocal causation. With these limitations, researchers have ignored the likely possibility that any environmental variable (say, home ownership) is reciprocally related to a given policy variable (say, property tax levels or quality of urban services). If we begin, however, with the assumption that environment-system interchanges are reciprocal, all three paradigms can be used to explain the relationship between some public policy variable and some environmental variable. We hasten not to promise more than we can, at this early stage, deliver. We promise only this: some attention to the theoretical problem in a practical context; the presentation of one (among several) methods for dealing with the reciprocity problem; and the exploratory application of the method to some urban policy data in the Canadian and American context.

METHODOLOGY (1)

The reasoning behind the statistical method used in this paper is presented verbally in this, the first part of the methods section. Readers who are, in V. O. Key's words, petrified by the sight of a figure unless it is preceded by a dollar sign or wrapped in a bikini, are urged to read this section. Those who are somewhat mathematically oriented may be interested in the more formal explanation of the method—two stage least squares regression analysis—presented in the second section.

Consider the case of the downward trend in public transit ridership, followed by decreased service. It is a common argument that increasing income levels enable people to buy more cars and, therefore, lessen their dependency on public transportation. In this context, income has an independent effect on the *modal split* (the proportion of people riding public transit).[8] Ridership habits subsequently affect the service levels since transit authorities are quick to reduce the service if a line is not paying for itself. This whole argument might be expressed diagrammatically as in Figure 1. But we are also interested in whether changes in service levels affect the modal split. This is, if transit service is improved will more people ride it? This is not an idle question in light of the anti-expressway and pro-public transit controversies of the 1960s and 1970s (Lupo, Colcord, and Fowler, 1971).

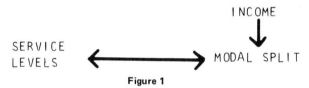

Figure 1

Relationships have been found between service and modal split, but without proper research, one can infer whatever one likes from such relationships. If one is in favor of letting personal preference for the car hold sway, then one might say that a decrease in ridership will properly cause a decrease in service. If one wishes to see cars discouraged in urban areas, one may want to argue that by increasing service an increase will be produced in ridership.[9] (And, conversely, of course, that decreases in service will discourage ridership.) The car lover will retort that people can never be persuaded to leave their cars. How can the empirical problem be investigated?

The obvious reasoning is to vary service levels in some way which is independent of modal split: for instance, if we change service levels in spite of the modal split, then we can see if there is any change in the modal split. What the reasoning implies is that in trying to untangle this reciprocal relationship it is fruitless to try to improve service levels without some kind of outside impetus like a government grant or political protest—whatever it is, it needs to be independent of the actual ridership, just like income. If it is not independent, the true impact of service levels on ridership can never be unraveled. Our new model would look like Figure 2.

The logical structure of the argument is similar to econometric methods using variables that are independent of interrelated variables which are the focus of an analysis. The verbal explanation masks something, however: one can *compute* the statistics describing a relationship whether or not the assumptions for the technique have been met. Previous research has assumed that public policy is a dependent variable, that the feedback arrow discussed by Easton is insignificant. [10] If in fact outputs affect inputs, then researchers have inferred a different link than there really is between environment and public policy.

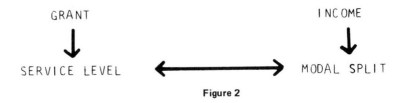

Figure 2

METHODOLOGY (2)

Ordinary least squares (OLS) yields coefficients which are inconsistent [11] when variables are reciprocally related. The problem may be stated as follows. A relationship between two interval scale measures can be estimated by a regression equation:

$$Y = a + bX + e \tag{1}$$

Data are collected for measures Y and X, and a and b are estimated by finding the straight line of (1) which minimizes the square of the distance between the line and the data plotted on an ordinary coordinate system. This method is called OLS. Then, given a number of assumptions, one can estimate a Y value from any X value, according to the structural relation shown in (1). The estimate is never perfect—in fact, in the social sciences it is typically quite imperfect—and the error in the estimation is represented by e. In order for OLS to yield unbiased and consistent estimates of a and b, two assumptions must be correct: the expected value of e must be 0 and there should be no relationship between X and e. These assumptions, however, do not hold when there is a reciprocal relationship between X and Y. Take the following simplest example:

$$Y_1 = a_1 + b_1 Y_2 + e_1 \tag{2}$$

$$Y_2 = a_2 + b_2 Y_1 + e_2 \tag{3}$$

Substituting (3) into (2) gives

$$Y_1 = a_1 + b_1(a_2 + b_2 Y_1 + e_2) + e_1$$

Thus, Y_1 turns out to be in part a function of e_2, which violated OLS's second assumption for (3). The same could be shown for the relationship between Y_2 and e_1 in (2).

Generally speaking, structural relations are seldom of the type of (2) and (3). Usually an analyst has quite a few more variables involved in his theory than just two reciprocally related variables. In addition, the model defined by (2) and (3) has coefficients which are not identifiable, which for practical purposes means that any number of different values of the a's and b's could produce the same values of Y_1 and Y_2. Usually theories include certain kinds of variables which help the analyst find unique estimates of the a's and b's. These so-called exogenous and predetermined variables are ones which a theory can safely assume are independent of the effects of Y_1 and Y_2 and thus unrelated to e_2 and e_1.

Suppose a theory included just one additional exogenous variable X_1, which is in the structural equation for Y_1 and by assumption independent of Y_2 and therefore of e_2. X_1 may of course be correlated with Y_2, but only because of its structural relationship to Y_1. The structural model would look like this:

Equations		Causal Diagram
$Y_1 = a_1 + b_1 Y_2 + b_3 X_1 + e_1$	(4)	
$Y_2 = a_2 + b_2 Y_1 + e_2$	(5)	

The method used in this research, two-stage least squares (TSLS) regresses Y_1 on X_1 obtaining an estimated Y_1 of Y_1. This new variable has been "cleansed" of its relationship with e_2, since it was generated solely by X_1, which is by assumption independent of e_2. Consistent estimates of a_2 and b_2 can then be obtained by the regression of Y_2 and Y_1 (the second stage).

However what about a_1 and b_1? Y_2 has not been cleansed of its relationship with e_1. That is, substitution of (4) into (5) would show that Y_2 is indeed related to e_1. Suppose our theory included another exogenous or predetermined variable, X_2. This would give us the following model:

Equations		Causal Diagram
$Y_1 = a_1 + b_1 Y_2 + b_3 X_1 + e_1$	(6)	
$Y_2 = a_2 + b_2 Y_1 + b_4 X_2 + e_2$	(7)	

X_2 could be used to generate a Y_2, which would be unrelated to e_1, just like X_2. Consistent estimates could then be made of a_1 and b_1 using Y_2 in (6) instead of Y_2.

As it turns out, (6) and (7) define a structure for which the coefficients can be exactly identified. In such a situation, a variety of econometric techniques yield the same results (Johnston, 1963: 234). When the structural equations contain more than just two exogenous variables, and we have what is called an over-identified model, TSLS is often used because it is a convenient way of pooling the additional information.[12]

This whole effort entails, in effect, "manufacturing" a set of structural relations from methodological exigencies. One would hope, of course, that one can start with a theory that leads to a testable model, although this is often not possible. What is important for the moment, however, is that if our theory includes X's which meet the proper assumptions, it is possible to evaluate the link between two reciprocally related variables. This is nothing new for econometricians, but it has some interesting implications for political scientists.

AN APPLICATION

THE PROBLEM

We begin by rejecting the assumption that "inputs" cause "outputs" in any simple one-way fashion, and we explicitly entertain the possibility of reciprocal causation between socioeconomic characteristics of cities and their policy choices. One issue which figures in all three paradigms—Socioeconomic Determinism, Economic Development-Policy Impact, and Rational Economic Man—is the relationship between the home-ownership patterns of a community and the levels of its taxes and expenditures. There is clear evidence in both the United States (Froman, 1967; Lineberry and Fowler, 1967) and Canada (Fowler and Lineberry, 1972a) that the correlation between home ownership and fiscal levels in cities is strong and negative. Borrowing from the Socioeconomic Determinism paradigm, one might explain the negative relationship in terms of the vocal opposition to higher taxes by the penny-pinching home owner. Lineberry and Fowler (1967: 712) observe, upon finding this strong negative relationship between owner occupancy rates and public expenditures, that "no doubt self-interest (perhaps private regardingness) on the part of the home owner, whose property is intimately related to the tax structure of most local governments, may account for part of this relationship."

There is, however, another side to the causal coin. Home ownership is also deeply implicated in both the Economic Development-Policy Impact and the Rational Economic Man paradigms. As sociologists of the Chicago School have pointed out (Burgess, 1929: 114-117), a city's commercial and industrial core tends to push residential areas further and further out as the city grows. Land at the center becomes so expensive that only high-rise apartments are financially possible as residences in the core area (Bourne, 1971). These growth pressures are not, however, entirely a product of the private sector, for at least two reasons. In the first place, the pattern of the home ownership is, in accordance with the Economic Development-Policy Impact paradigm, a function of urban policies affecting land use. Municipalities have found it advantageous to allow developers to assemble blocks of single-family dwelling units in core areas which are razed for large-scale land-intensive developments paying higher taxes than owner-occupied homes. These higher taxes are reflected, of course, in higher expenditures to service high-density areas and may also explain in part the negative correlation between fiscal levels and the incidence of owner occupancy. More generally, because the Economic Development-Policy Impact paradigm is so well etched in the minds of most local politicians, we should be surprised if policy were not related to a crucial economic characteristic such as home ownership. Metropolitan Toronto politician Paul Hunt observed of development (Toronto *Star*, 1970: 70):

> It's all very well for an elite, feather-headed crowd of comfortable pseudo-academics to take a negative attitude toward the growth of the city, but without development we're going to have unemployment, housing shortages, and no way of justifying the expansion of public transit or and other public services.

Another Toronto official, Alderman Fred Beavis, continued in the same vein:

> The same kind of people who are making all kinds of demands for better services, such as subways and cultural facilities, are saying we shouldn't have development. You can't have it both ways.

South of the border, a San Francisco area councilman observed that (Eyestone, 1971: 63):

> We need development of an adequate commercial center in which revenue can be obtained to alleviate the tax burden on the property owner. We have to develop some type of realistic commercial development which will produce revenues.

The public sector can be assumed to affect the incidence of home ownership for a second reason, one derived from the Rational Economic Man paradigm. People are hypothesized to move about the metropolitan areas specifically because of the package of goods and services offered to them by the public sector. Unquestionably, in such cities as New York and Newark, deteriorating services and ever-spiraling tax rates combine to drive out the home owner. Taxes in Newark "are confiscatory. Homeowners pay property tax of 9.63 dollars per 100 of assessed valuation. Since homes in the city are assessed at close to 100 percent of their real worth, a homeowner with a home valued at $20,000 must pay almost $2,000 in taxes. And it may get far worse" (Washington *Post*, 1972: 10). Some empirical effects of the level of service and tax levels on home ownership and property values is provided by Wallace Oates. Oates' (1969: 960) proposition was:

> If consumers, in their choice of locality of residence, do consider the available program of public services, we would expect to find that, other things being equal (including tax rate), gross rents (actual or imputed) and,

therefore, property value would be higher in a community the more attractive its package of public goods.

He discovered that property values were negatively related to the tax rate and positively related to expenditures per pupil on education. This suggests some credence for the Rational Economic Man paradigm in linking local public policy to property ownership and property value.

The problematic relationship between public policy on the one hand and home ownership on the other suggests a textbook case of reciprocal causation problems. For any observed correlation we can identify logical explanations derived from three contending paradigms. The problem, however, is not to describe the complexity, but to untangle it. In hypothesizing that the relationship between home ownership and municipal policy (here measured by the per-capita levels of expenditures and taxes) is reciprocal, we shall attempt to determine the nature of the relationship going each way.

THE DATA

The data for our test are derived from a larger study of comparative urban fiscal policy in Canada and the United States. As the variables and data sources are described in detail elsewhere (Fowler and Lineberry, 1972), we pass over them briefly here. Public policy is measured by city expenditures and city taxes, both expressed in per-capita terms. Homeownership is measured, fortunately, by straightforward census data on the percent of a city's dwelling units which are owner-occupied. Because of the inherent difficulties in matching sample information from two separate polities, we thought it prudent to rely on two Canadian samples to compare with our single American sample. Neither Canadian sample by itself offered the range of data available for our sample of American cities over 50,000 in population. The two thus complement each other. The smaller Canadian sample consists of Canadian cities over 50,000 population in 1966 (N = 19), and the larger one consists of all Ontario and British Columbia cities over 25,000 in 1966 (N = 45). To minimize distortions derived from a large sample of American cities, we confined our attention to a one-third sample (N = 90) of U.S. cities on which a full data-set was available.

Three explanations of the persistent negative relationship between owner occupancy and public spending seem plausible: (1) larger numbers of homeowners vote more frugal councilmen into office to keep taxes and spending down; (2) more spending and higher taxes eventually force out homeowners, who are replaced by more profitable (both for the city and the developer) multiple-family dwellings; and (3) better services, bought with higher taxes and expenditures, elsewhere, lead the homeowner to choose a different community in which to live. Each explanation can readily be matched to a common paradigm—Socioeconomic Determinism, Economic Development, and Rational Economic Man. The first explanation assumes owner occupancy is the independent variable, the second and third that it is the dependent variable, so that any analysis of the link would need to make use of additional variables independent of the endogenous variables homeownership and municipal spending policy. The equations we use are given in Table 1.

The "caps" are the variables which have been estimated by regressing that variable (H, T or E) on the exogenous variables in the analysis.

It was felt that both spending and taxation should be included in an examination of the relationship between homeownership and municipal policy. On the other hand, it is not possible to untangle the (probably) reciprocal nature of the relationship between taxation and spending, so separate sets of structural equations were formulated for taxation and expenditure.

Some of the assumptions about the exogenous variables should be explained, in part to show that they are in fact exogenous. "Percent Catholic," like "Population," is essentially a demographic given. There is not much that city governments can do to influence the percentage of Catholics living in their

TABLE 1

Structural Equations

Key:

H = % owner occupied housing
T = taxation per capita
C = % Catholic
I = median income per capita
G = intergovernmental grants per capita
E = expenditures (total) per capita
P = log of population

U.S.

$$H = a_1 + b_1 T + b_2 C + b_3 I + e_1 \tag{1}$$
$$T = a_2 + b_4 H + b_5 C + b_6 G + e_2 \tag{2}$$

$$H = a_1 + b_1 E + b_2 C + b_3 I + e_1 \tag{1}$$
$$E = a_2 + b_4 H + b_5 C + b_6 G + e_2 \tag{2}$$

Ont.-B.C.

$$H = a_1 + b_1 T + b_2 C + b_3 I + e_1 \tag{1}$$
$$T = a_2 + b_4 H + b_5 C + b_6 G + e_2 \tag{2}$$

$$H = a_1 + b_1 E + b_2 C + b_3 I + e_1 \tag{1}$$
$$E = a_2 + b_4 H + b_5 C + b_6 G + b_7 P + e_2 \tag{2}$$

CANADA 50,000

$$H = a_1 + b_1 T + b_2 C + b_3 I + e_1 \tag{1}$$
$$T = a_2 + b_4 H + b_5 C + b_6 G + e_2 \tag{2}$$

$$H = a_1 + b_1 E + b_2 C + b_3 I + e_1 \tag{1}$$
$$E = a_2 + b_4 H + b_5 C + b_6 G + b_7 P + e_2 \tag{2}$$

jurisdiction.[13] Although governments have tried to restrict populations of cities, they have been notoriously unsuccessful. Thus it is not unreasonable to assume percent Catholic independent of "Owner Occupancy." Similarly, it is doubtful that "Median Income" is affected by owner occupancy, let alone by municipal outlays.

"Grants" as an independent variable is somewhat more problematic. Matching grants, it would seem, would be as much dependent on spending as vice versa. Our line of reasoning was as follows. First, while grants may have uniform criteria, they are a small (U.S.) or minute (Canada) portion of total revenues. Second, evidence from several sources (Pidot, 1969; Fowler and Lineberry, 1972a) indicates that grants have a stimulative rather than merely an additive effect on local spending in the U.S. In other words, city governments respond to grant money, not vice versa.

FINDINGS

Table 2 reports the equations with the estimated coefficients. The cap on a variable means it was estimated first using all the exogenous variables in the set of two equations. The errors in estimation were so large in the Ontario-B.C. sample with respect to the relationship between owner occupancy and expenditure that we decided not to include those statistics.

The coefficients of multiple correlation are not large; it is likely that higher ones could be obtained with more or different sets of variables. Nevertheless, some conclusions may be inferred from the above equations if we convert the

TABLE 2

Regression Equations

United States (N = 88)

H = 44.1 - .752T - .068C + .123I		$R^2 = .38$
T = 745 - 2199H + .695C + .895G		$R^2 = .33$
H = - 3.22 - .568E - .021C + .117I		$R^2 = .36$
E = 695 - 2060H + .712C + .574G		$R^2 = .30$

Ontario-B.C. (N = 45)

T = - 341 - 691H - .280C + .071G		$R^2 = .28$
H = .508 - .902T - .366C + .162I		$R^2 = .29$

Canada (cities over 50,000) (N = 19)

H = 2.58 - .003E - 1.53C + .050I		$R^2 = .58$
E = - 13.6 - 219H - .158C + 1.45G + 44.8P		$R^2 = .75$
H = - 7.72 - .127T - 2.58C + .051I		$R^2 = .56$
T = - .062 - 179H - .135C + .505G		$R^2 = .52$

regression coefficients into a form which makes them more comparable. Multiplying the coefficients of the H's, T's, and E's by the ratio of the standard deviation of the independent variable to the standard deviation of the dependent variables will give us standard or beta coefficients, which indicate how many standard deviations the dependent variable changes for every standard deviation change in the independent variable. Table 3 reports these coefficients.

As Table 3 indicates, there is a strong relationship both ways between Canadian home ownership and fiscal policy. In the United States, however, public spending seems to have more effect on homeownership than vice versa. These findings do not allow us to distinguish among the utility of our three paradigms, but they do present a multiplicative explanation for the two-way relationship between home ownership and public fiscal policy. The findings do enable us to state, however, that the use of OLS or the unicausal assumption of the Socioeconomic Determinism paradigm will produce misleading results.

From policy-makers' perspectives, the regression equations indicate that an increase in taxation is associated with a decrease in homeownership, other things, of course, being equal. The first equation in Table 2, for example, suggests that an increase of, say, $10 per capita in tax incidence produces a decrease of about .7% in owner occupancy. What the equations do not tell us, to be sure, is the appropriate paradigmatic explanation for such consequences. It is possible that the decrease might be a function of irate taxpayers moving elsewhere (the Rational Economic Man). Or, more subtle economic changes may be set in motion by fiscal policy (the Economic Development paradigm).

TABLE 3

The Relationships (Beta Coefficients) between Owner Occupancy and Spending and Taxation in Canadian and American Cities: A Comparison of TSLS and OLS*

	TSLS		OLS
	$\hat{T} \rightarrow \hat{H}$	$\hat{H} \rightarrow \hat{T}$	$\hat{H} \rightarrow \hat{T}$
US	- .92	- .35	- .20
Ont.-B.C.	- .87	- .91	- .39
Canada (over 50,000)	- .71	- .98	- .86
	$\hat{E} \rightarrow \hat{H}$	$\hat{H} \rightarrow \hat{E}$	$\hat{H} \rightarrow \hat{E}$
US	- .69	- .21	- .27
Ont.-B.C.	Not Computed		- .46
Canada (over 50,000)	- .40	- 1.10	- .69

*The notation T → H means that T is the independent and H the dependent variable, corresponding to one of the regression equations reproduced in Table 2.

SOME IMPLICATIONS

The limited causal impact of homeownership on policy in the U.S. could cast doubt upon the conventional wisdom that homeowners are all political nega- tivists, ready to pounce upon municipal officials who dare up the tax ante. The issue, of course, is not whether citizens protest tax rates, but whether the protests are effective. Some well-to-do urbanites may eschew the "voice" option in favor of the "exit" option, in Hirschman's (1970) terms.[14] Other citizens, less well-off and trapped in the core city by virtue of economic or racial discrimination, may find exit unavailable and voice inefficacious (Parenti, 1970).

Having found some support in both polities for a policy $--\rightarrow$ environment causal linkage, we are still left with the problem of choosing between the Economic Development-Policy Impact paradigm and the Rational Economic Man paradigm, both of which posit a causal arrow going the same way. The former would suggest the impact of policy on homeownership directly, perhaps because high taxes discourage ownership or because governmental land acquisi- tion policies reduce the number of single-family dwelling units. The Rational Economic Man paradigm would suggest the indirect effect of policy on environ- ment, operating through the residential choices of families seeking an optimal service-tax mix. Unfortunately, neither our data nor our methodology permit a clear choice between these paradigms. We think, however, that there is ample evidence against an uncritical acceptance of Tiebout's municipal-services-market filled with mobile citizen-consumers. The most obvious empirical limitation on the model is the financial inability of low-income citizens to "vote with their feet." Even among the affluent, however, the Tiebout model seems overdrawn. In an effort to explore the behavior of economic man, Barlow, Brazer, and Morgan (1966) studied the economic choices of the affluent. They found that half of the affluent Americans—annual incomes over $10,000—believed that their state and local taxes were higher than in other areas where they might live, but that only one-sixth "had thought of moving in order to save taxes and only one-sixth of that sixth said they probably would move" (Barlow, Brazer, and Morgan, 1966: 169). Similar evidence about the effects of taxation policies on firms has been reviewed by Due (1961), who concluded that location shifts are only minimally a function of fiscal policies of state and local governments. In the face of such evidence, we doubt that the Rational Economic Man model operates with the full force and simplicity implied by Tiebout and his defenders.

To be sure, the Economic Development-Policy Impact paradigm has been subject to challenge as well. A decade ago, Banfield and Wilson (1963: 343-344) observed that "whatever may be the effect of city politics on the scope and character of local government activities, it seems to make little or no difference in the general standard of living." More recently, Banfield (1970: 14) has attacked even more sharply the view that public policy can improve the urban condition. Norton Long (1972: 130) eloquently describes how little interest municipal bureaucracies—and political scientists—have in the impact of public policies. Says Long: "We still await a study of New Haven, not one that deals with Mayor Lee as a minor league prince in the writing of some political science Machiavelli, but one that tells us what the millions spent achieved, for good or ill in the lives of the people of New Haven."

Political and other social scientists have just begun to debate the actual impact of public policy on problems in the urban environment. A variety of evidence (Coleman, 1966; Campbell and Ross, 1968) seems to demonstrate that the impact of public policy is not so simple nor so efficacious as was once assumed. It seems essential for social scientists to advance on both fronts, that is, studying both the effects of socioeconomic variables in determining the content and levels of urban policy as well as the impact of policies on the socioeconomic environment. Such has been the principal burden or our argument.

Naturally, our findings are too tentative to constitute any practical guide to public policy. Our arguments, our methods, and our conclusions are suggestive, but hardly definitive. Realistically speaking, any two-variable model violates reality by omitting myriad other causal factors. Not the least of these, in the present context, is the impact of race on the housing market, at least in the United States. Land prices, density patterns, transportation networks, and a score of other elements can affect the relationship between public policy and homeownership. Unless these variables can be specified, we shall remain unable to specify more general relationships between policy outputs and environmental changes. All we claim to have done here is to analyze, from a reciprocal perspective, the fact that "owner occupancy rates and fiscal outputs are negatively correlated." In our American sample, we found less evidence for the Socioeconomic Determinism paradigm, but a clear relevance of the Economic Development-Policy Impact and/or the Rational Economic Man paradigms. In the Canadian sample, on the other hand, we suggested a genuine case of reciprocal causation with homeownership levels and fiscal outputs conjointly influencing one another. Perhaps in this paper we have done more to raise issues than resolve them. But if policy analysis ignores the fundamental issues of reciprocity, we shall continue to misstate empirical relationships and fail to capture the theoretical richness of the transactional Eastonian model which inspired policy analysis in the first place.

NOTES

1. For instance, see Campbell and Sacks (1967), Dawson and Robinson (1963), Dye (1966), and Lineberry and Fowler (1967). An excellent review of this research is contained in Hofferbert (1972).

2. For instance, see Davis and Harris (1966) and Zisk (1972). Eyestone's (1971) work on policy leadership in Bay Area cities shows a familiar pattern. Although he recognizes the presence of reciprocal causation among his variables (p. 103), most of his analysis takes policy as dependent. He suggests, for example, that budgets affect councilmanic attitudes (89 ff.), but his causal modeling assumes that budgets depend upon council attitudes (137-144, 176-177).

3. Dye (1972) stresses the importance of "policy impact," but one reviewer (Whittington, 1972) accuses him in the final analysis of "brutally" refusing to "view policy outputs as *causes.*"

4. The passage from Banfield (1965: 7) cited above also presages policy impact analysis by suggesting that "the third link might be established by showing a causal connection between the content of city government policy and the quality of life in the city."

5. See, e.g., Campbell and Sacks (1967), who found an R^2 of .914 between six independent variables and metropolitan expenditures.

6. The non-economist will readily agree that the principal difficulty of the Tiebout hypothesis is the imperfect "fit" between the theory of free markets and perfect mobility and their reality. But for an excellent critique by an economist, see Thompson (1965: 259-263).

7. Curiously, some political scientists who worked originally with the Socioeconomic Determinism model have recently pursued just as vigorously the Economic Development-Policy Impact model. Contrast, e.g., Dye (1966) with Dye (1971 and 1972); or Sharkansky (1967a) with Sharkansky (1967b); Lineberry and Fowler (1967) with Lineberry and Sharkansky (1974).

8. "Modal split" in the following argument refers to the proportion of people riding public as opposed to private transit. If the modal split is, say, 30%, it means that 30% of all trips are made via public transportation systems. This example is, like all cases of reciprocity, a dynamic model and may be dealt with using differential equations, which, however, also entail difficulties of estimation (Blalock, 1970: chapters 5 and 6).

9. A study which assumes ridership is the dependent variable is Metropolitan Toronto and Region Transportation Study (1965: 54 ff.).

10. For a discussion of the feedback loop in urban political analysis, see Fowler and Lineberry (1972b).

11. An estimate is inconsistent when it remains too large or too small no matter how large the sample.

12. As we have emphasized, TSLS is one of several alternative strategems for the investigation of reciprocal relationships. In our own model, for example, TSLS or instrumental variables may be used. Given the simplicity of our models, there is no need to spell out the reduced form of the equations. In a more complex TSLS procedure the reduced form must be estimated as a part of the first step. On the procedures and assumptions of TSLS, see Christ (1966).

13. Interestingly, "percent Catholic" has a persistent relationship with "spending" in the United States, and consistently positive in all studies; the relationship between "Catholic" and "spending" in Canada is just as consistently negative. For evidence and commentary on these contradictory findings, see Fowler and Lineberry (1972a).

14. For an application of Hirschman's theory to choices of protest versus mobility under conditions of urban dissatisfaction, see Orbell and Uno (1972).

Chapter 11

NATIONAL DEFENSE AND LEGISLATIVE DECISION-MAKING

JON CAULEY

and

ROBERT B. SHELTON

College of Business Administration
Arizona State University

National defense is perhaps the most overworked example of what has come to be called a "pure" public good. However, defense expenditures are a nation-wide public good only in their "consumption" aspects, for in the production of this good, private incomes are generated that are geographic-specific. This latter aspect of defense expenditures is critical to some areas of the United States which are major beneficiaries of defense spending. Competing for defense expenditures has meant continued employment for many congressional constituencies. In no other area of the public sector have the political and the economic system become more entangled.

In view of this entanglement, the purpose of this paper is to investigate dynamic interactions between the economic system and the political system with specific reference to the implications that these interactions hold for cyclical and secular defense expenditure trends. The paper is divided into three parts. In part one a model of legislative decision-making is specified. This model begins with a calculus of the individual legislator and is followed by an analysis of coalitions and logrolling. The second part of the paper tests for possible relationships between the legislative decision-making process and defense expenditures.

AUTHORS' NOTE: The authors would like to thank Herbert Kaufman for his helpful suggestions on earlier drafts of this paper. William Arney provided assistance regarding the computer programing. We are also grateful to the University of Colorado Computer Center for computer time. Of course, the authors assume full responsibility.

Defense-expenditure cycles are found to exist. In addition, the second part of
the paper investigates the structure of temporal associations between defense-
expenditures and two key macro-variables that are specified in the legislative
decision-making model as connecting links between the economic system and
the political system. The third and final portion of the paper examines the
findings of part two within the context of part one. Conclusions are drawn
regarding political and economic interactions as they concern defense-
expenditure patterns.

A MODEL OF LEGISLATIVE DECISION-MAKING

The following analysis is based on the standard assumption of vote maximization on the part of the individual legislator, in which the legislator is viewed as
attempting to maximize the likelihood of his reelection (Buchanan, 1967;
Downs, 1957). The legislator is assumed to be faced with a decision regarding
the provision and mix of government defense and nondefense goods in his
district. That is, the strategy of the legislator is assumed to be that of deciding
the optimum mix of public defense and nondefense goods, while at the same
time providing this mix in an optimal fashion for maximizing votes received.[1]

Any given legislator would, if no constraints were placed on him, desire to
spend all of the revenues received by the legislature in his district. Of course,
there are many constraints placed on each legislator, and these constraints
dictate how much of the revenues he can expect to gain for spending in his
district.[2] The ability of a legislator to obtain government expenditures in his
home district will be referred to as his "power function," and any given
legislator's power function can be expressed as some fraction of the total
"power" of all legislators.

In view of the above discussion, we may proceed to investigate the "legislative" decision-making process itself. It is within this context that the limits of a
legislator's maximizing behavior are specified. An analysis of the legislative
environment must begin by building on the structure of coalitions and, as well,
by hypothesizing certain qualitative functional relationships between coalitions
and aggregate economic variables.[3] Following Anthony Downs, we define a
coalition as "a group of individuals who have certain ends in common and
cooperate with each other to achieve them" (Downs, 1957: 24). However, our
definition includes coalition sizes from one individual to n individuals (that is,
one legislator up to and including all members of the legislature).

The basic motivation for this analysis is to better understand the government
expenditure process, especially defense expenditures with the underlying
assumption being that government expenditures are a function of logrolling. We
may state this assumption as follows:

$$G = G(\beta, V, L) \qquad (1)$$

Where G is a government expenditure function, β is some fixed payment (that is, a prior budget commitment), V is government expenditures made on a non-logrolling basis, and L is our logrolling variable.

Actually this functional division for government expenditures somewhat resembles Tullock's now famous division between "Kantians" and "Maximizers" (Tullock, 1959: 571-579). Our V term represents government expenditures that are made when a majority of the legislators agree without making vote-trading agreements (for example, disaster relief for a flooded region). However, our attention in the remainder of this paper will focus on the logrolling aspects of the expenditure process and the basic assumption will be that increases in L lead to increases in G, or notationally:

$$G_L > 0 \qquad\qquad\qquad (2)$$

The analysis regarding the effects of coalitions on logrolling will be divided into two parts: first, the effect of GNP and the interest rate on coalition size; and secondly, the effect of these variables on the number of coalitions.

COALITION SIZE

The coalition (C^s) is hypothesized to be a function of the externalities (E) of the project. The term "externalities" here refers to the number of districts involved directly in the provision of the government goods and services.[4] For example, if the goods are to be provided in one district alone, then the externalities of the project are limited to one district and the coalition size would be one.[5] If the project involves provision in 12 districts, then the natural coalition size will be 12. Now, it is assumed that, ceteris paribus, a legislator would prefer to have a project concentrated wholly in his district with no externalities. There are two reasons for this assumed behavior. First of all, the larger the coalition size the less flexibility the individual legislator has in the disposition of projects within his district. For example, it is difficult to build a dam that goes through 16 districts, and a legislator might have to propose a new highway that may be less desirable in terms of vote production in his district. Second, there is the problem of "voter comparison." If a voter looks around and sees only projects that all other districts have, then the impact of those projects will be lessened. The effect of coalition size on vote production is shown in Figure 1. As the coalition size increases from C^1 to C^6, the increase in expenditures in the district, for some particular project, produces fewer votes at each and every expenditure level.

The key question that arises is: What determines the size of the project proposed by any legislator? That is, what determines the value of the externalities associated with a given proposal? We hypothesize that the externalities are a function of tax revenues and the government borrowing rate of interest. Since,

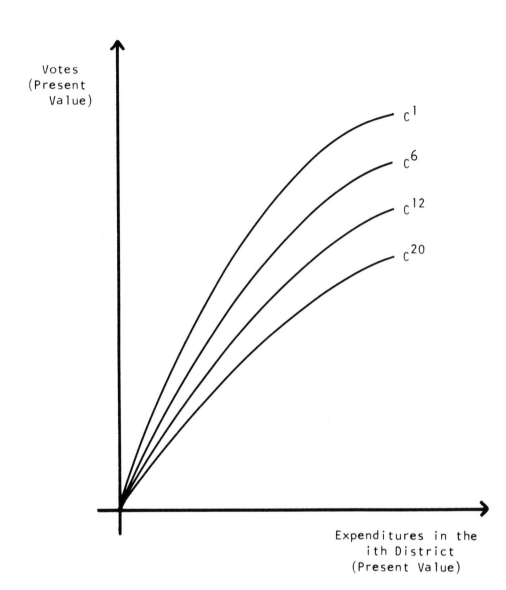

Figure 1

at any given tax rates, tax revenues are a function of the tax base, we may state that coalition size is a function of some aggregate economic indicator called Y.

It is assumed that the coalition size varies inversely with the size of Y and directly with the interest rate. As aggregate economic activity increases and therefore revenues, there is less pressure placed on each legislator to find projects that involve larger coalitions as he can more likely expect passage of more specialized expenditures for his home district.[6] Likewise, as the costs of capital projects increase (for instance, as interest rates go up) the individual legislator will tend to propose projects that involve more districts.[7] Notationally, we may summarize these propositions as follows:

$$C^S = C^S (E) \tag{3}$$

since $E = E (T, r)$, and $T = T (Y)$ we may write

$$C^S = C^S (T (Y), r). \tag{4}$$

We now may state our assumptions on derivatives:

$$C_Y^S = C_T^S T_Y < 0 \tag{5}$$

and

$$C_r^S > 0. \tag{6}$$

THE NUMBER OF COALITIONS

The number of coalitions formed during any legislative period is the next crucial variable that must be examined before we turn our attention to the legislative logrolling process. It is clear that any given legislator will attempt to satisfy more constituents with government consumer expenditures and investment projects as his control over these projects increases. Therefore one would expect a legislator to be a member of more coalitions with larger resources at his command. That is, the number of projects will be much more varied in that the vote maximizing legislator will attempt to appeal to more and more people in his district. Hence, the greater aggregate economic activity and therefore the greater the tax revenue received, the larger the number of coalitions that will be formed. On the other hand, the higher the cost of investment projects due to increases in the interest rate, the smaller the number of projects that will be proposed for adoption by the decision-making body.[8]

We may summarize our assumptions about the number of coalitions in the following manner:

$$C^N = C^N (T (Y), r) \tag{7}$$

and

$$C_Y^N = C_T^N T_Y > 0, \tag{8}$$

$$C_r^N < 0. \tag{9}$$

We are now in a position to state succinctly some basic propositions on the relationship between coalitions and the logrolling process.

COALITIONS AND LOGROLLING

Logrolling is essentially a process of "deal" making in that an individual, or groups of individuals, makes agreements with other individuals or groups of individuals. The "deals" involve agreements between the parties to trade support, and therefore votes, on legislative proposals. The outcome of the logrolling process, for our purposes, is an amount of money appropriated. It includes not only the number of agreements, but also the size (in terms of dollars) of each agreement. This will involve an analysis of the effect of coalition size and number on the size and number of agreements made.

The size of coalitions will obviously affect the logrolling process. The larger the size of a coalition, the larger the pool of resources (votes) available to achieve the necessary votes for making the appropriation. In terms of size of the appropriation, we shall assume that the larger the coalition size, the larger coalition expenditure.

The number of coalitions will have a great impact on the number of "deals" made and therefore on the logrolling process and the dollar volume of the process. It is assumed that, ceteris paribus, the greater the number of coalitions, the larger the dollar volume in dollars of logrolling.

We may summarize the above statements as follows:

$$L = L(C^S, C^N), \tag{10}$$

That is, logrolling (L) is assumed to be a function of the coalition sizes and the number of coalitions and by utilizing the results from equations and propositions (3) through (9), we may analyze the indirect effects of changes in Y and r on the function L by investigating the signs of the relevant partial derivatives. These partial derivatives are as follows:

$$L_Y = L_C S \, C_Y^S + L_C N \, C_Y^N \gtrless 0, \tag{11}$$

depending on whether

$$\left| L_C N \, C_Y^N \right| \gtreqless \left| L_C S \, C_Y^S \right|$$

since

$$L_c N C_Y^N > 0$$

and

$$L_C{}^S C_Y{}^S < 0;$$

$$L_r = L_C S \, C_r^S + L_C N \, C_r^N \gtreqless 0, \tag{12}$$

depending on whether

$$\left| L_C N \, C_r^N \right| \gtreqless \left| L_C S \, C_r^S \right|$$

since

$$L_C S \; C_r^S > 0$$

and

$$L_C N \; C_r^N < 0.$$

LEGISLATIVE DECISION-MAKING, LOGROLLING, COALITIONS, AND DEFENSE EXPENDITURES

The key to analyzing the effects of changes in income and the interest rate on logrolling, then, depends upon the relative magnitude of the changes in the number of coalitions and the changes in the size of coalitions. In terms of the present investigation, however, we are not so much interested in general logrolling, but logrolling that is specifically related to defense expenditures. To focus on defense-expenditure related logrolling, the logrolling component is broken into two segments under the assumption they are separable and additive: a defense-expenditure segment and a nondefense—expenditure segment. Notationally, this proposition is expressed as follows:

$$L_y = L_y^d + L_y^w \tag{13}$$

$$L_r = L_r^d + L_r^w \tag{14}$$

The interest is in the signs of L_y^d and L_r^d, the defense-expenditure related logrolling. In the remaining analysis it is assumed that the signs of these two derivatives are greater and less than zero respectively (that is, $L_y^d > 0$ and $L_r^d < 0$). This is an extremely plausible assumption. In general, the size of defense coalitions will change slowly over time since defense-project externalities will not, as a rule, fluctuate violently in the short run (that is, the pattern of defense installations and employment in districts does not change rapidly). Furthermore, given that defense projects are interconnected in their production processes, it would be very difficult for defense-beneficiary legislators to react by proposing district-specific projects, regardless of how great the increase in aggregate economic activity. Therefore, it is reasonable to expect that increased opportunities for defense-related logrolling generated by increased aggregate economic activity will manifest themselves in greater coalition numbers relative to coalition size. The same proposition holds true for increases in the interest rate. Hence, changes in the magnitude of income on defense-related logrolling through the changes in the number of defense coalitions are going to be greater than the changes in the magnitude of income on logrolling through the changes in the size of the defense coalitions. Again, the same proposition holds true for changes in the interest rate although the direction of inequality is reversed.

In part two, these results will be utilized to specifically analyze the dynamics of defense expenditures. For the moment, however, it will be of interest to look at the legislative decision-making process in conjunction with defense expenditures from a more general viewpoint. In particular, a test is made in an attempt to detect any systematic relationships between the legislative decision-making process and defense expenditures.

A TEST FOR LEGISLATIVE DEFENSE-EXPENDITURE CYCLES AND TEMPORAL ASSOCIATIONS

Spectral analysis is employed to test for the existence of possible relationships between the legislative decision-making process and defense expenditures, set within the structural context of the economic system.[9] That is, we are not interested in the absolute level of defense expenditures, but rather its size relative to gross national product. As such, the relevant variable is defense expenditures expressed as a percentage of gross national product (that is, hereafter specified as D/GNP). More specifically, a spectral analytical test is an ideal empirical method for providing evidence of any regular or periodic variations in D/GNP that are associated with the political process.

Spectral analysis operates in the frequency domain, as opposed to classical econometric procedures which operate in the time domain (Fishman, 1969; Granger and Hatanka, 1964; Jenkins and Watts, 1969; and Nerlove, 1964: 241-286). In lieu of a typical time series plot (x), where x = f(t) and t = time, with spectral analysis the variance of an original time series is partitioned into variance components (V) that are plotted against various frequencies (F) (that is, V = g(F)). This function, which is the Fourier Transform of the autocovariance function (that is, the time domain representation of the series), is termed the power spectrum and it can be demonstrated that it specifies the contribution of individual frequencies (or cycles) to the total variance of the process. The importance of a particular cycle is indicated by a peak in the power spectrum and its height designates the relative importance of cycles (that is, the contribution of that frequency to the total variance).

Political cycles, if they exist, would be expected to occur at four- and/or two-year intervals corresponding to executive and legislative turnover.[10] These D/GNP, political cycles are not necessarily created by partisan politics although at the executive level this is undoubtedly a factor (for example, the "missile gap" issue in the 1960 campaign). In addition, contributions to cycles may be produced by congressional reluctance to pass large defense-expenditure increases toward the end of a presidential term in comparison to less reluctance initially. Furthermore, two-year cycles may be created when pro-defense legislators turnover as a result of being subjected to uncalculable and/or uncontrollable "voter wrath" due to developments such as constituency misreading, changing power relations among colleagues, and voter ignorance.

In Figure 2, the power spectrum (or variance) of the time series D/GNP[11] is plotted with respect to individual frequencies (called frequency bands). The frequencies can be translated into years by dividing them into one. Hence, in

GRAPH OF POWER AT EACH FREQUENCY BAND FOR D/GNP

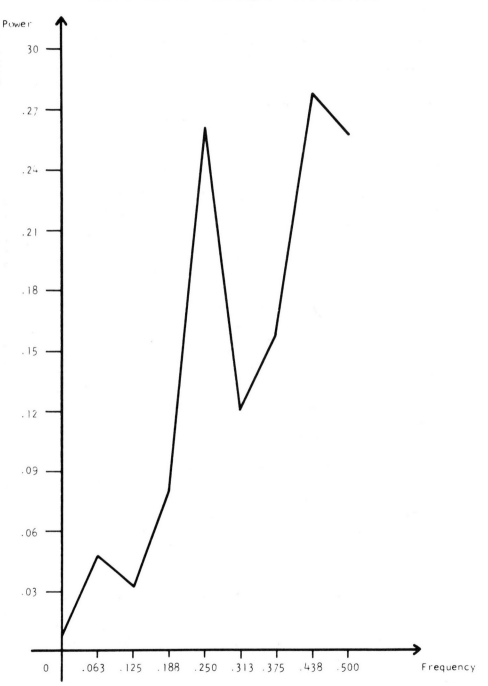

Figure 11

terms of years, the cycles of four and two years occur at .250 and .500 frequencies respectively. Strong evidence of a 2.38-year cycle and a four-year cycle is present since peaks of high power occur at frequencies corresponding to these periodicities. However, it is possible that the four-year cycle is being partially amplified by the approximate two-year cycle.[12] This same phenomenon may be contributing to the sixteen-year cycle.

In view of the above results, the purpose of this paper is to test for the existence of any regular and periodic associations between D/GNP, the interest rate, and gross national product. The unemployment rate is utilized as a proxy for cyclical changes in the size of gross national product, since the primary interest is in changes in the size of real gross national product. In addition, since gross national product is specified in the denominator of the independent variable, spurious associations may be produced with the alternative formulation.

On an a priori theoretical foundation there is a basis for postulating a causative structure and specifying D/GNP as the independent variable and the macrovariables as dependent variables. Research in the time domain by Bruce M. Russett provides supportive evidence for the above specification. Russett estimated the short-run impact of changes in D/GNP on other categories of gross national product and found these impacts to be quite considerable. Russett's work primarily focused on periods of high defense spending under the assumption that gross national product was approximately equal to gross capacity product (that is, the post-World-War-I period). Thus he found negative relationships between D/GNP and other macrovariables (Russett, 1969: 412-416; Russett, 1971: 29-50; and Hollenhurst and Ault, 1971: 760-763). However, assuming that gross national product is significantly below gross capacity product, and that all other conditions remain the same, a defense expenditure increase (that is, an increase in D/GNP) financed by "printing press money" would be theoretically expected to increase gross national product.

For the most part, during the period studied in this paper (1890 to 1958) real gross national product was below gross capacity product. In reality, of course, conditions are continuously changing that may alter or even cancel an impact of this nature. Furthermore, it is possible that impacts of this sort will not be direct in view of frictions associated with the dynamic adjustment process in a complex economy. As a result, lags of varying degrees may be involved. On the other hand, it is a possibility that associations between these two sets of series may be caused by other factors. Therefore, although D/GNP is specified as the independent variable in these tests, this specification is not necessarily intended to imply a comprehensive causative structure. In terms of interpreting the measure of variation in the dependent series explained by the independent series (D/GNP), this statement is an acknowledgment of the possibility that a portion of this variance may be explained by factors other than D/GNP. Thus, our primary concern is in the ex-post associative structure rather than the causative structure itself.

CROSS-SPECTRAL ANALYSIS

Cross-spectral analysis will serve to test for temporal associations, since it enables one to analyze relationships between two or more time series. In general, the concepts embodied in spectral analysis are similar to those in cross-spectral analysis. The cross-spectrum, however, is the Fourier transform of the cross-covariance between two time series. In practice, cross-spectral methods can indicate the degree of association between two time series at individual frequencies. The precise measure of association is signified by the coherency reading, which, when squared, is analogous to the coefficient of determination in regression analysis, defined at each frequency.

Even if two series are completely associated in terms of amplitude, they may be out of phase at different frequencies. Thus, cross-spectral methods enable the investigator to suggest lead or lag relationships between two time series through an interpretation of the phase spectrum. A particular phase estimate indicates angular displacement between two series that can be interpreted within the unit circle framework. In the case of a perfect sinusoidal function that repeats every four years, 360° on the unit circle would correspond to the completion of a four-year cycle. In the case of two of these functions, for example, a phase estimate of 180° would signify that either the first series lagged the second or that the second series lagged the first by two years (that is, the two series were completely out of phase).

The phase estimates, however, cannot be mechanically translated into lead-lag relationships.[13] Hence, they must be interpreted within the context of a theoretical structure. Therefore, in view of specifying D/GNP as the independent variable, if a phase difference is indicated it is assumed that the independent variable is lagged by the dependent variables.

In many instances, before implementing a spectral or cross-spectral test, two preliminary operations are performed on the data. First, it is necessary that the underlying processes being examined are covariance stationary because the results of spectral and cross-spectral analysis rest on this assumption. For example, a series which possesses a monotonic trend is non-stationary. Since most economic times series have a trend in mean, they must be detrended prior to analysis with spectral methods.

A series that exhibits trend may very well produce a spectrum characterized by the presence of high power at low frequencies. In fact, this is a criterion for evaluating whether or not trend has been removed from the series and the one used in this study. In particular, it is assumed that if high power at low frequencies was eliminated then the series had been detrended. There are, however, problems with this procedure since cycles that possess infrequent periodicity also produce high power at low frequencies and may be eliminated along with the trend. Since we are not interested in cycles of relatively infrequent periodicity in this study, this does not present a problem.

Non-stationary processes can be made stationary by a general process referred to as filtering. In the present instance, both a first and second difference filter were applied to all three series. The first-difference filter was sufficient to remove trend in all cases (that is, it eliminated high power at low frequencies).

Secondly, it is advisable to align each pair of series before a final cross-spectral analysis is applied (Mayer and Arney, 1974). This procedure is accomplished by determining the time lag (or lead) between two series at which the greatest cross-covariance occurs. In the case of D/GNP and the unemployment rate, the greatest cross-covariance occurred at zero lags. In the case of D/GNP and the interest rate, the greatest cross-covariance occurred at a lag of four years. Hence, these two series were aligned accordingly.[14]

RESULTS OF CROSS-SPECTRAL TESTS

The results of the cross-spectral tests are presented in Tables 1 and 2 below. The coherence estimates are perhaps the first cross-spectral statistic to look at. As a general rule of thumb for interpreting the coherence estimate, Granger and Morganstern (1963: 20) have provided the following classification scheme:

(1) Very high if many of the coherence values are above 0.95.
(2) High if some coherence values are above 0.80 with most of them above 0.50.
(3) Moderate if most coherence values are between 0.60 and 0.30.
(4) Low if few of the coherence values are above 0.40.
(5) Very low if the majority of the values are below 0.25.

Also, statistical tests are available and were applied (Bonomo and Schotta, 1969).

In Table 1, the cross-spectral estimates between the unemployment rate and D/GNP are presented. First, notice that at the cycle with periodicity of 3.20 years, a lag of seventeen hundredths of a year is indicated (that is, approximately 62 days). The interpretation of this lag is as follows. For cycles of 3.20 length, the unemployment rate reaches a peak approximately 62 days after D/GNP has reached a peak. In other words, after 62 days, the unemployment rate begins to drop (that is, aggregate economic activity begins to increase) in terms of its relationship with D/GNP.

At the cycle with periodicity of 2.66 years, the unemployment rate decreases after a lag of approximately 277 days. For cycles with periodicity of 4.00 and 2.28, aggregate economic activity increases after a lag of approximately one year with respect to D/GNP. Longer lags of approximately 3.82 and 7.66 years occur at cycles with periodicities of 8 and 16 years, respectively, and should be interpreted in the manner spelled out above.

The cross-spectral estimates between the interest rate and D/GNP are presented in Table 2. The shortest, significant lag at the .001 level occurs at a

TABLE 1

Cross-Spectra Between the Unemployment Rate and D/GNP

Years	Freq.	Amp	Phase	Coh	Coh^2	Lag
16	.063	.057	-172.3°	.967	$.935^{a}$	7.66
8	.125	.073	171.8°	.973	$.947^{a}$	3.82
5.33	.188	.095	135.2°	.921	$.842^{a}$	2.00
4.00	.250	.046	97.9°	.912	$.832^{a}$	1.09
3.20	.313	.046	19.1°	.730	$.533^{a}$	0.17
2.66	.375	.020	-102.9°	.706	$.498^{a}$	0.76
2.28	.438	.023	166.4°	.806	$.650^{a}$	1.05
2.00	.500	.014	0.0°	.432	.187	

a. Indicates coherence is significant at the .001 level.

(See Appendix A for data sources.)

TABLE 2

Cross-Spectra Between the Interest Rate and D/GNP

Years	Freq.	Amp	Phase	Coh	Coh^2	Lag
16	.063	.066	$- 23.7^{\circ}$	.743	$.552^{a}$	6.05
8	.125	.010	$- 65.6^{\circ}$	.698	$.487^{a}$	6.46
5.33	.188	.006	171.1°	.407	.166	
4.00	.250	.011	$- 43.4^{\circ}$	.562	$.316^{b}$	5.48
3.20	.313	.011	-119.9°	.541	$.293^{b}$	6.07
2.66	.375	.016	$- 94.9^{\circ}$	.744	$.554^{a}$	5.70
2.28	.438	.004	-152.6°	.355	.126	
2.00	.500	.001	0.0°	.176	.031	

a. Indicates coherence is significant at the .001 level.

b. Indicates coherence is significant at the .05 level.

(See Appendix A for data sources.)

2.66-year cycle and its length is approximately 5.70 years. As before, the interpretation is that the interest rate reaches a peak 5.70 years after D/GNP has reached a peak. Two other associations that are statistically significant at the .001 level are indicated with periodicities of 16 years and 8 years. The relevant lags are 6.05 and 6.46 years, respectively. Of course, these relationships between D/GNP, the unemployment rate and the interest rate have implications for defense-expenditure logrolling and they will be analyzed in the next part of the paper.

SYNTHESIS AND CONCLUSIONS

It remains to interpret the findings presented in part two within the framework of the legislative decision-making model. In particular, there are a number of interesting implications regarding cyclical and secular patterns in defense spending that will be developed.

To begin with, if one is willing to make the assumption that there is a correlation between pure "pork barrel" legislation and single-district legislation (or legislation involving only a few districts) then it can be seen that the magnitude of pork barrel, defense-legislation will be affected indirectly through changes in the macrovariables in the manner described in part one. Furthermore, the empirical results presented in part two can be utilized to test for the existence of these effects.

More specifically, we have seen in part two that D/GNP increases are associated with lagged increases in aggregate economic activity (that is, decreases in the unemployment rate). Recalling our assumption that $L_y^d > 0$, the implication is that increases in aggregate economic activity will result in an increase in the dollar value of defense-related logrolling. In general, this phenomenon will tend to ratify initial defense-expenditure increases. The analysis of part two indicates that six lagged ratifications of this sort will be forthcoming over a period of approximately eight years. Two of these will take place within the first year and serve to ratify both executive and legislative defense-expenditure increases vis-a-vis stimulating defense-related logrolling.

Three additional ratifications, which fall within a four-year boundary, will follow. First, a one-year ratification will again serve to stimulate defense-related logrolling on both an executive and congressional plane. The two-year ratification will serve to ratify congressional defense-related logrolling, followed by an approximate four-year ratification producing conditions favorable for executive proposals related to defense-expenditures. In addition, an approximate eight-year lag is a potential contributor to an initial four-year executive cycle.

This process of cyclical ratification, viewed in isolation is suggestive of an upward, long-run or secular trend in defense expenditures. Indeed, a number of authors have suggested that logrolling leads to over-spending. For example, Russett (1970) points out that "it is well known that, from the point of view of marginal costs and gains to the entire community, the pork barrel leads to excessive spending." Gordon Tullock (1959) has made this same argument from a deductive point of view.

However, just as there are "ups" in aggregate economic activity, there are also "downs" that tend to produce the reverse effect on the dollar value of defense-related logrolling. If the structure of these relationships is completely symmetrical, then the effects will cancel out and an upward secular trend will not be produced. Furthermore, the results of part two indicate an interest rate effect that comes into play. Since we assumed $L_r^d < 0$, this effect will operate to dampen initial increases in defense expenditures. However, these dampening effects come after a number of ratifications associated with increases in aggregate economic activity as well as less frequently. As such, we would expect them to be of secondary importance, not only with respect to the "ups" but also the "downs."

Thus the ultimate result of these dynamic processes rests upon the nature of the symmetrical properties associated with aggregate economic activity and its impact on defense-related logrolling. Is there any reason to believe, within the context of our knowledge of the legislative decision-making process as it pertains to defense expenditures, in an unsymmetrical case and, if so, in what direction would the bias occur?

There are a number of reasons to believe that there would indeed be a bias and that this bias would be in favor of increased defense expenditures. First of all, over the period of this study, this is an empirically observed fact (Russett, 1970). In addition, it is well known that once a project is initiated it tends to create its own momentum. This appears to be especially true with respect to defense expenditures (Russett, 1970). Moreover, as noted previously, defense expenditures tend to be of a localized nature and as such will not produce inter-jurisdictional externalities to the extent that nondefense expenditures will, especially welfare expenditures. Viewed within the context of the voter-comparison phenomenon, this feature of defense-expenditures will serve to strengthen vote-production functions of defense-beneficiary legislators relative to nondefense-beneficiary legislators. Over the long-run, this situation will tend to work against "dovish" legislators and in favor of "hawkish" legislators. Furthermore, hawk power functions will tend to be increased relative to non-hawks, as they move through the seniority system obtaining greater power over funds.

In view of the above and in terms of a secular viewpoint, we may not, in fact, be observing a strictly up-and-down process with respect to the defense expenditure cycles. Since we removed trend before performing the spectral analysis, it is possible that these cycles may be representative of a series of growth processes [15] created, at least in part, by the features of the legislative decision-making process depicted above.

This secular, upward trend in defense expenditures undoubtedly can be explained by additional factors. The present analysis, however, suggests an important contributing phenomenon associated with dynamic interactions between the economic and political systems. The dynamics of interactive processes connecting the economic system and the political system are extremely complex and this paper has only explored one aspect of the topic with respect to implications regarding the structure of defense expenditures. It goes without saying that a great deal more research is needed in the area, not only in relation to the defense-expenditure issue but for the multitude of other critical issues which are affected by these processes.

NOTES

1. In most cases, a particular defense or nondefense good will be of an intermediate nature and therefore give rise to a vector of joint products. It is the optimal provision of these vectors of joint products associated with defense and nondefense goods that the legislator is ultimately striving for.

2. These constraints would include such things as seniority, committee assignments, his ability to make "deals," and the like.

3. The analysis will not be cast in game theoretic or simulation techniques, the way much of the recent work in this area has been conducted, because all strategic aspects of the problem will be ignored.

4. The coalition size refers to a "natural" coalition in that no members have been "bought" into the coalition. We are, of course, overcoming the problem of preference revelation in a coalition, since it is assumed that votes are proportional to expenditures, which are directly measurable.

5. In fact, we might say the externalities are effectively internalized.

6. There is, in fact, a fundamental tradeoff faced by any legislator. As pressures increase for the legislator to find projects which involve larger coalitions he must calculate the costs in terms of votes lost in the home district, and we are therefore, in some sense discussing an "optimum" coalition size.

7. This will most likely, though not necessarily, mean smaller per-district capital expenditures.

8. It might appear, on first glance, that the number of coalitions should be made a function of the size of coalitions as well, and this would be true if the number of proposals and coalitions any member could join were fixed. However, since this is not the case, we cannot expect this direct relationship to exist.

9. Spurious cycles could have been produced if the variation in gross national product was large relative to defense expenditures. However, the evidence indicates that this is not the case. See Russett (1971).

10. Members of the House and one-third of the senators are potential turnover candidates every two years.

11. The time series was detrended to remove high power at low frequencies. A brief discussion of detrending is given below.

12. The approximate two-year cycle may be a harmonic of the four-year cycle. See Jenkins and Watts (1969: 19-21).

13. There are additional problems with interpreting the phase statistic which have not been resolved. See Granger (1969: 424-438) and Hause (1971: 213-217).

14. Any phase estimates must be adjusted with respect to lags (or leads) before interpretation.

15. For a good discussion of this phenomenon see Boulding (1966: 210-215).

APPENDIX A: DATA AND SOURCES

The data used in this study covered the period from 1890 to 1958. The defense expenditure data was taken from: U.S. Bureau of the Census, *Historical Statistics of United States, Colonial Times to 1957* (Washington: U.S. Government Printing Office, 1960), and *Historical Statistics of the United States, Colonial Times to 1957; Continuation to 1962 and Revisions*—Series HS 350 and HS 356. The Gross National Product data was taken from: U.S. Department of Commerce and Bureau of the Census, *Long Term Economic Growth—1860-1965*, Statistical Compendium—ES4—No. 1, Series A-7. The unemployment rate and the commercial paper rate were also taken from the above source, Series B1/B/2 and B69, respectively.

SECTION IV

CONCLUSION

THREE PATHS TO WHO GETS WHAT, WHEN, HOW

JOHN McCAMANT

The contributors to this volume were thirsting for the testable, as Kenneth Boulding suggested in his introduction, but it is also true that the theoretical literature on public expenditures provided very uncertain guidelines on what needed to be tested. The propositions tested in this volume have an ad hoc and eclectic quality to them that reflects the absence of any overall theory to guide research. Bringing the work of economists and political scientists together added even greater diversity than would have been found within the bounds of a single discipline. Yet one of the basic causes for the absence of a unified theory is the division of labor between economists and political scientists, when what is needed is a true political economics. Both disciplines have logical tools and concepts to contribute, and without the contributions of both, any theory would be incomplete. In this conclusion, we wish to suggest a way to organize the propositions found in this volume into a more unified theory of public expenditures.

The various hypotheses proposed and implied by the contributors to this work fall logically into three categories, each of which can be considered as a causal path between the environment and the budget decision. Any change in the environment which affects public resource allocation will operate through one or more of these paths, which taken together exhaust the logical possibilities. The first path is the *revenue path*. Different factors in the environment will determine the revenue available to the government, and the revenue available will influence the pattern of public expenditures. The second path is the *opportunity cost path*. The government is faced by prices of market goods, finance, and personnel, which reflect their opportunity costs within the society, and since these prices will affect how much of a public good or service can be delivered with any given expenditure, the government must take these prices into account. The third path is the *aggregate utility function path*. A number of different factors will affect the preferences of individuals, or their utility functions, and a system of collective choice will aggregate these utility functions into a set of community preferences, giving differing weights to different individuals' utility functions.

The three paths combine in the allocation decision, which then affects the provision of governmental services, goods, and investments, which in turn impacts on the environment. The full cycle is portrayed in Figure 1. Fowler and Lineberry discuss the importance of taking into account this reciprocal pattern of causation—which is particularly important in measuring and testing relationships. Nevertheless, we will concentrate our attention in this conclusion on the part of the cycle from the environment to the allocation decision, which has been the primary concern of nearly all of the studies in this volume.

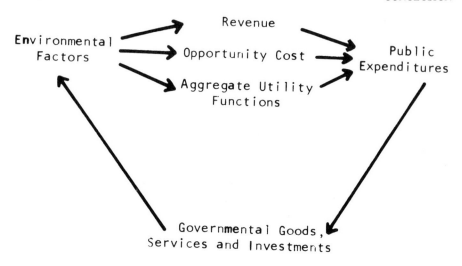

Figure 1

THE ENVIRONMENT-GOVERNMENT ALLOCATION-ENVIRONMENT CYCLE

Before discussing each of the three paths, we want to show why two contenders for a theory of public expenditure, the incremental theory and the level of production theory, while not proved wrong, did yield certain anomalies which made them at best incomplete. The incremental theory (Davis, Dempster, and Wildavsky, 1966) states that previous expenditures are the major determinant of current expenditures. Ames and Goff tested the theory in Latin America and found that previous expenditures correlated positively with current expenditures in each case, but the correlation was much lower for defense than for education and much lower in some countries than in others. Something more is clearly needed to explain why the correlations vary so enormously.

The other theory that proved inadequate or incomplete is the theory stating that levels of production are a major determinant of expenditures. The causal interpretation of this relationship is even less adequate than for the incremental theory, and its sole foundation rests on associations found, primarily between variables within the states of the United States. The associational analyses by Danziger, Abolfathi and Park, Ames and Goff, and Peters and Hennessy yield very inconsistent results. Sometimes they found associations between levels of production and expenditures and sometimes not. Ames and Goff even found a negative rather than a positive association when they regressed changes in gross domestic product and total expenditures together against changes in education and defense expenditures measured as a percentage of GDP. There is certainly no direct correspondence between levels of production and expenditure levels.

Neither the incremental theory nor the level of production theory provide consistent results in their present form. The relationships are far more complex than these simple theories suggest. The three-paths theory of the budget decision can subsume both of these earlier and simpler theories within it and may account for the anomalous results.

The amount of revenue available to a government influences, first of all, how much it will spend and, secondly, what proportions it will spend on different items. That how much is spent depends on how much there is to spend is not as tautological as it may sound. It competes with the idea that need or demand for public goods determines how much is spent. We want to emphasize that the amount of revenue often comes first, after which allocations are decided. Danziger's findings on the decisional process in two English boroughs substantiated the importance of this causal path. Budget-makers confessed they were very uncertain on the needs or demands of the community and relied on the finance officers to tell them how much to spend.

We also suggest that as governmental revenue goes up, the government will spend proportionately more on some items than on others. Ames and Goff found that both defense and education expenditures went up quite rapidly with expanded total expenditure, but other expenditures went up less rapidly. Some expenditure items are absolutely essential in small quantities, but additional quantities may not be useful. Other expenditure items may be less important in small quantities, but their usefulness may continue with additional quantities. Expenditures will be proportionately greater on the former when little revenue is available and proportionately greater on the latter when much revenue is available. Income elasticity of demand differs between items of expenditure made by governments as it does for individuals.

The amount of revenue available to a government is a function not only of the level and kind of production in a country but also of its tax system (referring to both laws and their application). Given any particular tax system, changes in production will bring more or less automatic changes in governmental revenue. However, the changes will be different in different tax systems. Revenue will go up more rapidly than production in some tax systems and less rapidly in others. Revenue change will also depend on the type of production that is changing. Several authors in this volume have suggested that the importance of levels of production for government allocations is through the effect on revenue, but none have taken into account the different impacts of different kinds of production and of different tax systems. The tax system is the problematic variable, for no theory exists for explaining differences in tax systems. Since production patterns change only slowly and tax systems rarely change, revenue ordinarily changes only incrementally—contributing to the incremental pattern of expenditures.

Curiously, in this volume the revenue question was raised by political scientists. The economists concentrated their attention on the question of opportunity costs, a concept ignored by our political scientists. The possibility that one government might spend more (or less) on some goods and services because its prices (opportunity costs) were lower does not seem to have occurred to most political scientists. The problem is less obvious because there is no market to set prices on governmental goods and services. Because there is no market, particularly an international market, for governmental goods and services the opportunity-cost structure varies enormously. In some poor countries construction equipment may cost twice (at market exchange rates) what it does in an industrial country, but a teacher may cost only one-twentieth as much as in an industrial country. These input costs will make some governmental goods and services relatively much cheaper or more expensive than others in one country as opposed to another.

The effect of opportunity costs or prices on government expenditures is uncertain—depending as it does on the price elasticity of the good or service. For some items, the government will spend more as the price goes up in order to maintain the same level of use. For others, it will lower its expenditure, judging the items not worth the cost.

Cauley and Shelton raised the question of opportunity cost in their discussion of the influence of unemployment and interest rates on government expenditures. High unemployment means that the social opportunity costs of additional government hiring is nearly zero. Interest rates affect the cost of investment goods and, they argue, will affect the proportion of investment goods to consumption goods provided by governments.

Sandler poses the question of the effects of a military alliance on defense expenditures. The alliance lowers the cost of defense by providing some of the good free through spillovers from the ally. In some small countries, the amount provided through the spillover may suffice, and that country will spend nothing on defense.

The associations found by Abolfathi and Park suggest a twist to the Sandler argument. Abolfathi and Park found that defense expenditures tended to be higher among those countries which received Soviet military aid or which had a high level of trade with the Soviet Union. This association may mean that lowering the marginal cost of defense (as opposed to the lowering of only average cost by the alliance) may increase expenditure of the good because defense is price elastic.

The giving of foreign aid of any kind provides a marvelous quasi-experiment for the study of price effects on public expenditures. Foreign aid lowers the opportunity costs of the programs funded vis-a-vis programs for which funds are not available; it lowers the cost of public investment vis-a-vis public consumption; and it lowers the cost of imported inputs vis-a-vis domestic inputs. Except for some rather loose descriptions of the results (McCamant, 1968), this phenemonenon has not been studied.

Economists often use the concept of the production possibilities curve, which indicates opportunity cost, in conjunction with a community indifference curve in order to determine how much of any item will be provided (see Sandler in this volume). The problem is that the community indifference curve is without empirical content and remains a mythical construction to establish equilibrium. Individual indifference curves do have empirical meaning, but it is logically impossible to add them together. At this point, the concepts and approaches of political science are necessary. The political process is the process whereby individual indifference curves, or utility functions, are aggregated into a community indifference curve. One must dip into the murky subjects of influence, power, authority, organization, and so on in order to aggregate individual utility functions in the third and most complex path to public expenditures.

The third path involves two separate steps. The first is to determine the individual utility functions for governmental goods and services. The second is to find out how different political processes aggregate these individual utility functions.

We use the concept of utility function instead of the political science concepts of public opinion and group interest because the utility function emphasizes the question of choice and its determinates and incorporates such useful logical tools as marginal utility and maximization.

Wagner applies the concept of the individual utility function to military expenditures. He points out that the value of military expenditures to an individual depends on the subjective probability that the expenditure will provide defense (prevent an attack or if attacked lead to the defeat of the attacker) and the value one places on being ruled by one's present government instead of a foreign government. He acknowledges that these factors are influenced by information (propaganda), and hence are subject to manipulation. Since many goods and services provided by government are, like defense, felt only indirectly or abstractly, the importance of information is even greater in the public sector than in the private sector (Bartlett, 1973).

Utility functions similar to that suggested by Wagner could be worked out for other goods and services provided by governments. After such functions are given empirical content and tested, we will be in a much better position to know how and why individuals value different public goods and services. But the big problem still remains: whose utility functions matter? And under what conditions?

Political scientists have worked on the question of whose utility function matters—though not nearly as much as would be expected, given the definition of politics as the authoritative allocation of values or who gets what, when, how (Mitchell, 1969)—but unfortunately, their ideas have not yet fallen together into a general parsimonious theory. Some political scientists emphasize masses, and some elites. Some are concerned with organization, and some with behavior. Some look at bureaucracies, and some at interest groups. Rather than go into these differences, which cover the whole field of political science, we will simply bring together the ideas presented in this volume and add that the whole subject needs much more comparative work.

Individual utility functions can not simply be summed because each person's utility function is weighted differently by the political process. The political process may give very little weight to some individuals' utility functions (for example, Indians in Guatemala) or in exceptional cases, give a weight of less than zero (Jews in Nazi Germany). It will give rather large weight to the utility functions of some prominent individuals (the Afrikaner Nationalists in South Africa). In order to simplify the task of estimating weights for different persons' utility functions, political scientists have classified individuals into broad categories or groups. The political importance of different groups depends on certain group characteristics (power resources), on the means used to exert influence by the group (violence, votes), and on the power structure of society (democracy or dictatorship, hierarchical or equalitarian).

Peters and Hennessy, in examining Swedish expenditures over the last hundred years, emphasize the importance of social and political mobilization of workers and other lower-class groups through urbanization, unionization, and voting. Mobilization, they argue, increased the importance of the utility functions of lower-class groups, particularly in the critical period of 1900 to 1930, when the Swedish government initiated and expanded programs benefiting the lower classes.

Ames and Goff found that violent behavior was positively related to increases in edcuational expenditure in Latin America. Apparently, willingness to undertake strong action in support of preferences increases the weight of those preferences.

Rundquist and Ferejohn found that when allocating public works projects, legislative committees give greater weight to the preferences of constituents of committee members than to constituents of noncommittee members.

Hadden postulates that the community preference for any particular good or service increases with the establishment of a bureaucratic organization to provide that good or service. At that time, the bureaucrats' utility functions, which are always weighted heavily, are added to the utility functions of private citizens.

Danziger examined the bureaucratic processes in two English boroughs and found that they differed enormously. He proposed that different patterns of allocations might be due to the differences in bureaucratic processes or standard operating procedures of organizations. His investigations raise the larger question of the effects of program budgeting, benefit/cost analysis, and economic planning on the allocation of governmental resources.

The three paths of influence on the budget decision outlined above do not yet amount to a theory. Sufficient data exist in this volume to establish that each path is important, but we do not yet know what factors in the environment affect changes in the values of intervening variables of the three paths. Nor do we know how important each path is relative to the others. Bringing these concepts together, however, allows us to discuss the effects of different environmental factors on governmental expenditure in a more sophisticated way and to pose critical questions for research.

We can now go back to the question of the relationship between levels of production and governmental resource allocation. Because many variables intercede between GNP and expenditures, it is not surprising that the correlations between these two variables were so inconsistent. The complexity of the relationship can be illustrated by tracing out the effects of one kind of change in production on one kind of governmental expenditure. Consider how an increase in manufacturing will affect educational expenditure levels through these three paths.

In countries where the government is highly dependent on taxation of imports, the development of manufacturing through import substitution will tend to lower government revenues. It will also change the cost structure by increasing the demand for, and hence wages of, trained personnel such as teachers while lowering the cost of manufactured goods. Growth of manufacturing will also alter utility functions and the way they are aggregated. Urbanization as well as the need for skills will increase the utility of education for the average person. The concentration of workers in one place will also make their mobilization and politicization easier, which will increase the weight given to their utility functions in the aggregate utility function.

The combined effects of an increase in manufacturing on educational expenditure would be contradictory. Revenue available for all expenditures would go down; costs of education would go up; and demand for education would go up. These contradictory effects may cause increased tension in society, and the only way to resolve the problem would be to change the tax system. If tax changes are not possible, the government may suffer a loss of legitimacy and an increase in oppositional violence.

The outline for a theory presented in this conclusion has not yet taken care of the lack of "an integrated framework which can weave these studies into a comprehensive image of a total world system," mentioned by Boulding in his introduction. We have limited ourselves to a small part of the total, that concerned with governmental resource allocations. We have indicated how certain political and economic concepts might be fitted together to form a theory of government expenditures. The outline may provide some guide to the routes we should take in order to quench our "thirst for the testable."

BIBLIOGRAPHY

ABOLFATHI, F. (1973) "Defense expenditures in the Persian Gulf: inter-state and international factors in the Iraqi-Iranian arms races (1950-1969)." Department of Political Science, Northwestern University (March), mimeo.

AKINS, J.E. (1973) "The oil crisis: this time the wolf is here." Foreign Affairs 51, 3 (April): 462-490.

ALBRECHT, U. (1972) "The study of international trade in arms and peace research." Journal of Peace Research 2: 165-178.

ALLEN, R.G.D. (1968) Statistics for Economists. 3rd rev. ed. London: Hutchinson.

ALLISON, G. (1971) The Essence of Decision. Boston: Little, Brown.

——— (1969) "Conceptual models and the Cuban missile crisis." American Political Science Review 58 (September): 689-718.

ALMOND, G. (1969) "Political development: analytic and normative perspectives." Comparative Political Studies 7 (January): 447-470.

ALT, J. (1971) "Some social and political correlates of county borough expenditures." British Journal of Political Science 1 (June): 49-62.

AMES, B. (1973) Rhetoric and Reality in a Militarized Regime. New York: Sage Papers in Comparative Politics (Fall).

AMES, B. and E. GOFF (1973) "A longitudinal approach to Latin American public expenditures." Paper presented at the American Political Science Association meeting, New Orleans (September).

ANDERSON, C.W. (1967) Politics and Economic Change in Latin America: The Governing of Restless Nations. Madison: University of Wisconsin Press.

ANDERSSON, I. (1957) A History of Sweden. Translated from the Swedish by Carolyn Hannoy. London: Weidenfeld & Nicholson.

AQUILONIUS, K. (1942) "Det Svenska folkundervisningsvasendt 1809-1860" in V. Frederikkson (ed.) Svenska folkskolans historia. Stockholm: A. Bonniers.

ARKHURST, F.S. [ed.] (1972) Arms and African Development: Proceedings of the First Pan-African Citizens Conference. New York: Praeger.

BAILEY, J. (1973) "Public budgeting in Colombia: disjointed incrementalism in a dependent polity." Department of Government, Georgetown University (July).

BALOYRA, E. (1974) "Democratic and dictatorial budgeting" in Sinding and Coleman (eds.) Studying Politics in Latin America. New York: Dodd, Mead.

——— (1973) "Budget analysis: methods and issues with application to Venezuela." Presented at the American Political Science Association meeting, New Orleans (September).

BANFIELD, E.C. (1970) The Unheavenly City. Boston: Little, Brown.

——— (1965) Big City Politics. New York: Random House.

——— and J.Q. WILSON (1963) City Politics. Cambridge: Harvard University Press and MIT Press.

BANKS, A. (1971) Cross-Polity Time Series Data. Cambridge: MIT Press.

BARBER, J.D. (1966) Power in Committees. Chicago: Rand McNally.

BARKER, E. (1945) The Development of Public Services in Western Europe, 1660-1930. London: Oxford University Press.

BARLOW, R., H. BRAZER, and J. MORGAN (1966) The Economic Behavior of the Affluent. Washington: Brookings Institution.

BARTLETT, R. (1973) Economic Foundations of Political Power. New York: Free Press.

BAUER, R.A. and K.J. JERGEN (1969) The Study of Policy Formation. New York: Free Press.

BAUER, R.A., I. POOL AND L.A. DEXTER (1963) American Business and Public Policy. New York: Atherton Press.

BEER, F.A. (1972) "The political economy of alliances: benefits, costs, and institutions in

NATO." Sage Professional Papers in International Studies. Beverly Hills: Sage Publications.

BENOIT, E. (1973) Defense and Economic Growth in Developing Countries. Lexington, Mass.: D.C. Heath.

BILL, J.A. (1972) The Politics of Iran: Groups, Classes and Modernization. Columbus: Charles E. Merrill.

BLALOCK, H. (1970) Theory Construction. Englewood Cliffs, N.J.: Prentice-Hall.

――― (1964) Causal Inferences in Non-Experimental Research. Chapel Hill: University of North Carolina Press.

BLOOMFIELD, L.P. and A. LEISS (1969) "Arms transfers and arms control" in J.C. Hurewitz (ed.) Soviet American Rivalry in the Middle East. New York: Praeger.

BOADEN, N. (1971) Urban Policy-Making. Cambridge, England: Cambridge University Press.

――― and R. ALFORD (1968) "Sources of diversity in English local government." Public Administration (London) 47 (Summer): 203-24.

BOARD, J. (1970) The Government and Politics of Sweden. Boston: Houghton Mifflin.

BOLLENS, J.C. and H.I. SCHMANDT (1965) The Metropolis: Its People, Politics, and Economic Life. New York: Harper & Row.

BONOMO, V. and C. SCHOTTA (1969) "Statistical table for time series analysis." Technical Paper No. 69-1. Department of Economics, Virginia Polytechnic Institute (January).

BOULDING, K.E. (1966) Economic Analysis: Macroeconomics. New York: Harper & Row: 210-215.

BOURNE, L. (1971) "Apartment location and the housing market," pp. 321-29 in L. Bourne (ed.) The Internal Structure of the City. Toronto: Oxford University Press.

BRAYBROOKE, D. and C. LINDBLOM (1963) A Strategy for Decision. New York: Free Press.

BRAZER, H. (1959) City Expenditures in the United States. New York: National Bureau of Economic Research.

BRETON, A. (1970) "Public goods and the stability of Federalism." Kyklos 23 (Fasc. 4): 882-902.

――― and R. BRETON (1969) "An economic theory of social movements." American Economic Review 59: 198-205.

――― (1966) "A theory of the demand for public goods." Canadian Journal of Economics and Political Science 32 (November): 455-467.

――― (1965) "A theory of government grants." Canadian Journal of Economics and Political Science 31 (May): 175-187.

BRIGGS, F.E.A. (1962) "The influence of errors on the correlation of ratios." Econometrica 30 (January): 162-177.

BRUSEWITZ, A. (1951) Konoungmakt, herremakt, folkmakt: forfattingskampe i Svrige 1906-1918. Stockholm: Almquist & Wiksell.

BUCHANAN, J. (1968) The Demand and Supply of Public Goods. Chicago: Rand McNally.

――― (1967) Public Finance in Democratic Process: Fiscal Institutions and Individual Choice. Chapel Hill: University of North Carolina Press.

――― (1965) "An economic theory of clubs." Economica 32 (February): 1-14.

――― and G. TULLOCK (1962) The Calculus of Consent. Ann Arbor: University of Michigan Press.

BULLOCK, C. (1971) "The influence of state party delegations on House Committee assignments." Mid.J. of Pol.Sci. 15 (August): 525-546.

BURGESS, E.A. (1929) "Urban area," pp. 114-117 in T.V. Smith and L.D. White (eds) Chicago: An Experiment in Social Science Research. Chicago: University of Chicago Press.

CAMPBELL, A.K. and S. SACKS (1967) Metropolitan America. New York: Free Press.

CAMPBELL, D. and H.L. ROSS (1968) "The Connecticut crackdown on speeding: time-series data in quasi-experimental analysis." Law and Society Review 3 (March): 33-53.

CAPORASO, J. A. and R. DUVALL (1972) "Time and social change." Department of Political Science, Northwestern University, mimeo.

CARTER, J.R. (1969) The Net Cost of Soviet Foreign Aid. New York: Praeger.

CASTLES, F. (1973) "The political function of organized groups: the Swedish case." Political Studies 21 (March): 26-34.

CATER, D. (1964) Power in Washington: A Critical Look at Today's Struggle to Govern in the Nation's Capital. New York: Vintage Books.

CHILDS, M. (1966) Sweden, The Middle Way. New Haven: Yale University Press.

——— (1952) The Farmer Takes a Hand. New York: Doubleday.

CHRIST, C. (1966) Econometric Methods and Models. New York: Wiley.

CHOUCRI, N. (1971) "Applications of experimental econometrics to forecasting in political analysis. Unpublished paper, MIT, August.

——— and W.C. MITCHELL (1969) "Armaments behavior among competing nations, simulating the naval budgets of major powers: Europe 1870-1914." Department of Political Science, Stanford University, mimeo.

CLARK, J. (1969) "Environment, process, and policy: a reconsideration." American Political Science Review 63 (December): 1172-82.

CLARKE, R. (1972) The Science of War and Peace. New York: McGraw-Hill.

CNUDDE, C. and D. McCRONE (1969) "Party competition and welfare policies in the American states." American Political Science Review 63 (September): 858-66.

——— (1967) "Toward a communications theory of democratic political development: a causal model." American Political Science Review 61 (March): 72-79.

COLE, M. and C. SMITH (1938) Democratic Sweden. London: Routledge.

COLEMAN, J.A. (1966) Equality of Educational Opportunity. Washington: Government Printing Office.

COLEMAN, K. and J. WANAT (1973) "Models of political influence on federal budgetry allocations to Mexican states." Presented at the American Political Science Association meeting, New Orleans (September).

Congressional Directory (1958) and (1966) Washington: Government Printing Office.

Congressional Record (1936) 74th Congress, Second Session, House (April 9).

CRECINE, J. P. (1969) Government Problem-Solving: A Computer Simulation Model of Municipal Budgeting. Chicago: Rand McNally.

CYERT, R. and J. MARCH (1963) A Behavioral Theory of the Firm. Englewood Cliffs, N.J.: Prentice-Hall.

DAHL, R. (1967) "Evaluating political systems" in I. de Sola Pool (ed.) Contemporary Political Science. New York: McGraw-Hill.

DANTZIG, G. (1963) Linear Programming and Extensions. Princeton: Princeton University Press.

DANZIGER, J.N. (1974) "Budget-making and expenditure variations in English county boroughs." Ph.D. dissertation. Stanford: Stanford University Press.

DAVIES, B. (1968) Social Needs and Resources in Local Services. London: Michael Joseph.

DAVIS, O., M.A.H. DEMPSTER and A. WILDAVSKY (1966) "A theory of the budgetary process." American Political Science Review 60 (September): 529-47.

——— and G.H. HARRIS. (1966) "A political approach to a theory of public expenditures: the case of municipalities." National Tax Journal 19 (September): 259-275.

DAWSON, R.E. and J.A. ROBINSON (1963) "Inter-party competition, economic variables, and welfare policies in the American states." Journal of Politics 25 (November): 265-289.

DEARLOVE, J.N. (1973) The Politics of Policy in Local Government. London: Cambridge University Press.

——— (1970) "Interest groups and councillors in Kensington and Chelsea." British Journal of Political Science (London) 1 (June): 129-53.

DECKARD, B. (1972) "State party delegations in the U.S. House of Representatives–a comparative study." Journal of Politics 34 (February): 199-222.

DEUTSCH, K. (1966) "Social mobilization and political development" in J. Finkle and R. Gamble, Political Development and Social Change. New York: John Wiley.

――― (1963) The Nerves of Government. New York: Free Press.

DONOVAN, J. ed. (1972) U.S. and Soviet Policy in the Middle East, 1945-1956. New York: Facts on File.

DORFMAN, R., P.A. SAMUELSON and R.M. SOLOW (1970) Linear Programming and Economic Analysis. New York: McGraw-Hill.

DOWNS, A. (1957) An Economic Theory of Democracy. New York: Harper & Row.

DUE, J.F. (1961) "Studies of state-local tax influences on the location of industry." National Tax Journal 14 (June): 163-173.

DUPUY, T.N. (1970) The Almanac of World Military Power. 1st ed. Dunn Loring, Va. and Harrisburg, Pa.: T.N. Dupuy Associates and Stackpole Books.

――― and W. BLANCHARD (1972) The Almanac of World Military Power. 2nd ed. Dunn Loring, Va. and New York: T.N. Dupuy Associates and R.R. Bowker Company.

DURBIN, J. and G.S. WATSON (1950) "Testing for serial correlation in a least-squares regression." Biometrica 37: 409-415.

DYE, T.R. (1972) Understanding Public Policy. Englewood Cliffs, N.J.: Prentice-Hall.

――― [ed.] (1971) The Measurement of Policy Impact. Tallahassee: Florida State U.

――― (1966) Politics, Economics, and the Public. New York: Rand McNally.

EASTON, D. (1957) "An approach to the analysis of political systems." World Politics 9 (April): 383-400.

ELAZAR, D. (1972) American Federalism: The View from the States. New York: Thomas Crowell.

ERICKSON, K.P. (1970) Labor in the Political Process in Brazil: Corporatism in a Modernizing Nation. Unpublished Ph.D. dissertation, Columbia University.

EYESTONE, R. (1971) The Threads of Public Policy. Indianapolis: Bobbs-Merrill.

EZEKIEL, M. and K. FOX (1959) Methods of Correlation and Regression Analysis. New York: Wiley.

FAGIN, H. (1967) "The evolving philosophy of urban planning," in L.F. Schnore and H. Fagin (eds.) Urban Research and Policy Planning. Beverly Hills: Sage Publications.

FAUSTO, B. (1970) A Revolucao de 1930: Historiografia e Historia. Rio de Janeiro: Editôra Brasiliense.

FENNO, R.F. (1973) Congressmen in Committees. Boston: Little, Brown.

――― (1966) The Power of the Purse: Appropriations Politics in Washington. Boston: Little, Brown.

FENTON, J. and D. CHAMBERLAYNE (1969) "The literature dealing with the relationships between political processes, socioeconomic conditions and public policies in the American states: a bibliographical essay." Polity 1 (Spring): 388-404.

FEREJOHN, J. (1974) Pork Barrel Politics. Stanford: Stanford University Press.

――― (1972) Congressional Influences on Water Politics. Ph.D. dissertation. Stanford: Stanford Univeristy Press.

FISHER, G. (1961) "Determinants of state and local government expenditure." National Tax Journal 14: 349-55.

FISHMAN, G. (1969) Spectral Methods in Econometrics. Cambridge: Harvard University Press.

FLANIGAN, W. and E. FOGELMAN (1971) "Patterns of democratic development: an historical comparative analysis" in J.V. Gillespie and B.A. Nesvold (eds.) Macro-Quantitative Analysis. Beverly Hills: Sage Publications.

FLEISHER, F. (1967) The New Sweden: The Challenge of a Disciplined Democracy. New York: McKay.

FOWLER, E. P. and R. L. LINEBERRY (1972a) "The comparative analysis of urban policy: Canada and the United States," pp. 345-368 in H. Hahn (ed.) People and Politics in Urban Society. Beverly Hills: Sage Publications.

––– (1972b) "Patterns of feedback in urban politics," pp. 361-367 in D. Morgan and S. Kirkpatrick (eds.) Urban Politics: A Systems Approach. New York: Free Press.

FRANK, LEWIS A. (1969) The Arms Trade in International Relations. New York: Praeger.

FREY, F. (1970) "Cross-cultural survey research in political science" in R. Holt and J. Turner (eds.) The Methodology of Comparative Research. New York: Free Press.

FRITSCHLER, A.L. (1969) Smoking and Politics: Policymaking and the Federal Bureaucracy. New York: Appleton-Century-Crofts.

FROLICH, N. and J. OPPENHEIMER (1971) An Entrepreneurial Theory of Politics. Ph.D. dissertation, Department of Politics, Princeton University.

––– (1970) "I get by with a little help from my friends." World Politics 23 (October): 104-120.

FROLICH, N. and O. YOUNG (1971) Political Leadership and Collective Goods. Princeton: Princeton University Press.

FROMAN, L.A. (1967) "An analysis of public policies in cities." Journal of Politics 29 (February): 94-108.

FRY, B. and R. WINTERS (1970) "The politics of redistribution." American Political Science Review 64 (June): 508-23.

FURTADO, C. (1968) The Economic Growth of Brazil: A Survey from Colonial to Modern Times. Berkeley: University of California Press.

GARWOOD, J.D. and W.C. TUTHILL (1963) The REA: An Evaluation. Washington: American Enterprise Institute.

GERWIN, D. (1969) "A process model of budgetary decision-making." Administrative Science Quarterly 14 (March): 33-46.

GLADE, W. and C. ANDERSON (1963) Political Economy of Mexico. Madison: University of Wisconsin Press.

GOLD, D. (1969) "Statistical tests and substantive significance." American Sociologist 4 (February): 42-46.

GOSS, C. (1972) "Military committee membership and defense-related benefits in the House of Representatives." Western Political Quarterly (June): 215-233.

Government of India, Planning Commission. (1965) Fourth five-year plan. Delhi: Government Printing Office.

GRAHAM, L. (1969) Civil Service Reform in Brazil: Principles vs. Practice. Austin: University of Texas Press.

GRANGER, C. (1969) "Investigating causal relations by econometric models and cross-spectral methods." Econometrica (July): 424-438.

GRANGER, C. and M. HATANKA (1964) Spectral Analysis of Economic Time Series. Princeton: Princeton University Press.

GRANGER, C. and O. MORGANSTERN (1963) "Spectral analysis of New York stock prices." Kyklos 16: 20.

GRANT, J.P. and S. SAMMARTANO (1973) "Growth with justice: a new partnership?" in Communique on Development Issues 18 (January).

GREENBERG, E. (1967) "Employment impacts of defense expenditures and obligations." Review of Economics and Statistics 69 (May): 205-210.

GREGORY, R.C. (1969) "Local elections and the 'rule of anticipated reactions.' " Political Studies (London) 17 (March): 31-47.

GRIFFITH, J.A.G. (1966) Central Departments and Local Authorities. London: Allen & Unwin.

GRILICKES, Z. and P. RAO (1969) "Small sample properties of several two-stage regression methods in the context of autocorrelated errors." Journal of the American Statistical Association 36 (March): 253-272.

HARDIN, R. (1971) "Collective action as an aggreeable n-prisoners' dilemma." Behavioral Science 16 (September): 472-481.

HASKEL, B.G. (1972) "What is innovation? Swedish Liberals, Social Democrats and political creativity." Political Studies 20 (September): 306-310.

HAUSE, J. (1971) "Spectral analysis and the detection of lead-lag relationships." American Economic Review (March): 213-217.

HAYES, M.D. (1973a) "Patterns of federal spending in Brazil: 1950-1967, an allocational policy analysis." Paper presented to Ninth World Congress, International Political Science Association, Montreal, Canada (August).

——— (1973b) "Ecological constraints and policy outputs in Brazil: an examination of federal spending patterns." Paper presented to Annual Meeting of the American Political Science Association, New Orleans (September).

HEAD, J.G. (1962) "Public goods and public policy." Public Finance 17 (Fall); 197-221.

HEARE, G. (1972) Trends in Latin American Military Expenditures: 1940-1970: Argentina, Brazil, Chile, Colombia, Peru and Venezuela. Department of State publication 8618 (December).

HECKSCHER, E.F. (1954) An Economic History of Sweden. Cambridge: Harvard University Press.

HECLO, H.H. (1972) "Review article: policy analysis." British Journal of Political Science 2 (January): 83-108.

HEIDENHEIMER, A.J. (1973) "The politics of public education, health and welfare in the U.S.A. and Western Europe: how growth and any reform potentials have differed." British Journal of Political Science 3 (July): 315-340.

HEMPEL, C. (1965) Aspects of Scientific Explanation and Other Essays in the Philosophy of Science. New York: Free Press.

HERSON, L.J.R. (1957) "The lost world of municipal government." American Political Science Review 51 (June): 330-345.

HICKS, J.R. and U.K. HICKS (1943) Standards of Local Expenditures. London: Cambridge University Press.

HIRSCHMAN, A.O. (1970) Exit, Voice and Loyalty. Cambridge: Harvard University Press.

——— (1958) The Strategy of Economic Development. New Haven: Yale University Press.

HOAGLAND, J.H. (1970) "Arms in the Third World." Orbis 14 (Summer): 500-505.

——— and J.B. TEMPLE (1965) "Regional stability and weapons transfer: the Middle Eastern case." Orbis 9 (Fall): 714-728.

HOFFERBERT, R.I. (1972) "State and Community policy studies: a review of comparative input-output analyses," pp. 3-72 in J.A. Robinson (ed.) Political Science Annual 3. Indianapolis: Bobbs-Merrill.

——— and I. SHARKANSKY (1969) "Dimensions of state politics. economics, and public policy." American Political Science Review 63 (September): 867-79.

HOLLENHORST, J. and G. AULT (1971) "An alternative answer to: who pays for defense?" American Political Science Review 75 (September): 760-763.

HUMPHREY, H.H. (1940) The Political Philosophy of the New Deal. Baton Rouge: Louisiana State University Press.

HUNTINGTON, S.P. (1969) "Arms races: prerequisities and results," pp. 15-33 in J. Mueller (ed.) Approaches to Measurement in International Relations: A Non-Evangelical Survey. New York: Appleton-Century-Crofts.

——— (1965) "Political development and political decay." World Politics 17 (April): 386-430.

HUREWITZ, J.C. [ed.] (1969) Soviet-American Rivalry in the Middle East. New York: Praeger.

ILCHMAN, W. and N. UPHOFF (1969) The Political Economy of Change. Berkeley: University of California Press.

International Monetary Fund (1971) International Financial Statistics. Washington, D.C.

ISARD, W. and J. GANSCHOW (n.d.) Awards of Prime Military Contracts by County, State, and Metropolitan Area of United States, Fiscal Year 1960. Philadelphia: Regional Research Institute.

JACOB, H. and M. LIPSKY (1968) "Outputs, structure and power." Journal of Politics 30 (May): 510-38.

JACOB, N. (1967) The Sociology of Development: Iran as an Asian Case Study. New York: Praeger.

JAGUARIBE, H. (1968) Economic and Political Development: A Theoretical Approach and a Brazilian Case Study. Cambridge: Harvard University Press.

JENKINS, D. (1968) Sweden and the Price of Progress. New York: Coward McCann.

JENKINS, G. and D. WATTS (1969) Spectral Analysis and Its Applications. San Francisco: Holden-Day.

JOHNSTON, J. (1972) Econometric Methods. 2nd ed. New York: McGraw-Hill.

JOSHUA, W. and S. P. GIBERT (1969) Arms for the Third World: Soviet Military Aid Diplomacy. Baltimore: John Hopkins University Press.

KAHIL, R. (1973) Inflation and Economic Development in Brazil 1946-1963. London: Oxford University Press.

KAISER, E.J. and S.F. WEISS (1970) "Public policy and the residential development process." Journal of the American Institute of Planners 36 (January): 30-37.

KEMENY, J.G. and J.L. SNELL (1962) Mathematical Models in the Social Sciences. Cambridge: MIT Press.

KEMP, J. (1969) "Strategy and arms levels, 1945-1967," pp. 21-36 in J.C. Hurewitz (ed.) Soviet-American Rivalry in the Middle East. New York: Praeger.

KENWORTHY, E. (1970) "Coalitions in the Political Development of Latin America," pp. 103-140 in S. Groennings, E.W. Kelley, and M. Leiserson (eds.) The Study of Coalition Behavior. New York: Holt, Rinehart & Winston.

KNAPP, J. (1973) The Advance of American Cooperative Enterprise. Chicago: Enterprise Publishers.

LAFER, C. (1970) The Planning Process and the Political System in Brazil, A Study of Kubitschek's Target Plan—1956-1960. Ithaca: Cornell University, Latin American Studies Program, Dissertation Series, Number 16.

LAFFERTY, W.M. (1971) Economic Development and the Response of Labor in Scandanavia: A Multi-Level Analysis. Oslo: Universitetforlaget.

LAMBELET, J.C. (1971) "A dynamic model of the arms race in the Middle East 1953-1965." General Systems Yearbook 14: 145-67.

LANCHESTER, F.W. (1916) Aircraft in Warfare, The Dawn of the Fourth Arm. London: Constable.

LA PALOMBARA, J. (1968) "Macrotheories and microapplications in comparative politics." Comparative Politics 1 (October): 52-78.

LASSWELL, H.D. (1968) "The future of the comparative method." Comparative Politics 1 (October) 3-18.

LEE, M.L. (1970) "Impact, pattern and duration of new orders for defense products." Econometrica 37:1 (January): 153-164.

LINDBLOM, C. (1959) "The science of muddling through." Public Administration Review 19 (Spring): 79-88.

LINDGREN, H. (1970) Social Planning in Sweden. Stockholm: Swedish Institute.

LINEBERRY, R.L. and E.P. FOWLER (1967) "Reformism and public policies in American cities." American Political Science Review 61 (September): 701-716.

LINEBERRY, R.L. and I. SHARKANSKY (1974) Urban Politics and Public Policy. 2nd ed. New York: Harper & Row.

LISKE, C. and B.S. RUNDQUIST (forthcoming) Policy Making on the Military Committees.

LOEHR, W. (1973) "Collective goods and international cooperation: comments." International Organization 27 (Summer): 421-430.

LOFTUS, J. (1969) The End of Liberalism. New York: Norton.

——— (1968) Latin American Defense Expenditures: 1930-1965. Santa Monica: Rand Corporation.

LONG, N. (1972) The Unwalled City. New York: Basic Books.

——— (1967) "Political science and the city" in L.F. Schnore and H. Fagin (eds.) Urban Research and Policy Planning. Beverly Hills: Sage Publications.

LOWI, T. (1967) "Machine politics: old and new." Public Interest (Fall): 83-92.

——— (1964) "American business, public policy, case-studies and political theory." World Politics 16 (July): 677-714.

LUPO, A., F. COLCORD AND E.P. FOWLER (1971) Rites of Way: The Politics of Highway Construction in Boston and the American City. Boston: Little, Brown.

LYON, K. (1970) "Some of the economic effects of subsidizing rural electrification." Ph.D. dissertation. Chicago: University of Chicago Press.

MACRIDIS, R. (1968) "Comparative politics and the study of government: the search for focus." Comparative Politics 1 (October): 79-90.

MARGOLIS, J. (1955) "A comment of the pure theory of public expenditure." Review of Economics and Statistics 37 (November), reprinted in R.W. Houghton (ed.) (1970) Public Finance. Harmondsworth, England: Penguin Books: 184-188.

MASOTTI, L. and D. BOWEN (1965) "Committees and budgets: the sociology of municipal expenditure." Urban Affairs Quarterly 1 (December): 39-58.

MASTERS, N. (1961) "Committee assignments in the House of Representatives." American Political Science Review 55 (June): 345-357.

MAYER, L. (1972) Comparative Political Inquiry. Homewood, Ill.: Dorsey.

MAYER, T. and W.R. ARNEY (1974) "Spectral analysis and the study of social change," pp. 27-28 in Costner (ed.) Sociological Methodology. San Francisco: Jossey-Bass.

MAYHEW, D. (1972) "Congress: an interpretive essay." Unpublished essay.

McCAMANT, J. (1968) Development Assistance in Central America. New York: Praeger.

MERRILL, K.E. (1960) Kansas Rural Electric Cooperatives. Lawrence, Kan.: Center for Research.

MERTON, R. (1957) Social Theory and Social Structure. New York: Free Press.

Metropolitan Toronto and Region Transportation Study (1965) Model Split Analysis.

MIHALKA, M. (1973) "Arms races in the Third World." Paper presented at the Annual Meeting of the Midwest Political Science Association, (April).

MILSTEIN, J.S. and W.S. MITCHELL (1968) "Dynamics of the Viet Nam conflict: a quantitative analysis and predictive computer simulation." Peace Research Society (International) Papers 10: 163-213.

MITCHELL, W.C. (1969) "The shape of political theory to come: from political sociology to political economy," in S.M. Lipset, Politics and Social Sciences. London: Oxford University Press.

MONTGOMERY, G.A. (1939) The Rise of Modern Industry in Sweden. London: P.S. King.

MOORE, B., Jr. (1966) Social Origins of Dictatorship and Democracy: Lord and Peasant in the Making of the Modern World. Boston: Beacon Press.

MOSER, C.A. and W. SCOTT (1961) British Towns. London: Oliver & Boyd.

MOSTELLER, F. and D.P. MOYNIHAN [eds.] (1972) On Equality of Educational Opportunity. Cambridge: Harvard University Press.

MUELLER, D.C. (1971) "Fiscal federalism in a constitutional democracy." Public Policy 4 (Fall): 567-594.

MURPHY, J. (1974) The Empty Pork Barrel. Indianapolis: Heath.

NASCIMENTO, K. (1966) 'O aumento de vencimentos do fucionalism federal em 1963," pp. 37-86 in Amaral and Nascimento, Politica e Adminstracao de Pessoal, Estudo de dois Casos. Rio de Janeiro: Fundacao Getulio Vargas.

NEEDLER, M. (1968) Latin American Politics in Perspective. Princeton: Van Nostrand.

Bibliography

[295]

NERLOVE, M. (1971) "Further evidence on the estimation of dynamic economic relations from a time series of cross sections." Econometrica 39 (March): 359-382.

——— (1964) "Spectral analysis of seasonal adjustment procedures." Econometrica (July): 241-286.

New York Times (1967) May 29: 13.

NEWCOMBE, A. and J. WERT (1972) An Inter-Nation Tensiometer for the Prediction of War. Toronto, Canada: The Canadian Peace Research Institute.

NISKANEN, W.A. (1971) "Bureaucracy and representative government. Chicago: Aldine-Atherton.

NORDLINGER, E. (1970) "Soldiers in mufti: the impact of military rule upon economic and social change in the non-Western states." American Political Science Review 64 (December).

——— (1969) Latin America: The Hegemonic Crisis and the Military Coup. Berkeley: University of California, Institute of International Studies, Politics of Modernization Series 7.

NRECA (1970) Rural Electric Facts. Washington, D.C.

——— (1959) Rural Electric Facts. Washington, D.C.

NUN, J. (1967) "The middle-class military coup," pp. 68-118 in C. Veliz (ed.) The Politics of Conformity in Latin America. London: Oxford University Press.

OATES, W.E. (1969) "The effects of property taxes and local public spending on property values: an empirical examination of tax capitalization and the Tiebout Hypothesis." Journal of Political Economy 77 (November-December): 957-971.

O'DONNELL, G.A. (1973) Modernization and Bureaucratic-Authoritarianism: Studies in South American Politics. Berkeley: University of California, Institute of International Studies, Politics of Modernization Series, 9.

OLIVER, F.R. and J. STANYER (1969) "Some aspects of the financial behavior of county boroughs." Public Administration (London) 47: 169-84.

OLSON, M. (1971) "Increasing the incentives for international cooperation." International Organization 25 (Autumn): 866-874.

——— (1967) "Collective goods, comparative advantage, and alliance efficiency," pp. 25-48 in R.N. McKean (ed.) Issues in Defense Economics. New York: National Bureau of Economic Research.

——— (1965) The Logic of Collective Action. Cambridge: Harvard University Press.

——— and R. ZECKHAUSER (1966) "An economic theory of alliances." Review of Economics and Statistics 48 (August): 266-279.

ORBELL, J. and T. UNO (1972) "A theory of neighborhood problem-solving: political action vs. residential mobility." American Political Science Review 66 (June): 471-489.

OSTROM, V., C.M. TIEBOUT and R.O. WARREN (1961) "The organization of government in metropolitan areas: a theoretical inquiry." American Political Science Review 55 (December): 831-842.

PARENTI, M. (1970) "Power and pluralism: a view from the bottom." Journal of Politics 32 (August): 501-530.

PAULY, M. (1970) "Optimality, public goods and local government: a general theoretical analysis." Journal of Political Economy 78 (May) 572-585.

PAYNE, J. (1965) Labor and Politics in Peru. New Haven: Yale University Press.

PEACOCK, A.T. and M. WISEMAN (1961) The Growth of Public Expenditures in the United Kingdom. Princeton: Princeton University Press.

PERLMUTTER, A. (1969) "The praetorian state and the praetorian army: toward a taxonomy of civil-military relations in developing polities." Comparative Politics 3 (April): 382-404.

PETERS, B.G. (1974) "The development of social policy in France, Sweden and the United Kingdom," pp. 257-292 in M. Heisler (ed.) Politics in Europe. New York: McKay.

――― (1972a) "Politics and economic effects on the development of social expenditures in France, Sweden and the United Kingdom." Midwest Journal of Political Science 16 (May).

――― (1972b) "Public policy, socioeconomic conditions and the political system: a note on their developmental relationship." Polity 5 (Winter): 277-284.

――― and T.M. HENNESSEY (1973) Theory and Concept Formation in Comparative Analysis: The Emergence of Public Policy. New York.

PIDOT, G. (1969) "A principal components analysis of the determinants of local government fiscal patterns." Review of Economics and Statistics 51 (May): 176-188.

PRYOR, F.L. (1968) Public Expenditures in Communist and Capitalist Nations. Homewood, Ill.: Irwin.

PRZEWORSKI, A. (forthcoming) "Per capita or sin capita: a note of caution." American Political Science Review.

――― and H. TEUNE (1970) The Logic of Comparative Social Inquiry. New York: Wiley-Interscience.

PULSIPHER, A. and J. WEATHERBY (1968) "Malapportionment, party competition, and the functional distribution of governmental expenditures." American Political Science Review 63 (December): 1172-82.

PUTNAM, R. (1967) "Toward explaining military intervention in Latin America." World Politics 20 (October): 83-108.

RA'ANAN, U. (1969) The USSR Arms the Third World: Case Studies in Soviet Foreign Policy. Cambridge: MIT Press.

RAIFFA, H. (1968) Decision Analysis: Introductory Lectures on Choices Under Uncertainty. Reading, Mass.: Addison-Wesley.

Rajasthan State Electricity Board (1970-71) Annual Report. Jaipur, India: RSEB.

RAKOFF, S. and G. SCHAFFER (1970) "Politics, policy and political science: theoretical alternatives." Politics and Society 1 (November): 51-57.

RANNEY, A. (1968) "The study of policy content," Chapter 1 in A. Ranney (ed.) Political Science and Public Policy. Chicago: Markham.

RASMUSSEN, W. D. and G. BAKER (1969) "Programs for agriculture 1933-1965," pp. 69-88 in V. Ruttan et al. (eds.) Agricultural Policy in an Affluent Society, New York: Norton.

REDFORD, E.S. (1969) Democracy in the Administrative State. New York: Oxford University Press.

RICHARDSON, L.F. (1960) Arms and Insecurity: A Mathematical Study of the Causes and Origins of War. Pittsburgh: Boxwood Press.

RIVERS, L.M. (1969) Congressional Record (daily edition). H4767. Washington: Government Printing Office.

ROSE, R. (1973) "Models of governing." Comparative Politics 4 (July): 465-496.

ROSENAU, J.N. (1967) "Foreign policy as an issue area" in J.N. Rosenau (ed.) Domestic Sources of Foreign Policy. New York: Free Press.

ROSENSTEIN-RODAN, P.N. (1963) "Notes on the theory of the 'Big Push,'" pp. 143-150 in T. Morgan (ed.) Readings in Economic Development. Belmont, Calif.: Wadsworth.

ROSENTHAL, A. (1967) The Social Programs of Sweden: A Search for Security in a Free Society. Minneapolis: University of Minnesota Press.

ROSTOW, W.W. (1960) The Stages of Economic Growth. Cambridge: Cambridge University Press.

RUDDLE, K. and P. GILLETTE (1972) Latin American Political Statistics (September). Los Angeles: Latin American Center.

RUGGLES, R. and N. RUGGLES (1956) National Income Accounts and Income Analysis. New York: McGraw-Hill.

RUMMEL, R.J. (1972) Dimensions of Nations. Beverly Hills: Sage Publications.

――― (1970) Applied Factor Analysis. Evanston: Ill.: Northwestern University Press.

RUNDQUIST, B.S. (1973) "Congressional influences on the distribution of prime military contracts." Ph.D. dissertation. Stanford: Stanford University Press.

RUSSETT, B.M. (1971) "Some decisions in the regression of time-series data," pp. 29-50 in J.F. Herdon and J.L. Bernd (eds.) Mathematical Application in Political Science 5. Charlottesville: University of Virginia Press.

––– (1970) What Price Vigilance? New Haven: Yale University Press.

––– (1969) "Who pays for defense?" American Political Science Review 63 (June): 412-426.

––– (1968) "Modernization and comparative politics: prospects in research and theory." Comparative Politics 1 (October): 37-51.

RUSTOW, D. (1955) The Politics of Compromise. Princeton: Princeton University Press.

SACKS, S. and A.K. CAMPBELL (1964) "The zoning game." Municipal Finance 35: 140-149.

SAFRAN, N. (1969) From War to War: The Arab-Israeli Confrontation, 1948-1967. New York: Pegasus, Bobbs-Merrill.

SAMUELSON, P. (1954) "The pure theory of public expenditure." Review of Economics and Statistics 36 (November): 387-389.

SAMUELSSON, K. (1968). From Great Power to Welfare State: 300 Years of Swedish Social Development. London: Allen & Unwin.

SANDLER, T. and R. SHELTON (1972) "Fiscal federalism, spillovers and the export of taxes." Kyklos 25 (Fasc. 4): 736-753.

SCHAAR, S.H. (1967) "The arms race and defense strategy in North Africa: the military potential of Algeria, Morocco, and Tunisia." American Universities Field Staff Report Service, North Africa Series 13 (December): passim.

SCHLESINGER, J.A. (1966) Ambition and Politics. Chicago: Rand McNally.

SCHMITTER, P.C. (1971a) Interest Conflict and Political Change in Brazil. Stanford: Stanford University Press.

––– (1971b) "The Portugalization of Brazil," in A. Stepan (ed.) Authoritarian Brazil. New Haven: Yale University Press.

––– (1971c) "Military intervention, political competitiveness and public policy in Latin America: 1950-1967," pp. 425-506 in Janowitz and van Doorn (eds.) On Military Intervention. Rotterdam: Rotterdam University Press.

SCHNEIDER, R. M. (1971) The Political System of Brazil: The Emergence of a 'Modernizing' Authoritarian Regime, 1964-1970. New York: Columbia University Press.

SCOBIE, I. (1972) Sweden. New York: Praeger.

SEIDMAN, H. (1970) Politics, Position, and Power: The Dynamics of Federal Organization. New York: Oxford University Press.

SELLERS, R.C. (1971) "Economic theories of public policy: resource-policy and need-policy linkages between income and welfare benefits." Midwest Journal of Political Science 15 (November): 722-740.

––– (1970) "Environment, policy, output and impact: problems of theory and method in the analysis of public policy": 61-80 in I. Sharkansky (ed.) Policy Analysis in Political Science. Chicago: Markham.

––– (1968) The Reference Handbook of the Armed Forces of the World. 2nd ed. Garden City, N.Y.: Sellers & Associates.

SHARKANSKY, I. (1970a) Public Administration: Policy Making in Government Agencies. Chicago: Markham.

––– (1970b) The Routines of Politics. New York: Van Nostrand-Reinhold.

––– [ed.] (1970) Policy Analysis in Political Science. Chicago: Markham.

––– (1969) The Politics of Taxation and Spending. Indianapolis: Bobbs-Merrill.

––– (1968) Spending in the American States. Chicago: Rand McNally.

––– (1967a) "Economic and political correlates of government expenditures: general tendencies and deviat cases." Midwest Journal of Political Science 11 (May): 173-192.

––– (1967b) "Government spending and public services in the American states." American Political Science Review 61 (December): 1066-1077.

SHIBATA, H. (1971) "A bargaining model of the pure theory of public expenditure." Journal of Political Economy 79 (January/February): 1-29.

SHOUP, C.S. (1964) "Standards for distributing a free governmental service: crime prevention." Public Finance 19 (Winter): 383-392.

SINDING, S. (1974) "The impact of political participation on public expenditures: the case of Chile" in Sinding and Coleman, Studying Politics in Latin America. New York: Dodd, Mead.

SINGER, M.R. (1972) Weak States in a World of Powers: The Dynamics of International Relationships. New York: Free Press.

SKIDMORE, T.E. (1967) Politics in Brazil, 1930-1964: An experiment in Democracy. New York: Oxford University Press.

––– and P. SMITH (1970) "Notes on quantitative history, federal expenditures and social change in Mexico since 1910." Latin American Research Review 1 (Spring): 71-86.

SMOKER, P. (1967) "The arms race as an open and closed system." Peace Research Society (International) Papers 7: 41-62.

STEPAN, A. (1971) The Military in Politics: Changing Patterns in Brazil. Princeton: Princeton University Press.

STINCHCOMBE, A. (1968) Constructing Social Theories. New York: Harcourt, Brace.

Stockholm International Peace Research Institute (SIPRI) (1972) Yearbook of World Armaments and Disarmament. New York: Humanities Press.

––– (1971) The Arms Trade with the Third World. New York: Humanities Press.

––– (1969) Yearbook of Armaments and Disarmament. New York: Humanities Press.

STROM, G. (1973) "Congressional policy-making and the federal waste treatment construction grant program." Ph.D. dissertation. Urbana: University of Illinois.

Sweden, Ministry of Finance (1972) The Swedish Budget 1972/73. Stockholm: Goteborgs offsettryckevei.

TAYLOR, C.L. and M. HUDSON (1972) World Handbook of Political and Social Indicators. New Haven: Yale University Press.

THAYER, G. (1972) The War Business: The International Trade in Armaments. New York: Discus Books.

THOMPSON, W.R. (1965) A Preface to Urban Economics. Baltimore: Johns Hopkins University Press.

TIEBOUT, C.M. (1968) "A pure theory of local expenditures," pp. 355-366 in S. Greer, D.L. McElrath, D. Minar, and P. Orleans (eds.) The New Urbanization. New York: St. Martins.

TILTON, T. (forthcoming) "The social origins of liberal democracy: the Swedish case." American Political Science Review.

TOMASSON, R. (1970) Sweden: Prototype of Modern Society. New York: Random House.

Toronto Star (1970) December 12: 17.

TRIBE, L.H. (1972) "Policy science: analysis or ideology?" Philosophy and Public Affairs 2 (Fall): 66-110.

TUFTE, E. (1969-70) "A note of caution in using variables that have common elements." Public Opinion Quarterly 33 (Winter): 622-25.

––– (1969) "Improving data analysis in political science." World Politics 21 (July): 641-57.

TULLOCK, G. (1959) "Some problems of majority voting." Journal of Political Economy 57: 571-79.

UNITED NATIONS, Secretary-General (1971) Economic and Social Consequences of the Arms Race and Military Expenditure. New York: UN Document No. A/8469/Rev.1.

United States Department of Agriculture (1973) Farm Income Situation. USDA (July). Washington: Government Printing Office.

––– (1969) Agricultural Statistics. Washington: Government Printing Office.

––– (1946) Agricultural Statistics. Washington: Government Printing Office.

University of Minnesota Department of Agricultural Engineering (1928?) The Red Wing Project of the Utilization of Electricity in Agriculture. Minneapolis: University of Minnesota.

VAN DYKE, V. (1960) Political Science: A Philosophical Analysis. Stanford: Stanford University Press.

VAN YPERSELE DE STRIHOU, J. (1968) "Sharing the defense burden among Western allies." Yale Economic Essays 8 (Spring): 261-320.

VERBA, S. (1972) "The foundations of modern Sweden: the swift rise and fall of Swedish liberalism." Political Studies 20 (March): 42-59.

––– (1967) "Some dilemmas in comparative research." World Politics 20 (October): 111-127.

VERNEY, D. (1957) Parliamentary Reform in Sweden 1866-1921. Oxford: Clarendon Press.

VITAL, D. (1969) "Back to Machiavelli," pp. 144-157 in K. Knorr and J.N. Rosenau (eds.) Contending Approaches to International Politics. Princeton: Princeton University Press.

VOEVODSKY, J. (1969) "Three studies on wars." Peace Research Reviews.

WAINSTEIN, L. (1971) "The Dreadnought gap," pp. 153-169 in K. N. Waltz and R. J. Art (eds.) The Use of Force: International Politics and Foreign Policy. Boston: Little, Brown.

WARREN, R. (1964) "A municipal services market model of metropolitan organization." Journal of the American Institute of Planners 30 (August): 193-204.

Washington Post (1972) December 10:10.

WEAVER, J.L. (1973) "Assessing the impact of military rule: alternative approaches," pp. 58-116 in Schmitter (ed.) Military Rule in Latin America: Function, Consequences, Perspectives. Beverly Hills: Sage Publications.

WEIBULL, J. (1970) Sweden, 1918-1968). A lecture delivered at the University College, Scandinavian Department, London (December 12, 1968).

WEIDENBAUM, M.L. (1966) "Measurement of the economic impact of defense and space programs." American Journal of Economics and Sociology 25 (October): 415-426.

WESTERFIELD, B.H. (1966) "Congress and closed politics in national security affairs." Orbis 10 (Fall): 737-753.

WHITTINGTON, M.S. (1972) Review. Canadian Journal of Political Science 4 (December): 380.

WILDAVSKY, A. (1964) The Politics of the Budgetary Process. Boston: Little, Brown.

–––, O. DAVIS, and M.A.H. DEMPSTER (1966) "A theory of the budgetary process." American Political Science Review (September): 529-547.

WILENSKY, H.L. and C.N. LEBEAUZ (1958) Industrial Society and Social Welfare. New York: Russell Sage.

WILKIE, J. (1970) "On methodology and the use of historical statistics."

––– (1967) The Mexican Revolution: Federal Expenditures and Social Change Since 1910. Berkeley: University of California Press.

WILLIAMSON, O.E. (1967a) "The economics of defense contracting: incentives and performance" in R.N. McKean (ed.) Issues in Defense Economics. New York: Columbia University Press.

––– (1967b) "A rational theory of the budgetary process." Papers on Non-Market Decision-Making 20: 71-89.

WILSON, J.Q. [ed.] (1968) City Politics and Public Policy. Cambridge: Harvard University Press.

WIZELIUS, I. [ed.] (1967) Sweden in the Sixties. Stockholm: Almquist & Wiksell.

WOLFSON, M. (1968) "A mathematical study of the Cold War." Peace Research Society (International) Papers: 107-112.

WOOD, R. C. (1964) 1400 Governments. Cambridge: Harvard University Press.
——— (1958) Suburbia. Boston: Houghton Mifflin.
ZISK, B.H. (1972) "Local interest politics and municipal outputs," pp. 231-254 in H. Hahn (ed.) People and Politics in Urban Society. Beverly Hills: Sage Publications.

NOTES

NOTES

NOTES

NOTES